The Impact of Technology on Long-Term Health Care

Edited by John M. Grana and David B. McCallum

The Impact of Technology on Long-Term Health Care

Edited by John M. Grana and David B. McCallum

Project HOPE
Center for Health Affairs
Millwood VA 22646

The Project HOPE Center for Health Affairs is a private, nonprofit policy center that provides objective research and policy analysis to help develop solutions for problems in the U.S. health system. Founded in 1982 as part of Project HOPE, the international health organization, the Center has a special interest in the role of the private sector and state and local governments in moderating the rise of health expenditures.

Library of Congress Cataloging-in-Publication Data
Main entry under title:

The impact of technology on long-term care.

  Based on a workshop held in Millwood, Va., Feb. 16–18, 1983 and sponsored by the Office of Technology Assessment and others.
    1. Long-term care of the sick—United States—
Congresses. 2. Aged—Medical care—United States—
Congresses. 3. Technology assessment—United States—
Congresses. I. Grana, John M., 1948–   .
II. McCallum, David B., 1943–   . III. United States.
[DNLM: 1. Health Services for the Aged—United States—
congresses. 2. Long Term Care—in old age—
congresses. 3. Technology, Medical—congresses.
WT 30 I34 1983]
RA644.6.I47   1985   362.1'9897'00973   85-28438
ISBN 0-930177-02-9
Published by the Project HOPE Center for Health Affairs
Project HOPE, Millwood, VA 22646

International Standard Book Number 0-930177-02-9
Library of Congress Catalog Card Number 85-28438

Printed and bound in the United States of America.

Typeset and printed by Braun-Brumfield, Inc., Ann Arbor, Michigan.

Contents

Summary of Issues, Major Points of Discussion, and Major Findings

John M. Grana and David B. McCallum

The growth in the number of those 65 and older, and particularly the increase in those beyond age 75, has profound implications, not least for social policy. The pressure of these changes on population structure is gradual but inexorable. Hence, attention to the rational development of new products, services, and programs to meet the needs of the changing population, as well as the adaptation or elimination of existing ones, must be an objective of federal policy. This interaction between technological change and an aging population presents both opportunities and challenges for individuals and society.

The need to consider the implications for federal policy of the changing age structure of the U.S. population, combined with rapid technical change anticipated in the future, led to a request by the House Select Committee on Aging and the Senate Special Committee on Aging to the Office of Technology Assessment to study the impact of technology on aging in America. The study was also endorsed by the House Education and Labor Committees.

The assessment evaluated some of the policy implications for developments in biomedical and health care technologies which can affect the number of persons 65 and over and their functional capacity, developments in housing and living arrangements and in the workplace, and long-term care for a growing elderly population. (Office of Technology Assessment, *Technology and Aging in America*, U.S. Congress, Washington, D.C., October 1984.) As part of this assessment, the Office of Technology Assessment, Project HOPE, The National Health Policy Forum, and The National Academy of Science's Project on an Aging Society sponsored a workshop on the Impact of Technology on Long-Term Care. The workshop was held at

1

the international headquarters of Project HOPE in Millwood, Virginia, February 16-18, 1983.

Its first focus was on long-term care for the elderly population, rather than the mentally retarded or developmentally disabled. The other focus of the conference was on technology. Technology was defined broadly to encompass a broad range of aspects, from organized delivery systems, respite care, and financing schemes, to social services programs, housing alternatives, devices for managing incontinence, home security systems, and information management technologies. Hardware, such as computers and other electronic devices, are often neglected in planning for long-term care; the workshop explored ways in which these technologies can be applied to reduce the need for long-term care services, improve the productivity of services, and assist in planning. Within this framework, the conference focused on four topics which would best reveal guidelines, concerns, and options under the present opportunities and constraints of the long-term care system: organization, financing, assessment, and prevention.

The conference was structured to provide ample time for presentation and discussion in both small and large groups. It was hoped that participants would enumerate as many approaches to care of the elderly as possible and explore how these relate to the application of technology to long-term care. Participants were chosen for their expertise in long-term care issues or in related areas. The broadly based group of participants identified alternative strategies, their impact, and the incentive structure which affects them.

The following summarizes both the issues and discussions of this workshop to provide an overview of critical points and relationships.

I. Ethical Considerations as a Framework for Long-Term Care Decisions

Long-term care (LTC) in the U.S. has been shaped by many different forces and individuals, in and out of government. John Iglehart notes that historically, the roots of the American welfare state stem fundamentally from the Great Depression, which discredited unregulated capitalism and eroded Americans' faith in individual responsibility. Iglehart believes that long-term care today represents a classic example of the dilemma facing this country as it moves from individual responsibility toward more collective structures.

The policies of the federal government toward the elderly have been focused primarily on making life better for the majority. U.S.

policy for the elderly has been primarily an income policy; its emphasis has been on retirement. Even the one federal health insurance program for the elderly, Medicare, has been an extension of retirement insurance. Medicare protects the retiree against the cost of an episodic illness which is believed to be unbudgetable and cannot reasonably be met by a regular monthly pension. Yet Medicare was not designed to cover the cost of long-term care for the chronically ill; it presently pays for only approximately 2 percent of the total money expended on nursing home care in the United States. Instead, the federal government chose to finance long-term nursing care on a means-tested basis through the state administered, but federally subsidized medical program, Medicaid.

Medicare pays for medical services, primarily those that are prescribed by physicians. If a person needs help with household tasks for shopping, home repairs, or transportation, Medicare will not pay the bill. It is a medical program favoring a more sophisticated technology than may be needed and more highly qualified professionals than may be necessary.

Recent initiatives and programs designed to address long-term care issues at the state level represent a positive development in the quest for new approaches that will ultimately provide the elderly with more alternatives to institutionalized care. Technologies are developing in three broad areas to achieve this goal and to control the cost of long-term care: alternative methods of paying providers which emphasize greater cost-consciousness; gate-keeping mechanisms to restrict access to costly institutionalized services; and targeting community based care to high risk individuals. Yet the outcome of the application of these technologies is uncertain, because they are being applied in the context of conflicts that we have never resolved: the individual versus the collective; the private sector versus the state.

Many decisions in long-term care require us to consider values and tradeoffs between various segments in our society. Samuel Gorovitz developed an ethical context for such discussions. He points out that the development of goals for a long-term care system is often impeded by an artificial distinction between "us," the planners and taxpayers, and "them," the disabled and frail consumers of long-term care. This illusion of separate constituencies distorts the way we think about the issues. A more useful way of addressing the question is to ask who is entitled to what, at whose expense, recognizing that over our lifetimes we play the roles of taxpayer, neighbor, family member, wage earner, and, if we live long enough, eventual recipient of long-term care.

Gorovitz considers three moral perspectives that might be used to deal with the conflicting values that influence decisions about long-term care. The first, the "consequentialist" view, suggests adoption of that action which produces the best consequences (outcomes), usually maximizing human happiness and minimizing suffering for the greatest number of people. This perspective, which dominates public policy debate, fails, however, to resolve conflicts between societal interests and individual rights when these are not complementary. For example, cost-benefit analysis reflects the belief that a consideration of the consequences ought to determine what we choose to do. But it is notoriously biased in resolving resource allocation dilemmas in favor of persons who can contribute most to the national product. By contrast, the "non-consequentialist" perspective looks not to the consequences of an action but applies an absolute standard to the action itself. This perspective is exemplified by the traditional moral maxim that one should never treat others as means only, but should always respect them as ends unto themselves. This perspective, however, fails to take account of the potential social costs of strict compliance with the moral imperative. Maximization of the autonomy of persons in need of longterm care may require massive investments that would be prohibitive from the societal point of view.

A more recent moral viewpoint is the "Rawlsian" perspective, which seeks actions based on principles that are fair and just regardless of the decisionmaker's role in society. The principles of a just society are those that would be mutually acceptable to rational persons negotiating under circumstances in which no distinctions among people can be made. Not knowing whether we will be a recipient of long-term care, a provider of such care, or simply a taxpayer supporting such care, helps us to make decisions concerning the structure of long-term care that transcend the parochialism of personal interests. Transcending the "we versus them" perspective may help us gain a broader sense of what is fair and just.

Long-term care is a good example of people in competing roles negotiating for resource allocation. A good way to approach long-term care issues is to adopt the different perspectives of decisionmakers, each acting to maximize the probability of certain ends, in the context of the incentives created by the system. As Bob Kane points out, there has been a series of individual decisions, but no master plan: each decision maker has focused on an expedient solution to a particular problem, resulting in the current patchwork of programs and services. Kane urges identification of the "big decisions," which set the goals and performance objectives for the system. These goals and objectives should guide decisions made by the various partici-

4

pants in implementing the long-term care process. Kane proposes that these system decisions include what are the paramount goals of long-term care; whose money will we spend; what is the appropriate time frame to measure success and reevaluate decisions; how will quality be defined; how well can we target services; and whether there should be a joinder of acute and long-term care.

The decision makers that influence the use of LTC services include the client and his family, providers of care (most notably the physician due to the necessity to certify medical needs), institutional administrators, the recently added case manager, and the policy maker. All these participants in the process respond from their individual perspectives to incentives and disincentives provided by reimbursement mechanisms and eligibility criteria, based on the amount of information available to them and the degree of urgency at the time decisions must be made.

II. The Need for Care and Prevention Strategies

The growth in the dependent elderly population is likely to continue over the short run. The size of this population and its functional status will affect the demand for LTC.

In her overview of the health implications of aging in America, Karen Davis provided a demonstration of computer-assisted statistical projection techniques for health services planning and policy analysis. Since projections of the need for care depend on a number of assumptions, this first step, a dynamic simulation which allows exploration of alternatives, illustrates how technology can contribute to improved policy formulation. Davis forecasts a tremendous growth over the next 20 to 50 years in persons (especially females) who will be single or living alone and at greater risk of needing long-term care. Under assumptions of constant prevalence of disability or functional disability per person of a given age-sex cohort, the need for assistance in functioning at various levels would grow dramatically. If recent trends continue, the proportion of all hospital patient days accounted for by people age 65 and over will increase from 38 percent in 1980 to 58 percent by 2000. This will impose serious strains on the long-term care system, and Davis suggests that we aim our biomedical research at cost-reducing and quality-of-life enhancing technologies, as well as pay a greater array of health care providers on a capitation basis. This should discourage unnecessary care, encourage lower cost methods of providing quality care, and reduce hospitalization. The technique of simulation applied to long-term care is a promising innovation in this field with positive implications for strategic planning and public resource management.

Prevention of disability is one factor which may reduce the demand for LTC. Robert Berg summarizes a wide variety of interventions presently available which, if applied broadly and with vigor, may prevent much disability in old age. Primary prevention strategies, secondary interventions or rehabilitative efforts are often neglected, adding greatly to dependence of aged persons and the consequent societal costs. Education of health professionals is important, but not a sufficient solution. Incentives for preventive medicine and coordination of health care need to be woven into the health care system. Berg describes in detail selected disorders which are responsible for much disability in old age and for which substantial gains may be achieved with sound preventive practice. In the area of primary prevention (the avoidance of disease), he lists successful interventions for dental health, atherosclerosis, falls and accidents, pneumococcal pneumonia, influenza, and tetanus. He also lists secondary and tertiary interventions for detection, treatment, and rehabilitation in the areas of psychological health, physical health and function, and independent living.

The discussion group at the workshop expanded on some of the issues raised by Berg. The need for education of health care providers in gerontology and health promotion was discussed. It was agreed that lack of interest in these areas on the part of health care providers has been due mainly to a cure versus care/rehabilitation orientation, lack of payment for preventive services, and traditional attitudes regarding aging. Continued and increased funding in support of educational efforts in aging as they pertain to prevention was advocated. Institutional disincentives to promote wellness and health behavior were also discussed, including funding regulations, reimbursement and level of care (sickness) criteria, and the attitudes of staff members in favor of enforced dependency.

It was felt that there was a strong need to differentiate approaches required by differences in sub populations (for example, along ethnic and socioeconomic lines). The discussants put together a list of examples of technologies to encourage life-style changes, including health education, pre-retirement planning, life-span planning, use of media, exercise, nutrition, health information dissemination, support system development and protection, permitting and facilitating meaningful roles, and peer counseling. Examples of specific preventive technologies were listed, including use of computers in nursing homes, vaccines, risk factor analysis, programs to prevent medication mismanagement, sensory loss detection, instruction on body mechanics to prevent hip fractures, and sheltered workshops in nursing homes. Discussants felt there was a need for research regarding the quantification of prevention effects and measures of wellness in addition to illness prevention, even if cutting back of current initiatives was necessary in order to pay for this kind of research.

Changes in financing options for institutions were suggested which would reorient the current process-focused system to a focus on outcomes. Inclusion of a fixed benefit (for example, $200 per annum) in the Medicare package for prevention was also suggested. For purposes of success in the political arena, it was felt that early offerings should be targeted to already motivated groups to increase the chances of success and visibility.

III. Assessment Technologies

Assessment technologies provide a means of critically evaluating client needs. T. Franklin Williams noted that the extensive and growing need for long-term care services has created general agreement that "approaches and procedures are necessary which will help assure that each person in need of such services will have his/her specific needs identified in order that services appropriate to those needs can be provided and also that adequate planning for, administration of, and financing of such services can be accomplished." Since governments are involved in the reimbursement for long-term care provided to the functionally dependent elderly, assessment can serve a "gate keeping" function for long-term care services as well as to assure that the patient does not receive unnecessary services.

In existing institutional and community program evaluation and planning, two types of assessment technology appear: clinical assessment and clinical judgement, and the use of standardized assessment protocols. These technologies prompt a series of basic questions about the acquisition, interpretation, and use of assessment data:

1. What are the common and different characteristics of various assessment protocols for different domains of information? How thoroughly have these protocols been tested for reliability, for validity, for comparative usefulness?
2. In what different ways may assessment protocols assist in clinical management decisions in long-term care screening, diagnosis, monitoring, and prognosis? Are different types of protocols needed for different roles?
3. What are the roles of standardized assessment protocols in the long term care of individual patients? Are assessment instruments

to be viewed in the same sense as other diagnostic technologies such as laboratory tests, as adjutants to clinical decision-making?
4. Is there a tendency to substitute the use of protocol results for clinical judgement? When, if ever, is this justified?
5. What are the potential values of scoring systems for assessment of protocol data, and what are the potential losses through such use?
6. To what extent can standardized protocols be used, instead of clinical judgement, in management and planning decisions about long-term care? What are the potential hazards in such use?

These and other questions were addressed by the discussion group. Consensus developed against the use of scale scores or an algorithm in specific decisions. As Williams concludes, assessment information must be incorporated as any other objective data as adjuvants to arriving at a clinical judgement; it is not a substitute for clinical judgement. Scoring or scaling of assessment findings may have some value in monitoring changes in functional status and in group data for management and planning purposes; but the aggregation of disparate elements will normally obscure the specific details which should be addressed in the clinical care process.

The process of moving from assessment to a decision about how much of what kind of service the client is eligible for is vitally important. The need for service depends on the functional capacity of the client and his or her social resources. Assessment of functional capacity should include assessment of physical and mental capabilities, environment, and motivation. Concern was expressed by the discussion group that the inherent tension of using assessment to discover needs for services and to ration, control and direct the allocation of resources could result in a usurpation of individual decision-making. Some discussants argued that the team assessment approach with multiple inputs preserves the ability of the client to make decisions. There was a consensus that multidisciplinary units are needed in assessment, but that branching decisionmaking processes be endorsed for cost containment reasons. It was agreed that there was no sense in performing elaborate assessments if options for services are not available.

It was pointed out that state-of-the-art assessment processes are wide open to litigation if people are denied benefits. An analogy was drawn with the difficulties present in the assessment of work disability claims. Concern was also expressed as to the role of the medical profession and hospitals in assessment because of improper incentives to identify problems amenable to medical intervention. It was noted that social functioning and client resource assessment is underdeveloped compared to the assessment of activities of daily living. There was concurrence also that no adequate measure of cognitive functioning exists.

IV. Hardware/Devices and Innovative Programs

Ruth Bennett proposed that for the elderly residing in the community, bottom-line needs are those which must be met to keep them out of an institution; at a higher level, meeting needs may mean providing that which improves (or maintains) quality of life. For the institutionalized elderly, needs are defined quite differently or, perhaps, oppositely. Bottom-line needs are those which must be met to improve (or maintain) the quality of life; at a higher level, meeting needs may mean providing that which facilitates discharge from the institution.

Bennett notes that among the community residing elderly, 20 percent need assistance for mobility, and 43 percent have functional limitations which restrict their activities. Those requiring any assistance represent approximately 30 percent of the elderly. She notes too that mental illness is a major problem among the elderly. The National Council on Aging reports that one of four suicides in the United States is committed by persons 65 and over; that 3 million older persons, 13 to 15 percent of the older population, are in immediate need of mental health services; and that 7 million elderly live in conditions conducive to the development of mental illness and about 5 percent suffer from dementia, some of which is treatable.

There are a wide range of programs to meet the long-term care needs of the community based elderly, and also a variety of organizations to assist families caring for the elderly in the community. The list of services is so vast and our information is so poor, however, that at this point it seems virtually impossible to understand what is going on in the community to meet both bottom-line and higher level care needs. New technological developments are regularly being added to this list; alone or in combination, these also might meet the bottom-line needs of community residing elderly and help prevent institutionalization.

About 4.2 percent of the people over age 65 and 9.2 percent of those over age 74 are in long-term care institutions. The proportion of nursing home residents discharged to private residences varies dramatically across states depending on the availability of single-level dwellings, the presence of willing families, the availability of unoccupied apartments, home care and other community based services, and favorable weather conditions. At present, however, the presence of combinations of these factors remains rather limited, and the need for nursing home care, or care in similar settings, remains strong. A recent survey of innovative programs in long-term care institutions performed by Bennett provides a clearer picture of programming for the elderly in long-term care institutions. It was found that the number of programs in an institution correlated with institutional size. Many of the institutions were found to have multiple programming. Three of the more popular programs were a rehabilitation program, a physical activity program, and a community linkage program.

A wide range of hard technologies to meet the needs of the elderly also are found in long-term care institutions. Some forms of technology are used to meet higher level needs of the institutionalized elderly to prepare patients for discharge, such as tilt tables, hydraulic bath-lifts, and cooking and cleaning utensils. Other forms of technology are used in institutions to meet lower level needs, to maintain individual skills, or to improve the quality of life in institutions, such as bedsore and incontinence devices. Bennett calls for more descriptive studies, experimental evaluations of programs, and the systematic addition of new technologies which could result in the standardization of programs and better targeting.

V. Organization of Long-Term Care Services

The organization of LTC services has been more responsive to funding mechanisms and the desire to limit public expenditures than to needs-based planning efforts. For years, public financing bias in the Medicaid law has favored institutional care, and as a consequence, the range of covered services has been limited under Title XIX. Congress has attempted to rectify this through Section 2176 of the Omnibus Budget Reconciliation Act of 1981, adding a new provision to the Social Security Act, Section 1915 (C)(1) which authorizes the Secretary of Health and Human Services to waive most or all statutory provisions of Medicaid law which discourage or restrict coverage of home and community based long-term care. For the first time, states are able to provide under Medicaid services such as case management, homemaker, home health aide, personal care, adult day health care, habilitation, and respite care. An important regulatory requirement of the new law, however, is that the services offered under the waiver program must result in Medicaid expenditures which are lower than what they would have been without the waiver. This provision reflects the view that when home and community based care are provided, nursing home use will go down. The law is an attempt to reorient the organization of long-term care, reflecting the political view that home and community care are "better" than institutional care, and the desire to respond to this without increasing public outlays.

William Weissert points out, however, that results from a large number of studies show that there is little or no evidence that nursing home use is reduced by home and community based care, because the great majority of those who use noninstitutional services are at little or no risk of nursing home entry. Further, even among those who are at risk, the treatment is not effective; because the small group which does go into nursing homes has very short stays on average, savings from reduced institutionalization would be trivial. As a result, Weissert concludes that most patients use a noninstitutional service as an add-on rather than as a substitute for institutional care.

Another provision of the new law requires that those served by the waiver authority must be persons who, "but for the waivered services," would be in nursing homes. A recent study has shown, however, that noninstitutional services have not typically served that desperately dependent population which becomes the nursing home long-stayer. Consequently, Weissert contends that "unless the states choose to define their eligibility rules for home and community based care services in such a way as to limit use to those who fit this 'desperate need' model, they are not likely to meet the legislative goal of serving exclusively those who, 'but for' the waivered services, would be in nursing homes." Further, recent cut-backs in the Title XX Social Services Block Grant program provide strong incentives for states to do just the opposite and shift some of their block grant and state funded community care recipients onto the Medicaid roles.

Yet proof that states have been in violation of provisions of the new law will be difficult. The task of comparing what expenditures are with what they would have been without the waiver will be extremely complex. But even if the Health Care Financing Administration is successful in showing that its expenditures rose as a result of the waiver, advocates of home and community based care will argue that the lives of those who used community care are better off than they would have been without the community care. That is, they will argue that added expenditures are off-set by added benefits. Thus, use of home and community based care services is likely to grow and costs are almost certain to rise.

Diane Piktialis and James Callahan argue that home-based services should be considered on their own merit. Although they may be more expensive, that is, lead to higher total expenditures for long-term care, spending on homebased services can be controllable. They present for consideration the Massachusetts Home Care Program, a state-wide case management system which presently serves 41,000 older persons. The program was developed with state funds and operates without federal funding, waivers, or demonstration authority. The program approaches long-term care from a social rather than a medical perspective and places long-term care services within a family and social support context and uses medical services only for health maintenance and treatment of acute illness. Two independent studies identified the Home Care Program target group as being 6 percent of the Massachusetts noninstitutionalized elderly population; that is, those needing intensive supports to maintain relative independence. The Massachusetts Home Care Program accepts a large number of clients who are both functionally impaired and in need of formal support services. There is some indication that paid home care services may have substituted for informal care in three service areas. But it was found that home care clients are not "overconsumers" of care; existing home care clients have average service utilization levels that approximate those found in the community population.

Adjusting for income eligibility, the Department of Elder Affairs of Massachusetts has set a target goal for case load at about 5 percent of the noninstitutionalized elderly. By June, 1982 the case load figure represented 4.2 percent. Piktialis and Callahan note that as the case load began to approximate the overall state-wide target, the program experienced dramatic declines in overall growth rate. In light of this evidence, they conclude that even though the elderly subgroup is the largest and fastest growing segment of the long-term care population, a community based system of long-term care is both limited and controllable.

The discussion group expressed universal acceptance of the case management concept. They agreed that long-term care should be organized around a multiple set of points of access, which are largely based in social services agencies (but with hospital discharge linkage). There should be outreach and pre-nursing home placement screening. Assessment was seen as a means of giving service choice to patient and family rather than to physicians. Medical assessment is particularly important to evaluate the full range of patient needs.

Discussants felt that who controls care, in general, should be a matter for local decision, but that priority should be given to nonproviders. It was felt that control of funding (especially of social services) and source of funds should be under the auspices of the case management unit. It was felt that control over medical dollars by case management was seen as workable, but a conflict was anticipated.

A major conflict emerged over combining social and medical services. One point of view maintained that separate funding and operation of hospital, nursing home, and community-based care was politically important in order to protect the community based services. Another point of view linked these levels of care to encourage efficiency among higher cost services. The broadening spectrum of services offered by single providers, especially by nursing home chains, was noted. Simultaneous constraints placed on hospital and nursing home utilization have uncertain implications for long-term care organizations. The discussants felt that long-term care system development issues should be dealt with separately from solving problems in the nursing home industry.

VI. Financing Long-Term Care

William Pollak points out that current long-term care policy is best understood in the context of income maintenance or welfare programs, such as Supplemental Security Income (SSI), which insure that people can live independently by providing them with an income deemed sufficient to cover the cost of maintaining a minimal standard of living. Long-term care policy expresses that commitment when impairments, by elevating the cost of maintaining that standard of living, make the income maintenance programs inadequate. Most financing for long-term care comes through Medicaid; only a small fraction of long-term care financing comes from sources dissociated from welfare. Hence, there is a tendency to meet those standards at least public cost, whether or not that corresponds to least social cost and is efficient in the economist's sense. Therefore, despite the common rationale or justifications for public intervention in long-term care—such as responding to externalities, information problems, market failures, controlling monopolizing behavior, and redistributing social burdens in an equitable fashion—long-term care in this country is based on the welfare model.

The general restriction of benefits to institutional care (with small but increasing exceptions) is consistent with the notion of least public costs because the unattractive nature of nursing homes discourages use by potential residents and their families. The frail elderly and their families will provide substantial care themselves, and will resort to the institutional benefit only when they can no longer cope with the physical and/or financial demands of providing care at home. Although social costs would probably be decreased by a policy that makes more equal the subsidization of substitute forms of care, increased provision of noninstitutional care would probably increase public costs because of the expanded use of services by the frail and their families. But demographic and technical changes are creating growing needs, and unless we choose to neglect those needs, we will face large cost increases. Thus, we are faced with a financing problem.

Private insurance coverage for long-term care is something that many, and possibly most people, would like to purchase. But for many reasons the market is unlikely to respond to either the basic demands that would exist in the absence of any public long-term care, or to the much smaller demands for coverage of risks that are not met by a minimum living standards program of the type we now have. There is, therefore, a strong rationale for public intervention: a program of compulsory public insurance. Compulsion is needed to protect tax payers from the costs imposed by those who under voluntary arrangements would rely on a virtually certain back up program.

Since people would probably prefer benefits that complement what they feel family and friends can and should do, Pollak believes that while an "ideal" public program would grade benefits to assistance providable by the family, this grading of benefits by family situation rules out cash benefits, primarily because of moral hazard problems of family members distorting their work and other behaviors and stated preferences for purposes of eligibility. An in-kind long-term care benefit that includes noninstitutional services reduces to some extent the moral hazard dilemma. Cost sharing also should be an element in the financing of a broad benefit long-term care program, but must be income related in order to assure access for the poor. Residents of institutions should also, at a minimum, pay for housing, board, and other noncare costs that are not part of the (insured) long-term care risks. Informal care also should be subsidized to avoid the inefficiency of a service or in-kind program in which only formal services are subsidized. Distinguishing family assistance that is reasonably expected from family help that should be reimbursed, however, also raises moral hazard problems.

The discussion group accepted Pollak's notion that income maintenance characterizes most of the present long-term care system. The group focused on the financing of long-term care for the nonpoor. The group expressed doubts about the potential of some recent developments, such as life care and capitation demonstrations, to reach the mainstream. Serious obstacles were raised, such as the uncertainty of the cost of benefits that must be paid out in the future, and myopia on the part of buyers who are reluctant to pay now for a risk that is far off in the future. Since no one has developed private insurance on a large scale, there are no reasons presently to believe that it might be close to economic viability.

In the absence of private insurance, the group discussed what benefits should look like under the social insurance approach. The approach has had extensive experience in Europe, and is useful for personal care services. This is an efficient approach, but one which is likely to use more public funds. Another possible approach would be a block grant to local authorities which would leave the design of assessment, rationing, and provision up to the localities. A third possible approach would be capitation which would include acute care paid for under a Medicare voucher.

Discussants felt that the most feasible financing approach would be an addon to Medicare, with a focus on premiums paid by the elderly. Potential sources for these premiums would include home equity and the children of elderly. It was felt that the use of general revenues to finance this more comprehensive program was not feasible.

VII. Concluding Remarks

These papers summarize the current status of the application of technology, broadly defined, to long-term care of the nation's elderly, and provide a panorama of the future. Together they succeed in conveying the optimism which characterizes research in this field, despite predictions of overwhelming problems just around the corner. There appeared a shared sense that, with concerted research, planning, and effort, these obstacles can be overcome. There is belief in the ability of preventive technologies to alleviate much suffering, improve quality of lives, and postpone and prevent the use of some costly medical services. There is currently much activity in the community and in institutions with respect to the development and implementation of new technologies, both of the "hard" and the organizational kind. What is needed is more information dissemination and improved technology transfer; federal and private biomedical research should be redirected towards prevention and the reduction in the prevalence of chronic diseases.

Our ability to screen, assess, and target is improving rapidly; more work is needed, however, especially in the determinants of the social and psychological aspects of the lives of the elderly. Assessment technologies, when applied fairly and with sensitivity to the potential for abuse by agents responsible for funding long-term care, hold great promise for improved clinical decisionmaking, patient management, and control over utilization of long-term care services.

Home care has been demonstrated to be an effective intervention for many elderly. Major new federal subsidies have not been needed, and total expenses appear to be controllable. Home care does not supplant the need for residential options including nursing homes. The application of technologies to improve the efficiency and quality of care in these settings needs additional attention. Further discussions are needed on rationalizing our public funding sources to ensure a socially optimal distribution of scarce public and private resources among this and other long-term care technologies. Continued discussion is also needed to ensure that we are capable of dealing rationally and fairly with the ethical challenges which accompany these technological opportunities.

1

A Historical Perspective on the Evolution of Federal Long-Term Care Policy

John K. Iglehart

I have been charged within the framework of this Conference, and within the context of federal policy with looking at long-term care technology in the future—a somewhat intimidating challenge. Nevertheless, let me start by making several observations about the evolution of federal policy as it applies to this subject. I am defining technology very broadly to include any intervention, be it hardware, surgical procedure, a home health visit, a prescription drug, or a system of care.

Usually, of course, more than one technology is deployed to treat or manage a chronic condition or any affliction that prevents an older person from being independent. Fortunately, the overwhelming number of Americans who are over 65 do not have physical or mental limitations which require them to seek help from family or friends, or from social agencies, to perform the ordinary tasks of daily living. Nevertheless, demographic trends make it clear that future demand for long-term care will be substantial. The latest projections by the Bureau of the Census estimate that by the year 2050, almost 22 percent of the population is likely to be over the age of 65, up from the present rate of 11.5 percent. In addition, female life expectancy is projected to rise from the current 78.3 years to 83.6 years, and male life expectancy is projected to increase from 70.7 years to more than 75 years. As a consequence, the percent of the population that will be over 85 will grow from about 1 percent to more than 5 percent. The problem created by the increasing demand for long-term care will be exacerbated by another anticipated change in our demography: a reduction in the ratio of individuals of working age to individuals of retirement age. The ratio is projected to drop from its present level of 5.4 to 1 to 2.6 to 1 by the year 2050.

The policies of the federal government toward the elderly have focused primarily on making life better for the majority, i.e., those who are not, or at least not yet, in the unfortunate position of needing institutionalized treatment. Federal policy for the elderly also has been primarily an income policy. The emphasis has been on retirement: the provision of widows' and widowers' benefits under a nearly universal social security system; the establishment of a federal minimum floor for all the elderly under the SSI program; the promotion of private pension plan supplements to social security through tax incentives; and the establishment of quite generous career pensions for the military and employees of government at all jurisdictional levels. Even the one health insurance program for the elderly, Medicare, conceptually has been an extension of retirement insurance. Protecting the retiree against the cost of episodic illness is based on the notion that such costs are unbudgetable and cannot reasonably be met by a regular monthly pension. Medicare has not been designed to cover the cost of long-term care for the chronically ill, and is the primary source of payment for only 2 percent of the total money expended on nursing home care in the United States. The federal government chose very hastily in 1965 to finance long-term nursing care on a means-tested basis through the state administered, but primarily federally financed, Medicaid program.

Beginning with the Kerr-Mills Act in 1960, followed by the enactment of Medicare and Medicaid, federal policy accelerated the creation of a nursing home industry. Total national expenditures for nursing home care grew tenfold between 1965 and 1980, from $2.1 billion to more that $20 billion. The Department of Health and Human Services is currently projecting that nursing home expenditures will more than quadruple before 1990, reaching almost $82 billion. Of the $20.7 billion spent on nursing home care in 1980, about $9 billion was derived from private sources while $11.8 billion came from public payments. And perhaps most importantly for the future, Medicare fostered the development of the home health agency and is the major source of support for such agencies today.

Medicare is the largest federal program that purchases home health services. Home health agencies are, it is well to remember, medical agencies. The services are prescribed by physicians for the most part. But if all a person needs is help with household tasks or shopping, or home repairs or transportation, Medicare does not pay the bill. And that is in the major area where Medicare has supported efforts to keep the chronically ill at home and avoid institutionalization. It is limited by being a medical program; a program favoring a more sophisticated technology than may be needed and more highly qualified professionals than may be necessary for many long-term care patients.

What is needed, it seems to me and to a lot of others, is an integrated medical and social agency. And of course the challenge is how to get there. The struggle to redesign Medicare so that at least it more effectively meets the needs of the chronically ill has been a largely losing struggle thus far. It was a struggle even before concern over the soaring cost of medical care reached its present level. Perhaps that should come as no surprise because Medicare's benefit package, like most private health insurance upon which it was largely modeled, is the product of the late 19th and early 20th centuries when acute illness was the primary concern and when most patients either got well or died in a relatively short period of time. The role of behavioral, environmental and genetic risk factors in chronic disease, and the importance of periodic screening, patient counseling and early treatment in postponing the onset of disabling afflictions, were not well understood. Nor was the necessity of years of rehabilitation and long-term care for those who now survive an acute heart attack, a stroke, or other serious problem. The historical paradox of medical progress is that, while we may be successfully reducing mortality, the evidence is not yet in whether this is accompanied by a reduction or an increase in morbidity.

Federal policy has been very slow to recognize the technologies that prevent heavy service utilization, including periodic screening and counseling, as an essential aspect of on-going primary care. Eye or hearing examinations for eye glasses, hearing aids and preventive dental care are other inexpensive technologies which can help prevent the onset of chronic disabilities and diseases or minimize their severity. The antiprevention bias of most insurance programs, including Medicare, appears particularly egregious in view of the recent success of programs reducing or controlling hypertension, strokes or other cardiovascular conditions. In the words of the National Heart, Lung, and Blood Institute's 1981 Task Force report on arterial sclerosis: "The marked and continuing decline in mortality rates from coronary heart disease in the 1970's lends support to the concept that the epidemic onslaught of these diseases can be controlled and prevented."

The lack of attention to the needs of the chronic patient is thus one gaping hole in current federal policies for the long-term care needs of the elderly. Another need that must be addressed is a more rational sorting-out of roles between the several levels of government. There has been a great deal of discussion about which level of government should do what, but resolution seems nowhere in sight. The Reagan Administration has been very inconsistent in its policy toward Medicaid, the program which finances the bulk of long-term care purchased by the federal government. Early on, the Administration sought to cap federal expenditures in the program, and Congress rejected that approach. In its second budget year, the Administration reversed itself and proposed federalization of the program, assuming all of its costs in exchange for devolving cash assistance programs to the States. In its third-year budget, the Administration expanded federalization of Medicaid, leading the states and other interested parties to seriously question whether any force other than budget cutting really drives the Administration's policies towards Medicaid. This remark is not necessarily critical only of the current government's vacillation towards long-term care. It is probably fair to say that answers to the nation's long-term care dilemma have escaped Republicans and Democrats alike. At the state level, as states respond to the need to close budget deficits and to the new federal flexibility that is encouraging more experimentation with noninstitutional community based programs, an extraordinary array of approaches and programs designed to address long-term care issues is evolving. I think most of this represents a positive development, a searching for answers, a quest for new approaches that will ultimately provide the elderly with more alternatives to institutionalized care. At the moment, the clear emphasis of policy directions at the state level favors an effort to reduce or at least moderate future expenditures. This obviously is in tune with the most pressing issues facing many states: a serious shortfall in revenue. According to a paper delivered at a recent HOPE conference by Lawrence Bartlett of the National Governors' Association (Bartlett and Greenberg, 1985), states are moving in three broad areas to control the cost of long-term care: One, utilizing alternative methods of paying providers, with emphasis on greater cost-consciousness; two, instituting gatekeeping mechanisms to restrict access to institutionalized services; and three, targeting community-based care (client and case management programs) to high risk individuals. But no consensus exists amongst states on what directions to follow. Bartlett said,

> While there may be a general feeling that people should not necessarily be institutionalized, many states have indicated that they have no idea which specific services prevent institutionalization. Nor do they know whether or not such a program can be cost-effective. Almost uniformly, discussion with state officials reveals interest exists in developing community services for the elderly. But the service system is not well conceptualized.

Money, or the absence of it, and the medical model are driving most long-term care decisions today. We as a society must begin a process of more serious searching for priorities. Can we afford the medical model when what many elderly people need is not a medically dominated regimen but companionship, shelter, and enough income to live? The current issues in long-term care represent, in a manner of speaking, the clashing of concepts that we in this country have never dealt with comfortably or cleanly: The individual versus the collective; the private sector versus the state. The Great Depression qualified our belief in free enterprise, and along with it, faith in the individual's ability to take care of himself. Until the Depression, the consensus was that there was something wrong with those who could not take care of themselves. And while the Depression did not destroy our society or its belief in free enterprise, it tempered that consensus with a new social philosophy that called for greater intervention by the state. The conflict remains with us, and our long-term care problems represent but one issue in this conflict. This conference is one small step towards dealing with these issues. What we need are larger steps that demonstrate that we as a society have the compassion and the foresight to get on with the job.

References

The Elderly and Long-Term Care: Present and Future State Directions. Lawrence Bartlett and J.M. Greenberg, Paper presented at conference on "New Federalism and Long-Term Health Care of the Elderly," Project HOPE, Millwood, Virginia, December 9 and 10, 1982.

2

Ethical Issues In Long-Term Care

Samuel Gorovitz

We are here to consider the impact of technology on long-term care. Of course, the recipients of this care include the chronically ill and seriously handicapped of all ages, but I will focus on issues concerning the aged. By most measures, this is the major category of need for long-term care, and the category that is growing with alarming rapidity.

And the situation is indeed alarming. We have barely begun to deal with the problems posed by an aging population, problems which arise from a changing population structure, changing patterns of social organization, increased demographic mobility, a high divorce rate and the diffusion of social responsibility, the bureaucratization of social services, and even the successes of modern medicine.

These problems are well known. My objective here is to try to illuminate some of the moral premises of discussions of these matters, and to provide some points of view and concepts that may have heuristic value. It is perhaps useful to begin by asking what the goals of long-term care are.

Unless we know what aspirations are appropriate, it is hard to evaluate progress. Indeed, it is a widespread failing of our educational institutions that they focus primarily on the development of skills that are useful in achieving goals, without paying significant—let alone comparable—attention to the more fundamental problems of assessing and selecting among goals.

What is the point of long-term care? Is it to keep people alive longer, to make them more comfortable, to enrich their lives, to minimize their dependence on others, to minimize our investment in their continuing lives, to meet their needs? Each of these goals has something to recommend it, yet each can be in conflict with the others. What we decide to do will depend ultimately on how we evaluate these, and perhaps other, goals in respect to one another.

That process of evaluation requires us to make a number of increasingly difficult judgments. For example, one frequently hears reference to the needs of the incapacitated elderly and the chronically ill. But what are those needs? Of course we can identify certain basic needs of survival—food, shelter, emergency medical care. But is that all there is to human needs? We would all agree that much more is involved in a decent and humane sense of the needs of dependent persons, but it is less likely that we would agree on just how to expand the list.

Is it not a basic human need to live in a social environment that allows for gratifying interpersonal relationships? Granting that there is a difference between what people need and what they want, is it not a need that at least some of one's wants be achievable?

As we expand the conception of need that shapes our understanding of the goals of long term care, we also change—often in ways we do not fully anticipate—the social and economic consequences of pursuing those goals. As a result, it becomes unavoidable that even our sense of what is a need will reflect to some extent our awareness that meeting needs can be very expensive.

One way of putting the question is in terms of justice in intergenerational transfer—what do we owe to the elderly, and why? But that way of casting the question, although useful in some respects, also has the disadvantage of setting the issue in the language of "we" and "them," thus giving the illusion of a separation of constituencies that can distort the way we think about the matter. Perhaps a more useful way of casting the question is this: how should the burdens of providing long term care be distributed among recipients, families, and larger social groupings? Or, who is entitled to what, at whose expense?

In pondering these questions, we are wise to bear in mind that we do not play fixed roles over a lifetime; rather, we are each taxpayers, neighbors, family members, wage-earners, and potential recipients of long-term care.

I will describe briefly three moral perspectives that may be of use as you consider how to deal with the conflicting values that influence decisions about long-term care. The first is the consequentialist perspective. According to this view, the right thing to do is that which produces the best consequences—according to some standard of what counts as a good consequence. Usually the measure is taken to be human happiness, so that the right actions become those that maximize happiness and minimize suffering. That view is historically exemplified by the utilitarianism of John Stuart Mill, and has been a dominant influence in our moral thought and our public policy debates for the last hundred years.

The utilitarian mandate to produce the greatest good for the greatest number supports our inclinations to beneficence. It offers an explanation of why we should do good for others, even absent their request that we do so. But it is rife with difficulties, for there seem to be deep conflicts between the utilitarian concern with societal interests, on the one hand, and the need to protect individual rights, on the other. Even if more human happiness would in fact be produced by simply abandoning an aged and costly ancestor to whom we have clear commitments, it is unlikely that we would have any right to do so. Despite such problems inherent in consequentialist moral thought, most policy justifications are cast in precisely these terms. Policymakers focus on the outcomes of the choices before them, and cost benefit analysis is one of the tools that reflects the belief that a consideration of the consequences ought to determine what we choose to do.

The consequentialist view of morality does not go unchallenged, however. There is a tradition of moral thought, going back at least to the Ten Commandments, according to which the consequences are *not* the determinants of the moral standing of our actions. Rather, some actions are held to be morally required, and others forbidden, by virtue of the kinds of actions they are. Thus, we have a commandment to honor our fathers and mothers. It does not say: Honor thy father and mother, unless in the circumstances it turns out that more human happiness will result from your refraining from honoring them. Moral commandments do not have escape clauses, or footnotes restricting their range of applicability. They enjoin us to look not to the future, to what the consequences of our action will be, but rather to the actions themselves.

A leading proponent of such non-consequentialist morality was the 18th century German philosopher Immanuel Kant. He held that respect for persons as autonomous rational agents lies at the core of morality. He is perhaps best known for his Categorical Imperative, the most useful version of which states that one ought never to treat others as means only, but should always respect them as ends unto themselves. Such a principle precludes slavery, punishment of the innocent, and other forms of exploitation no matter what the potential societal benefits might be. These acts are wrong because of the kinds of acts they are, and one therefore need not even inquire into their consequences.

25

But this perspective, too, is laden with difficulties. First, it fails to guide us through many kinds of moral conflict. For example, Kant held that one must never lie, and that one must always keep one's promises. He is mute on the question of what one should do in that unfortunate—but all too common—situation in which one can keep one's promise only by the telling of a lie. Second, he fails to take any account at all of the potential social costs of strict compliance. To maximize the autonomy of those in need of long term care may require massive investments that would be disastrous from other points of view. Are we really to exclude all such matters from our deliberations?

From these two historically prominent moral perspectives, I now turn to a viewpoint propounded by John Rawls about a decade ago in his masterful book *A Theory of Justice*. For present purposes, I will draw one fundamental idea from its 87 sections, none of which is easy reading. I offer this idea as a useful heuristic for further deliberations.

Rawls holds that the principles of a just society are those that would be mutually acceptable to rational persons negotiating under a veil of complete ignorance as to their own identities, but in full awareness of the issues and facts of the outside world. Imagine that we pursue a more restricted agenda; we seek, behind just such a veil of ignorance, to decide how long term care should be structured.

As we discuss the matter, we will realize that certain policies will benefit some persons to the disadvantage of others. Thus, a policy of investing half the national wealth in the care of those now over 80 will perhaps do very nicely for them, but will be a disastrous policy for those just now approaching adulthood. How do you vote on such a policy, assuming that you are interested merely in doing as well for yourself as you can? That will depend, among other things, on your age. If you are 20, you'll be against it. But if you are 85, you will think it just fine.

Here is where the veil of ignorance has its effect. Since you know nothing that will distinguish you from anyone else, you have no idea of your age. You are thus required by the logic of the situation to favor only those policies that will be fair to you, no matter who or what you turn out to be when the veil lifts.

You will thus be moved to ask a somewhat different set of questions from those asked by the Kantian or by the Utilitarian. You will ask: What sort of community can I reasonably endorse, not knowing where I will fit into it? Not knowing whether I will be a recipient of long-term care, a provider of such care, or simply a taxpayer supporting such care—how do I want such matters to be handled?

I propose that we ask such questions from time to time over the course of this conference. Doing so can help us transcend the parochialism of our own perspectives and thereby gain a broader sense of what is fair and just.

I turn next to some observations that are more specifically linked to the agenda of this meeting. Advanced age can be a time of sublime tranquility, beyond ambition and its strains. I had the good fortune years ago to have Malcom Cowley as my teacher, and I find that he puts the point particularly well in his little volume, *The View From 80*:

> Those pleasures include some that younger people find hard to appreciate. One of them is simply sitting still, like a snake on a sun-warmed stone, with a delicious feeling of indolence that was seldom attained in earlier years. A leaf flutters down; a cloud moves by inches across the horizon. At such moments the older person, completely relaxed, has become a part of nature—and a living part, with blood coursing through his veins. The future does not exist for him. He thinks, if he thinks at all, that life for younger persons is still a battle royal of each against each, but that now he has nothing more to win or lose. He is not so much above as outside the battle, as if he had assumed the uniform of some small neutral country, perhaps Lichtenstein or Andorra. From a distance he notes that some of the combatants, men or women, are jostling ahead—but why do they fight so hard when the most they can hope for is a longer obituary? He can watch the scrounging and gouging, he can hear the shouts of exultation, the moans of the gravely wounded, and meanwhile he feels secure; nobody will attack him from ambush.

Old age can also be a time of ennobling activity. In "Ulysses," Tennyson wrote:

> Old age hath yet his honor and his toil;
> Death closes all: but something ere the end,
> Some work of noble note, may yet be done,
> Not unbecomming men that strove with gods.

He wrote that at 33, but let it guide his life for half a century more, and he published *Dmeter and Other Poems* in 1889 at the age of 80.

These reminders of the possibilities for tranquility and for accomplishment are important to keep in mind; they are useful antidotes to an overly pessimistic view. But they are not the whole story either. For there are both social and physical causes of the problems of the aged. And even in a utopian community in which the social problems have been overcome, there can come a time when a sanguine view seems out of place.

I think here of the contrast between my father, nearly eighty, and my grandmother, two decades older. My father practices law in Boston, as he has for over fifty-five years. He doesn't put in quite a full week any more, but he is still sprightly in his bow tie and as clever as they come.

My grandmother, in contrast, was nearing 100, in poor health even for her age, when she died. For some years, she had periods of lucidity with diminishing frequency. She lived in a world barely larger than her little space in a nursing home. She was uncomfortable much of the time, and had little sense of herself or her circumstances. But she had such readily available and superb medical care that there was no telling how long her deteriorating life might be preserved.

I'm not at all sure how we ought to respond to cases of that sort, but I am sure that we need to be thinking hard about them, for their numbers are increasing very rapidly—and we appear to be on the brink of advances in medical technology that will give the phrase "long term" an entirely new kind of impact. I'll say a bit more about that point in a moment.

First, however, I want to offer a few thoughts about some specific categories of technology. I do not refer here to the broad interpretation of technology according to which virtually any intervention can be viewed as a technology. I am thinking simply of the hardware.

Technology can be used in the context of long-term care in at least four different ways. It can be used to facilitate daily living; here I have in mind such objects as handrails, hearing aids, prosthetic devices, and the like. It can be used for more effective communication; alarm systems go into this category, as do telephones. It can be used to enrich the quality of life; computers may be central to this category. Finally, it can be an important aspect of medical intervention, in both chronic and acute care.

The availability of devices to facilitate daily living is largely a function of market phenomena. What is already developed is not widely enough known or distributed, but the situation may improve as the size of the market increases. That presupposes, of course, that there is a corresponding increase in purchasing power—and it would be imprudent to be overly sanguine about that point these days. If we want the impaired elderly to benefit from life-facilitating technologies, we cannot rest content with the development of those technologies. We must also strive to make them known to those whom they can help, and to ensure that economic barriers do not inhibit their use.

Communications technologies, too, are well developed, and can greatly increase the safety and independence of the elderly. Again, it is largely a question of cost and distribution—in addition to some psychological barriers to their acceptance. With regard to life-enhancing technologies, I suspect we have not yet scratched the surface. Life for the very old typically lacks the diversity of earlier years. It becomes dominated, on the one hand, by the basic needs of physical survival, and on the other hand, by behavior that is focused on the handling of information, be it keeping up with the news, providing an oral history within the family, reading Aristotle as Oliver Wendell Holmes is said to have done on his deathbed in his 90s, or simply enjoying the pleasures of reminiscing.

We need to ask how the revolutionary information-processing technology that surrounds us can be put to use in the service of these interests. I don't have in mind simply putting Pac-man games into nursing homes—although I understand that has now been done with some intriguing results in increased vitality of the residents. Books and magazines of all sorts could be made available at terminals on demand, with the text appearing on the screen in whatever size print and intensity of brightness were best suited to the individual reader. Friends in different locations could play games of chess or checkers, complete with commentary, by using terminals in interconnected systems. And so on. If the wizards of high technology could be briefly distracted from the lure of large markets, I suspect my little list of examples could be multiplied tenfold in short order.

Finally, I turn to those technologies that support medical intervention to save or prolong life. Where such intervention saves a life that would otherwise be lost, the result is a patient instead of a body—a patient who may be in need of long-term care. The intervention that makes such care possible, by making it possible, oftimes makes it necessary. Our successes in medicine thus increase the demand for medical care instead of reducing it.

I cite the case of Barney Clark—chosen as a case in point to illustrate the problems that loom before us, and especially that new sense of "long term" that we must begin to ponder, as I wrote in an editorial in the *Los Angeles Times*. We all rooted for Barney Clark—that medical pioneer, man of courage, and symbol of our desire to defeat our own mortality. But there is something deeply troubling in his experience, with ominous consequences for our future. Even if his artificial heart had kept working indefinitely without any further difficulty, and he had adjusted to his resulting life as well as could reasonably be hoped, the day would surely have come all the same when something else went awry. Imagine that you were one of Clark's doctors on that fateful day when, let us say, his kidneys failed. Would you have turned your back on this triumph of modern medical skill, and condemned him to the death that had been forestalled so dramatically? Or would you have sent him on to the dialysis unit, where kidney failure is just a problem to be solved, not a fatal deficiency?

The British Health Service would not dialyze anyone Clark's age; that's one way of keeping a lid on their national medical bill. But would we have been likely to let our Barney go like that, just to save the cost, after the emotional, intellectual, and financial investments that had already been made? We don't like the idea of making vital decisions on the basis of what the bill will be. We have a national policy of providing dialysis to anyone whose life can be saved that way, and would certainly not have discriminated against Clark just because he had a mechanical heart.

Fifteen years ago, with a prescience not unusual for him, Kurt Vonnegut wrote a little play called *Fortitude*. The heroine has been saved from death by modern medical technology. She's got a mechanical heart, and she's on dialysis. She has had her liver replaced by a newly developed artificial one. Her pancreas was custom-made. In fact, by the time that we meet her in the play, the only original equipment that she has left is her head—connected to a roomful of devices, monitors, and controls. Now *that's* medical progress! It's lucky for her that she's the widow of a billionaire.

I don't mean to suggest that we should simply put on the brakes and stop developing or applying advances in medical technology. But we do need to think very hard about the road ahead. I'd have dialyzed Barney Clark, too, if that's what he wanted. But I worry about how much of this sort of thing is for the best.

In principle, we can greatly reduce the costs of dialysis through an increased public awareness of the need to donate transplantable kidneys. And perhaps one day the artificial heart will be small, reliable, and of moderate cost. But something else—a liver or a pancreas—will then capture our attention in the front ranks of medicine's inexorable march forward. And the cost will matter, like it or not.

I don't know what the answer is to the problem of deciding how much is enough, but I do know we need to be thinking hard about finding it. Modern medicine is in its adolescence—delighted and awed by the rush of new powers that have come upon it almost overnight, and yet not old enough to have developed a seasoned, mature sense of just how to use those dazzling, irresistible, frightening, almost mysterious abilities.

That maturity of judgment won't come easily, and it probably won't come soon. Maybe it will take a few hundred years to develop. And maybe we'll be around to see it when it does. Or, at least, our heads will.

References

Cowley, Malcom. The View from 80. Penguin Books, Inc., 1982.
Gorovitz, Samuel. Editorial. Los Angeles Times. 14 January 1983.
Rawls, John. A Theory of Justice. Harvard University Press, 1971.

3

Acute and Long-Term Care: Decisions and Decisionmakers

Robert L. Kane

The criticisms of our current system of long-term care (LTC) include perverse incentives, high cost, fragmentation, inappropriate utilization, poor quality, dehumanization, over-reliance on institutions, inadequate coverage of basic services, and lack of imagination (Scanlon, Difederico, and Stassen, 1979; Somers, 1982; Vladeck, 1980; Mendelsohn, 1974; U.S. Comptroller General, 1979; White House Conference on Aging, 1982; Meltzer, Farrow, and Richman, 1981). Long-term care (LTC) in the United States appears as a series of individual decisions with no master plan or overall direction. It is the result of uncontrolled growth toward an unclear end. Each decisionmaker, focused on the particular problem of the moment, has created an ad hoc solution.

Although definitions of LTC vary, there are some common themes. The emphasis is on efforts to improve a person's ability to function autonomously; that is, to minimize reliance on another person to perform at least basic activities appropriate to some minimum standard of living defined by societal norms. The term implies that the care is provided over a sustained period but may be intermittent; i.e., it is continual but not necessarily continuous. The nature of the care, and hence of the caregiver(s), is usually left unspecified. Medical care is

Views expressed in this paper are the authors own and are not necessarily shared by Rand or its research sponsors.

certainly an important component, but so are a variety of other services provided by professionals and others.

This admittedly vague definition is not meant to obscure but to underline the amorphous nature of long-term care and hence the difficulties involved in making decisions about it. The lack of conceptual clarity has been compensated by programmatic definitions. Because the focus of most health care programs has been acute care, especially hospital care, long-term care has often been defined by exemption. Where LTC policies have been specifically created, they have focused on programs, especially those dealing with institutions. The result is a vague construct bordered by sharp bureaucratic definitions, many of which are based on professional bias rather than solid evidence.

Persons confronting such a system are likely to look for ways to meet their needs and achieve their ends. Their decisions will be shaped by their perceptions of the situation. In the absence of clearly articulated policy, these perceptions will vary widely.

I. Big Decisions

Several basic issues pertaining to long-term care policy can be identified. This should facilitate the discussion of concrete decisions made by the various participants in the LTC process.

The Goals of Long-Term Care. Definitions of LTC emphasize function in some form. Although loose terms like "dependency" and "autonomy" are used, the intent is usually clear: to maintain or enhance the individual's ability to function. This then becomes one candidate goal for LTC. Juxtaposed against this goal is the concern with cost and its corollary: reducing demand for costly services. This conflict is reflected in several papers at this conference. A project may be successful in improving function, but at the cost of using more resources, especially if it increases the survival rate.

The concept of functioning suggests two major components: the intrinsic capacity of an individual and the support afforded by the environment. The same individual may be functional in one setting and not in another. This is an important distinction embodied in the World Health Organization classification of impairment, disability, and handicap (World Health Organization, 1980). It implies a hierarchy of efforts (usually through medical intervention) first addressing the individual's innate capabilities and then moving to provision of the most supportive environment (usually a social function).

The phrase "least restrictive environment" found in LTC policies suggests an important concern about breeding dependency. Counteracting this caution is the concept of risk aversion. Encouraging vulnerable persons to do things for themselves means an increased risk of adverse effects; most institutions (including the family) will act to minimize such risks. This tendency is exacerbated by costs; it is generally easier and cheaper to do a task for someone than to encourage the person to do it himself.

Whose Money Will We Spend? The pervasive LTC policy in the U.S. today is to encourage the use of private over public resources. The obvious implication is to require economic dependency before help is given. Such a policy reduces the probability of rehabilitation by depleting the very sources needed to sustain the person in an independent state. It is important to appreciate that this social policy is not ubiquitous. Most developed countries provide LTC resources as an entitlement rather than as welfare; services are allotted on the basis of need rather than means (Kane and Kane, 1976).

The emphasis on private support extends beyond monetary coverage to the direct provision of personal services. The bulk of LTC has been given and continues to be given by family members and other informal caregivers. Any effort to press that resource harder (e.g., by direct payments or tax credits) threatens to provide unnecessary reimbursement or push these caregivers beyond their capacity.

The other pattern of emphasis in a system favoring private over public support is the individual. Recent efforts have focused on developing a private insurance market for LTC, an interesting reversal of historical financing trends.

Focus on individual responsibility is also reflected in a continuing interest in various preventive strategies designed to delay either disease or its consequences. There is mixed enthusiasm for such an approach. Some have raised accusations of "blaming the victim." Our evidence for the efficacy of prevention in the elderly is fairly weak, however. Despite the intuitive attraction of primary prevention, activities aimed at preventing an impairment from becoming a disability—secondary prevention—are likely to be more effective. If prevention has been successful, its success is reflected in decreasing mortality rates among the old; the signs of corresponding reductions in morbidity are harder to see (Colvez and Blanchet, 1981).

What Is the Time Frame? A program designed to reduce institutionalization usually involves initial and intermittent assessment and provision of services. The question of cost-effectiveness of this type of investment depends on how far one looks into the future. If the intervention is effective, its effects usually take some time to appear. To the extent that these effects are future benefits, the period of observation must be sufficient to allow the benefits to become evident. The shorter the time perspective, the more one encourages programs that deal only with those at immediate risk of expensive care. Such a philosophy is obviously antithetical to a preventive approach.

Long-term care is chronic care. To be timely, associated activities, including decisions, must recognize the continuing nature of the process. Because change is the norm, decisions must be reevaluated regularly. Interventions cannot be one-shot affairs. As the client's condition changes or the circumstances of care alter (e.g., through death or fatigue of a primary caregiver), the situation must be reassessed. Such a commitment to regular evaluation can be an advantage as well as an expense. If decisions such as nursing-home admission were considered transitory rather than permanent, more active efforts might be made to move institutionalized persons back into the community; more attention might be given to other solutions such as various forms of respite care.

What Is Quality? In an area like long-term care, where the product is ill-defined and the consumer characterized by vulnerability, the question of quality is difficult. Most long-term care requires a low level of technology. Several different types of services are interchangeable. Such a situation argues against exacting professional standards despite their allure as safeguards against exploitation. The emphasis would be more properly placed on outcomes that reflect the goals of improved functioning, but we must then be able to define these outcomes and measure them in a way that allows for reasonable expectations of achievement rather than astute selection of cases. An inability to obtain such data tends to emphasize less relevant measures and hence to discredit quality-enhancing regulations. The buyer of services, unable to assess quality, may simply decide that the cheapest care is the best. Such a result would place a client identified originally on the basis of vulnerability in an even more precarious position.

Where Are We Starting From? As in any service program, assessments of effectiveness in LTC must recognize the concept of marginal benefit. In a system already heavily biased towards institutional care and still further saddled with excess demand for LTC beds, how do we assess the value of deflecting persons to other forms of care? Where there is a queue for a bed, moving someone out means filling the bed with someone else and also providing new services. The net result seems to be addition rather than substitution of services.

Control of utilization requires rationing the availability of expensive services. In such a context, providing community services legitimizes an already established social policy. We can justify reducing the supply of beds if we can show that clients can be cared for elsewhere, but unless we reduce that supply (or hold it constant in the face of rising demand), we will not likely save money.

Acute and long-term care are already firmly entrenched. Programs are in place for both, complete with funding approaches, eligibility criteria, and target populations. We do not have the luxury of starting afresh, nor do we necessarily want to. We have made important strides and learned useful lessons. But any new approach will be shaped by existing programs. In the area of LTC, we have a welfare model; in acute care for the elderly, an entitlement benefit unrelated to income. It is not clear why one form of care should require poverty as a precondition, while the other does not.

How Well Can We Target Services? Allocation decisions about LTC services based on some principle of equity or efficiency require us to determine the vulnerability of individuals and the probability of their benefiting from various interventions. The current level of our knowledge does not seem to support such an approach. We can describe a spectrum of situations ranging from independence of any reliance on formal care at one end to dependence on institutional care at the other. Several points of transition are evident from experience to date: becoming dependent in one or more functions (needs), using the formal care system (demands), using the hospital, entering a nursing home. However, we know surprisingly little about the factors that predict transition from one state to another.

Perhaps the most work has gone into assessing the risk factors for entering a nursing home. Table 1 summarizes the results of research on that topic. In interpreting the table, it is important to appreciate the difference between finding characteristics that distinguish between institutionalized and noninstitutionalized groups and being able to assign a predictive value to these characteristics. For example, a recent study of such risk factors identified five significant characteristics, but taken together, they accounted for less than 10 percent of the explanatory power for predicting admission (Branch and Jette, 1982).

Our knowledge of risk factors is better than our understanding of their mutability. Risk factors can be used in two ways: (1) to identify vulnerable groups, and (2) to identify characteristics which, if altered,

Table 1
Risk Factors for Nursing Home Admission: A Summary of Selected Research

Source	Sample	Risk Factors
National Center for Health Statistics (1981)	Survey of nursing home residents in 1977 (compared to those age 65+ living in the community)	Age, female, white, unmarried
Vicente, Wiley and Carrignton (1979)	Nine-year follow-up of residents age 55+ in Alameda County, CA.	Age, poverty, white, lack of social support
Palmore (1976)	Twenty-year follow-up of residents age 60+ in Piedmont, North Carolina area	Unmarried, white
Weissert et al. (1980a)	One-year study of day-care recipients and controls in six sites	Primary diagnostic conditions, impairment prognosis, hospital outpatient or other ambulatory use
Weissert et al. (1980b)	One-year study of home-maker recipients and controls in four sites; patients were hospitalized for at least three days during the two weeks prior to the study	Primary diagnostic conditions, ADL prognosis, bed disability prognosis, hospital outpatient or other ambulatory use
McCoy and Edwards (1981)	National sample of welfare recipients age 65+	Age, functional impairment, white, living alone or with non-relatives, lack of social supports
Branch and Jette (1982)	Six-year follow-up of community sample aged 65+ in Massachusetts	Age, living alone, use of ambulation aid, mental deterioration, use of assistance in instrumental ADLs

can reduce vulnerability. Our information about the latter is scanty indeed. We appreciate the role of physical limitations and acknowledge the importance of social support, but are a long way from being able to quantify the effects of intervention to change either.

Our inability to define such interventions with precision does not mean we are impotent to make any predictions. There is a growing body of experience to suggest that we can intervene successfully with clients at different levels of risk (Rubenstein, Rhee, and Kane, 1982; Skellie, Mobley, and Coan, 1982; Quinn et al., 1982), but our relative imprecision means that we are at risk of haggling with various providers over selection criteria. This becomes critical when we think of any type of prepaid capitation system, but is also evident in accusations of market skimming for nursing-home admission.

In the face of incomplete information about the relationship between process and outcome in LTC, we may be wise, as mentioned before, to focus on outcomes. The reward systems devised should emphasize what is achieved rather than what is done. Such an approach is alien to our prevalent practices, especially in acute care, where we have historically paid on the basis of inputs. But even here, times are changing. In LTC, there is a very real possibility of framing a payment system that is based on achievable outcomes and adjusting for case mix (Kane et al., 1982; 1983 a and b). The process of articulating and defining outcomes will of itself improve the quality of our thinking about LTC. Such an approach has the further advantage of facilitating comparisons across modes of care.

Acute and Long-Term Care: One System or Two? To date, our policies have reflected the notion that acute and long-term care are separable. Common parlance, bureaucratic regulations, and funding mechanisms reinforce that perception. In practice, the distinctions blur, however. Patients move back and forth. Some providers work in both fields. As we look at options for cost containment through capitation, the relationships between the two systems are clear. Actions in one sector will certainly produce effects in the other, while separation enhances the potential for exploiting one at the expense of the other. For example, prospective reimbursement of hospitals creates obvious incentives to discharge patients early, even at the risk of admitting them to nursing homes. Hospitals or those responsible for acute care costs only are certainly not motivated to bear the costs of comprehensive assessment intended to forestall nursing-home placement. (With the implementation of DRGs, this will be even less likely.) Conversely, the nursing home is likely to move patients into hospitals whenever their care needs exceed the norm. Opportunities for more efficient operation are greater when there is no strict separation of acute and long-term care.

One mechanism for merging both types of care is prepaid capitation. Several efforts have been launched to explore the feasibility of such an approach. The rationale for pooling funds lies in the greater flexibility gained and the ability to realize savings from more intensive work in subsequent reductions in care needs. Flexibility includes the use of more diverse (hopefully less expensive) caregivers. This may involve substitution (e.g., nurse practitioners for physicians) or more effective involvement of informal support through, for example, unpaid caregivers. The principle of realizing savings is based on a belief that evaluation and attention to problems at an early stage will reduce later complications.

Capitated programs that effectively merge acute and long-term care have been more conceptual than real to date. Perhaps the most promising are those developed as Social Health Maintenance Organizations (SHMOs), but even there the promise is mitigated by reality. The constraints of third-party coverage have forced compromises such that the programs resemble Medicare with options rather than remarkably new approaches. We can point to only scattered innovations, such as On Lok in San Francisco, as encouraging exceptions to the rule.

II. The Differing Perspectives of Decisionmakers

Various persons make decisions that affect the fate of LTC clients. These include the client himself, his family, physicians, institutional administrators, case managers, government regulators, and policymakers. Even in the best case, each acts to maximize the probability of certain ends. These goals are not always clear and are often in opposition to those of others in the system. In a situation of uncertainty, like that of LTC, certain pressures take precedence. Often clinical decisions are made under great stress.

The configuration of the system provides various incentives, which, both consciously and not, influence the direction of these decisions. Table 2 outlines some of the factors that shape decisions affecting LTC clients. Clearly far more categories of decisionmakers can be listed beyond those shown, but these should be sufficient to illustrate the dilemmas.

We have already acknowledged that decisions must be made on the basis of imperfect information. We submit that the rational decision maker uses what data are available to assess the alternatives and to weigh the consequences, but rational decisionmaking is easier in theory than in practice. In most instances, a few factors assume paramount importance (Janis and Mann, 1977). In such cases, the incentives offered by the system of care, including the funding and remuneration structure, are likely to be critical elements.

The client and his family must decide whether to enter the care

Table 2
Differing Perspectives on Long-Term Care

Personnel	Role	Issues
Client and Family	User Payor	Demands Prognosis Incentives Anxiety Stress on Others Obligation Dignity

Physician	Provider
	Patient Advocate
		Patient needs and demands
		Probability of treatment's
		    benefit
		Economic reward (coverage)
		Time costs
		Pressure from family and
		    others
		Available resources, ease of
		    access

Hospital (or nursing home) administrator	Manager	Suitability of resource Demand for resource Payment Public Pressure Regulations
Case Manager	Client advocate Societal agent Risk sharer	Needs vs. demands Social support Prognosis Available care resources Available financial resources Assuming service provision

Policymaker	Program creator	Which group will benefit
		    most?
		Efficacy
		Cost
		What are important
		    outcomes?
		Political pressures
		Time frame

system. The seeking of formal aid represents a response to anxiety and a belief that assistance is necessary. The barriers to seeking service may be financial. Eligibility for one type of care over another will influence preferences. For example, the current Medicaid program offers an incentive to use nursing homes in cases of medical indigency because the costs are more predictable than home care, which requires exhausting personal resources anew each month.

Because Medicaid requires the individual to spend his resources before assistance is given, financial need can be more readily established prospectively for a service with a more easily estimated cost (e.g., a month in a nursing home) than for a service provided piecemeal (e.g., home care). Moreover the basis for calculating the fiscal responsibility for a spouse remaining at home may vary with the patient's disposition (U.S. Comptroller General, 1979).

In the United States at least, the decision to enter a nursing home is often a last resort after the stress on the family has produced exhaustion. The decision may be reached in an atmosphere of crisis when the threshhold of tolerance is passed. Such a setting produces mixed emotions of guilt and anxiety. These can contribute to suggestibility and acceptance of solutions that appeal to the outside decision maker as broker for the system and the client.

In many instances, clients are not key participants in decisions about their fate. Sometimes they are cognitively incompetent, but more often ignored as other actors take over. Their preferences may not be considered at all; large choices among alternative types of care or smaller choices about location, attributes, and amenities may not be offered. Too often the decision process does not explore possibilities, probabilities, and implications. Clients are not invited to express priorities about aspects of care or consequences they wish to maximize.

Physicians face conflicting roles in the decision paradigm. They are providers of some services and agents for others. They are the advocate of their patients but also the agents of society. The synthesis of these conflicts is frequently unsatisfactory. On the one hand, physicians must act as gatekeepers; they must certify the client's need for services—a means of rationing—but also seek the best package of services for their patient. If the regulations specify eligibility requirements, they may alter their description to meet them if it serves the interests of their patient.

The physician's power to label is critical. The implications of a diagnosis can dramatically alter a patient's future. Mild forgetfulness is very different from early senility. The physician should consider the probabilities of benefit and risk from any intervention. Such calculations require knowledge about prognosis and are susceptible to value judgments about the patient and his condition. These decisions can be moral agonies for both physicians and families. When should life support be discontinued? How far does one go in looking for an etiology when the diagnostic procedures involve risk and discomfort?

Few physicians have special training in the care of elderly patients; many may reasonably be expected to harbor common bias. There is an inherent advantage in making a dire prognosis because the penalties for error are less severe; at worst the physician is an accurate prognosticator and at best a potent therapist (Siegler, 1975). Concerns about malpractice enhance this risk aversion. In areas of uncertainty, one is likely to choose the more conservative course. Physicians are also susceptible to other pressures. In many cases, they stand to benefit from the decision or represent an institution with a vested interest. Reimbursement policies reward doing more. In the worst cases, elderly patients are exposed to high technology because technology is rewarded over compassion and concern. Monitoring devices and artificial life support systems have changed the American way of death to the point where we have created a new technology of dying in the hospice.

There are few direct rewards for careful consideration. Often this type of deliberation and the time spent in gathering both objective information and the preferences of various parties involved is not reimbursable. The easiest decision may thus appear the most attractive. If the pressures for some action are acute, the tendency toward such a course is exacerbated.

In general, the central role of physicians in the decisionmaking process is not reflected in the time spent with older patients (Keeler et al., 1982). When faced with questions of LTC, they are likely to be passive, yielding the ultimate decision to more active parties (Kane et al., 1979).

Institutional administrators act in accord with those factors that stand to benefit the institution. Although not devoid of compassion, administrators have an obligation to assess the impact of the decision on the institution. Often they must outweigh competing demands for the resource. If occupancy is low, they must balance the cost of an unused resource against the likelihood of finding a more suitable candidate. They will respond to incentives that assure adequate payment. In circumstances where payment is tied to some level of care, there is a natural incentive to seek those at the margin of the distribution, those clients in each group who will require the least care. Other considerations are the suitability of the resource to provide necessary services. Institutions, like most of the decisionmakers noted here, are averse to risk. This risk aversion may be reinforced by regulations, which put the institutions in jeopardy for taking on difficult cases.

Administrators must also reckon with the consequences of an action to deny care. They must find socially acceptable bases for such decisions. Faced with pressures to discharge a patient, they may readily encourage quick solutions regardless of later consequences. Because responsibility generally ends when the patient leaves, most distant considerations are of much less importance.

Case managers are relatively new on the scene. They may operate from a variety of different bases, each with its own set of incentives. The basic notion of the case manager is to provide a nonpartisan decisionmaker who can assess the situation on its merits. But the independence of the case manager is not always clear. In general, the authority carries with it some degree of risk-sharing. The case manager may control resources or access to them. Budgetary concerns may be very evident. Thus, many of the pressures faced by other decisionmakers are shared. In addition, the case manager may be even more sensitive to the questions of time than others because of a continuing responsibility for the client's course.

Ideally, the case manager should belong to neither the social nor the medical camp but should serve as a skilled neutral figure in combining the services of both to the client's greatest advantage. In practice, such disinterest is impractical. Most case managers come from a background of nursing or social work. Blending of services is a difficult task at best. In the present environment of multiple programs with differing eligibility criteria, the question often becomes less "What does the client need?" than "What can he get?"

Although the history of case management is short, there is growing enthusiasm for this role. For generous programs, it represents a means to control access and utilization, at least based on state-of-the-art assessment. For meager programs, it offers a client advocate who can maximize whatever assistance is available. Creatively done, case management involves blending of complementary care. Medical and social services are used to assure that the remediable is remediated and the residuum is managed in an environment most conducive to maximum functions. Professional services are coupled with informal care to benefit the client and preserve the continuing nature of care. In practice the result is usually short of the ideal, but at least there is an opportunity for a second consideration, a check in the system to see if something was overlooked and, perhaps most important, a commitment to reassess the situation at a later date.

Policymakers must be concerned with both large and small issues. Their task is possibly more difficult in a country like the United States. Our tradition of entrepreneurship and associated litigiousness have created a combative environment; any effort to regulate may easily set off a counterploy. They must thus clearly fix on their primary intent and anticipate how the strategic response to this proposed policy may move the target toward that goal. Such a combination of wisdom and gamesmanship would be hard to find in the protected reserve of theoretical academe. It is even less likely to emerge when the policies must be forged in an environment of politics and interest groups and continual concern about cost.

Policymakers must be clear about which group is intended to benefit primarily from the program and the extent to which others will be adversely affected, directly or not. A program of new or increased services offers advantages to some recipients and providers but at higher costs, which deprive some other sector. An effort to tighten controls may provide protection but provoke protest and may result in cosmetic changes only.

Political pressures can also become time pressures. Programs are constrained by a political clock that measures time in two-year intervals. Demands for results or at least the appearance of doing something to deal with a problem can prompt action that offers the appearance of activity and the hope of a fast benefit; the longer-term consequences are more likely to be heavily discounted, especially when they are uncertain and subject to influence by factors yet unknown.

There is constant danger of mis-specification of the problem. The solution proposed may not address the right issue. For example, enthusiasm for hospice care has frequently been based on its potential to save money. Some analysts point to the large amount of money spent on an individual in the last year of life to argue that changing patterns of terminal care will save money. However, in truth, most of the costs will already have been borne before the final stage of hospice care is initiated.

Although we profess our need for proof of efficacy, we rarely have such information. We usually rely on less exact evidence, appreciating that any social program will be implemented differently in different settings. The policymaker is no less risk averse than the other decisionmakers discussed. Modest success is generally accepted to avoid grand failure. Even for those more inclined to take large risks, the process tends to reduce risk of dramatic intervention through the inevitable need for compromise.

43

III. An Ideal Model

What would happen if we gave full rein to a rational decision maker designed to distribute services where they could do the most good? The underlying sequential decision tree prototype applied to LTC is shown in Figure 1. The process requires a good deal of information not currently available. Risk groups must be characterized on the basis of easily identified variables—both demographic and clinical. For each group, the probabilities of benefiting from a variety of interventions would be derived from empirical data. (The example is simplified to two alternatives). The outcomes are expressed in terms of definable benefits and costs.

This list of components is helpful to appreciate the gap between what is needed and what we have. Although we are by no means totally bereft of pertinent information, we have a long way to go. Progress has been made in developing measures to assess outcomes (Kane and Kane, 1981). As noted earlier, work is under way to identify risk factors. The growing body of experience with demonstration projects in various forms of LTC provides a basis for beginning to estimate the effects of interventions.

Even if we had an ideal model in hand, important questions remain. Issues of time frame must be clarified, especially the extent to which we value immediate benefits over future ones. There is probably no consistent answer to this question. Some people will opt to maximize near-term results; others prefer more distant goals (McNeil, Weichselbaum, and Pauker, 1978). There is even less clarity about the values we place on the variety of outcomes LTC might produce—from fundamental questions about the quality of life and the closely related issues of euthanasia to more abstract issues about the relative desirability of gains in one domain over another. For example, would one choose improved mobility at the cost of more pain or the risk of a fall? Work in this area is just beginning (Kane and Kane, 1982; Tversky and Kahneman, 1981), but the very process of articulating the issues is an important first step.

There is an alternative to the resource allocation approach. Society can begin with a different directive. We can aim to increase the care available to all persons and mobilize resources toward that end in a belief that more care is better, at least for some time to come, and a confidence that care purchased will be delivered. Such a policy places heavy responsibility on the government to make resources available and implies a conviction that such social services take precedence over other governmental responsibilities. The strategy is based on a trust in providers that they will behave responsibly (but

Figure 1
Decision Tree for Placement of LTC Patients

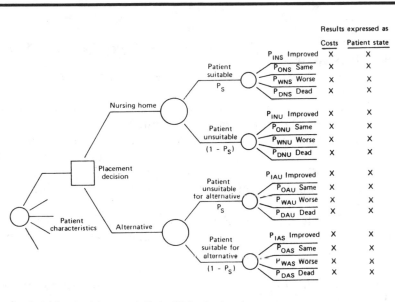

P_S = Probability of pt being more suitable for NH than for alternative
P_{IXY} = Probability of patient improving given a placement X and suitability Y (of placement)
P_{OXY} = Probability of patient staying the same given a placement X and suitability Y (of placement)
P_{WXY} = Probability of patient getting worse given a placement X and suitability Y (of placement)
P_{DXY} = Probability of patient dying given a placement X and suitability Y (of placement)

Source: Kane and Kane, 1980. Reprinted by permission of *The Gerontologist*.

not necessarily altruistically) to attend to the interests of their clients.

IV. Conclusions

1. Our society must clarify its position on long-term care of dependent persons.
2. The various decisionmakers need better information. At the very simplest level, clients need to know more about the options available to them. Clinicians and case managers need information with which to estimate the effects of interventions.
3. Decisions about the fate of individuals should not be made in a crisis mode.
4. Better information is needed on what different segments of society value with regard to aspects of long-term care, including outcomes. We may not like what we learn.
5. Research on the efficacy of clinical and social therapies is necessary if we are ever to choose rationally between alternative approaches. Such research must carefully consider specific subgroups at special risk.
6. People respond to incentives. In LTC, these incentives should direct care providers to achieving defined outcomes.
7. LTC should not be separated from acute care. Such a separation reduces flexibility, creates artificial barriers, and reinforces perverse incentives.

References

Branch, L.G. and Jette, A.M. A prospective study of long-term care institutionalization among the aged. American Journal of Public Health, 72:1373-1379, 1982.

Colvez, A. and Blanchet, M., Disability trends in the United States population 1966-1976: Analysis of reported causes. American Journal of Public Health, 71:464-471, 1981.

Janis, I. and Mann, L., Decision-Making: A Psychological Analysis of Conflice, Chocie and Commitment. New York: The Free Press, 1977.

Kane, R.A. and Kane, R.L., Assessing the Elderly: A Practical Guide to Measurement. Lexington, MA.: D.C. Health, 1981.

Kane, R.A., Kane, R.L., Kleffel, D., Brook, R.H., Eby, C., Goldbert, G.A., Rubenstein, L.Z., and VanRyzin, J., The PSRO and the Nursing Home, Vol. I. An Assessment of PSRO Long-Term Care Review. (R-2459/1-HCFA) Santa Monica, CA.: The Rand Corporation, 1979.

Kane, R.L. and Kane, R.A., Long-Term Care in Six Countries: Implications for the United States (80-1207). Fogarty International Center, NIH, Washington, D.C.: Government Printing Office, 1976.

Kane, R.L. and Kane, R.A., Alternatives to institutional care of the elderly: Beyond the dichotomy. The Gerontologist, 20:249-259, 1980

Kane, R.I. and Kane, R.A. (eds.), Values and Long-Term Care. Lexington, MA.: D.C. Health, 1982

Kane, R.L., Riegler, S., Bell, R., Potter, R., and Koshland, G., Predicting the Course of Nursing-Home Patients: A Progress Report. (N-1786 NCHSR) Santa Monica, CA.: The Rand Corporation, 1982.

Kane, R.L., Bell, R., Riegler, S., Wilson, A., and Keeler, E., Predicting the outcomes of nursing-home patients. The Gerontologist, 23:200-206, 1983a.

Kane, R.L., Bell, R., Riegler, S., Wilson, A., and Kane, R.A., Assessing the outcomes of nursing-home patients. Journal of Gerontology, 38:385-393, 1983b.

Keeler, E.B., Solomon, D.H., Beck, J.C., Mendenhall, R.C., and Kane, R.L., Effect of patient age on duration of medical encounters with physicians. Medical Care, 20:1101-1108, 1982.

McCoy, J.L. and Edwards, B.E., Contextual and socio-demographic antecedents of institutionalization among aged welfare recipients. Medical Care, 19:907-921, 1981.

McNeil, B.J., Weichselbaum, R., and Pauker, S.G., Fallacy of the five-year survival rate in lung cancer. New England Journal of Medicine, 299:1397-1401, 1978.

Meltzer, J., Farrow, F., and Richman, H., Policy Options in Long-Term Care. Chicago: University of Chicago Press, 1981.

Mendelsohn, M.A., Tender Loving Greed. New York: Alfred A. Knopf, 1974.

Palmore, E., Total chance of institutionalization among the aged. The Gerontologist, 16:504-507, 1976.

Quinn, J., Segal, J., Raisz, H., and Johnson, C., (eds.), Coordinating Community Services for the Elderly. New York: Springer, 1982.

Rubenstein, L.Z., Rhee, L., and Kane, R.L., The role of geriatric assessment units in caring for the elderly: An analytic review. Journal of Gerontology, 37:513-521, 1982.

Scanlon, W., Difederico, E., and Stassen, M., Long-Term Care: Current

Experience and a Framework for Analysis. Washington, D.C.: The Urban Institute, 1979.

Siegler, M.C., Pascal's wager and the hanging of crepe. New England Journal of Medicine, 293:853-857, 1975.

Skellie, F.A., Mobley, G.M., and Coan, R.E., Cost-effectiveness of community bazed long-term care: Current findings of Georgia's alternative health services project. American Journal of Public Health, 72:353-358, 1982.

Somers, A.R., Long-term care for the elderly and disabled: A new health priority. New England Journal of Medicine, 307:221-226, 1982.

Tversky, A. and Kahneman, D., The framing of decisions and the psychology of choice. Science, 211:453-458, 1981.

U.S. Comptroller General, Engering a Nursing HomeCostly Implications for Medicaid and the Elderly (PAD 80-12) Washington, D.C.: General Accounting Office, 1979.

U.S. Department of Health and Human Services, Public Health Service, National Center for Health Statistics, Characteristics of Nursing Home Residents, Health Status and Care Received: National Nursing Home Survey, United States, May-December 1977 (PHS 81-1712). Vital and Health Statistics, Series 13, Hyattsville, MD.: NCHS, 1981.

Vicente, L., Wiley, J.A., and Carrington, R.A., The risk of institutionali zation before death. The Gerontologist, 19:361-366, 1979.

Vladeck, B.C., Unloving Care: The Nursing Home Tragedy. New York: Basic Books, 1980.

Weissert, W., Wan, T.T.H., Livieratos, B., and Katz, S., Effects and costs of day-care services for the chronically ill: A Ramdomized Experiment. Medical Care, 18:567-583, 1980a.

Weissert, W.G., Wan, T.T.H., Livieratos, B., and Pellegrino, J., Cost effectiveness of homemaker services for the chronically ill. Inquiry, 17:230-243, 1980b.

White House Conference on Aging, Final Report of the 1981 White House Conference on Aging. Washington, D.C.: U.S. Department of Health and Human Services, 1982.

4

Health Implications of
Aging in America

Karen Davis

In the next 50 years the U.S. population over age 65 will increase markedly. Especially rapid increases in the numbers of the very old (over 85 years of age) are predicted. This changing demographic composition of the U.S. population has profound implications for the economic, social, and cultural character of the nation and is particularly important for the health sector. The elderly population on the whole is less healthy than younger members of society. The aged use more health services and have higher health expenditures. An increase in the number of people over the age of 65 and especially a major increase in the very old age groups means that more resources will be required to provide care for the aged.

Government budget expenditures will be greatly affected by this increase in the aged population. The federal government finances hospital, physician, and other acute care services for the elderly under the Medicare program. State and federal governments finance institutional long-term care services for low income elderly under Medicaid. At the time of this writing, these programs represent 9 percent of the federal budget. As the elderly population grows in size, expenditures on their health care are expected to grow dramatically if present policies continue. Further, it is widely recognized that existing programs fall far short of meeting all of the current health care needs of the elderly, especially for those who require assistance to enable them to live at home.

It is important, therefore, to look ahead to the changes that will occur in the next 20 to 50 years and design long-range policies that will assure the aged a right to live out their years in dignity and comfort, at an affordable cost to society.

IMPACT OF TECHNOLOGY

I. Computer-Assisted Policy Analysis and Simulation (CAPAS)

This paper will present results from a Computer Assisted Policy Analysis and Simulation (CAPAS) model developed at the Johns Hopkins School of Hygiene and Public Health with support from the World Health Organization, European Regional Office. This model provides a graphic display of the implications for the health sector of projected demographic trends in the elderly population, using an Apple II microcomputer. Projection models forecast the impact of the aging of the population on the health system. Policy analyses and simulations demonstrate the cost and impact of alternative strategies for caring for the elderly over time.

The computer generates population projections by age and sex for the United States under alternative mortality rate assumptions and analyzes the impact of the projected growth of the elderly population on health status, utilization of health services, and health expenditures. The model generates projections to the year 2000 for a comprehensive range of factors relating to health and aging, and to the year 2030 for a more limited array.

The results presented here are limited to those for the United States, although similar analyses have been performed for Canada and several Canadian provinces. Work is under way to extend the model to European countries to simulate policy alternatives addressing health needs of the elderly for interested European governments.

The U.S. data base for the CAPAS model is drawn from over 200 different sources, including the various surveys conducted by the National Center for Health Statistics, the Health Care Financing Administration, and the Bureau of the Census. The data base contains current information on demographic characteristics of the population, socioeconomic status, economy, labor force participation, social security, housing, social services, health status, health resources and service utilization, long-term care needs and utilization, and health expenditures.

Projections for future years are based on official government estimates of the prospective population by age, sex, and race cohort. The model incorporates the U.S. Bureau of the Census assumption of 400,000 immigrants annually, and a fertility rate of 2.1 children per woman ages 14-49. Mortality rates are based on projections by actuaries of the Social Security Administration by age, sex, race, and cause of death. These estimates predict a 36-percent decline in the age-adjusted death rate for the U.S. between 1978 and 2055. However, the CAPAS model permits alternative mortality rate assumptions for the

U.S. that assume a decline in overall mortality twice that of the official forecast, a decline one-half the rate of the official forecast, and no change in mortality rate. Unless otherwise noted, all results presented in this paper are based on the official Social Security Administration mortality rate estimates.

Projections of the impact of aging on the health system incorporate several methodologies. In those areas for which extensive studies have already been conducted, results are incorporated in the model. For example, projections of future physician supply are those of the Graduate Medical Education National Advisory Committee (GME-NAC; 1980).

Projections of health expenditures are based on econometric estimates of health expenditures by age group (65 and over, 19-64, and under 19) by type of service (e.g., hospital, physician, nursing home) for the historical period from 1965 to 1978. Log linear regressions of per capita health expenditures yield annual growth rates in constant dollars experienced over this period. These constant dollar annual growth rates are then applied to yield forecasts of per capita health expenditures by age group and type of health service.

Mortality rates by cause of death are likewise based on estimates by actuaries of the Social Security Administration (1982). For the most part these estimates suggest that trends of increase and decline in mortality rates by age and sex in the past 15 years will continue, but at a more moderate rate. The actuaries assume little further decline in mortality from infectious diseases, continued decline in mortality from degenerative diseases, and an increase in deaths from violent causes, principally among young adults.

Forecasts of morbidity levels in the U.S. population are based on the assumption that prevalence rates by age and sex cohort will stay constant over time. This is a controversial assumption. Kramer (1980) and Gruenberg (1977), for example, argue that the seriously disabled or chronically ill are now living longer due to the success of technical innovations, and that the prevalence rate of disabling and chronic conditions will therefore increase over time, by prolonging their average duration (see also Fries, 1980). Manton (1982), on the other hand, argues that there is no evidence that the average health status of the aged has declined in recent years, despite a very dramatic decline in mortality rates for the aged. In the absence of convincing evidence that would settle this controversy, the prevalence of disability or functional limitation per person of a given age-sex cohort is assumed to be constant over time. Thus, the total prevalence of disabling conditions in future populations is determined solely by the growth of population cohorts. These assumptions can be readily modified in the CAPAS model if evidence is obtained of superior predictive assumptions for some or all conditions.

Given the rudimentary state of development of projection methodologies, projections, especially those looking as much as 50 years into the future, must be viewed cautiously. Technological advances could markedly alter these forecasts. Fertility rates could continue to decline markedly or increase dramatically, affecting the size of the work force supporting the aged population. Increased immigration could take up the slack created by a declining younger native population.

Most importantly, these projections assume that current policies will continue unchanged. One of the major purposes of the CAPAS model, however, is to simulate how alternative policies could affect the future course of the health system. If alternative policies are adopted, current projections would not hold. Thus, postponement of retirement, redefinition of "old age" by physical condition rather than chronological age, promoting healthier lifestyles, or shifting resources toward noninstitutional care could all change the future course set forth here.

The CAP package permits policy analyses and simulations of alternative strategies affecting future trends. The versatility of the model and its graphic displays encourage the broad involvement of many individuals and groups in policy analysis and planning. For example, government officials can see how changing the financial structure for health programs will affect budgets over future periods. Mutual tradeoffs between prevention, biomedical research, health services, or other services can be explored. Epidemiologists can examine health trends under alternative mortality rate or morbidity assumptions. Health planners can estimate the need for physicans, or for hospital or nursing home beds, given demographic changes in the population.

II. Demography

In 1900, 4 percent of the U.S. population was age 65 or over. By 1980 this proportion had reached 11 percent, or 26 million people. By the year 2000, the aged population will reach 33 million people, or 12 percent of the U.S. population. As the post-World War II baby boom cohort reaches retirement, the aged population is expected to grow to 59 million or 19 percent of the population in 2030. (Unless otherwise cited, all figures quoted in this paper are generated from the CAPAS presentation.)

Exhibit 1
Total Population (In Millions) By Age Group And Sex

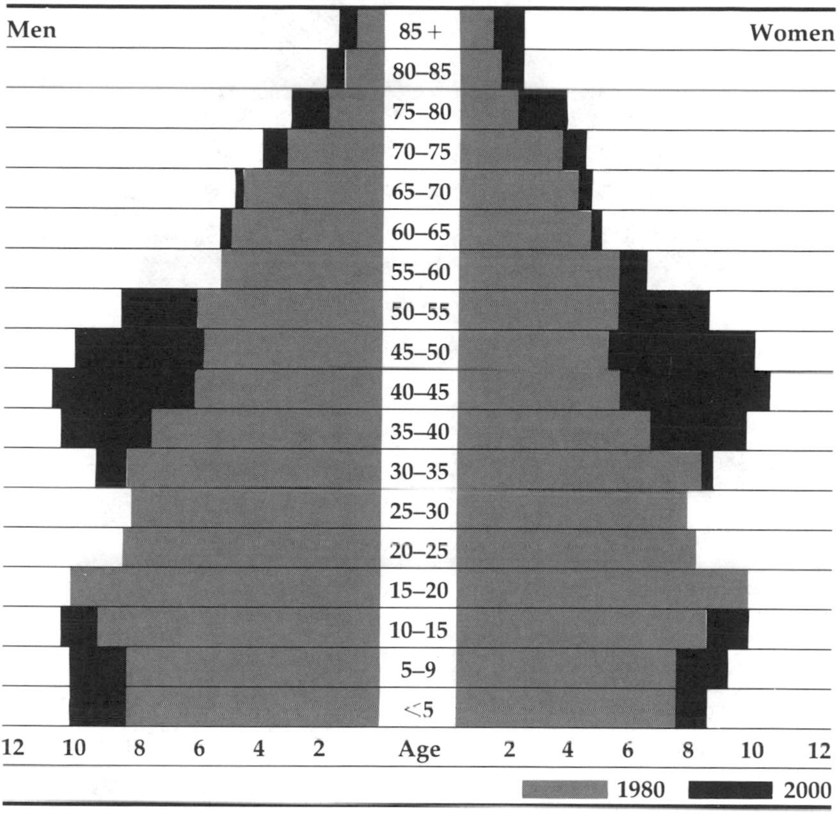

Men						Age Group						Women

Age groups (center column, top to bottom): 85+, 80–85, 75–80, 70–75, 65–70, 60–65, 55–60, 50–55, 45–50, 40–45, 35–40, 30–35, 25–30, 20–25, 15–20, 10–15, 5–9, <5

Men axis: 12 10 8 6 4 2   Age   2 4 6 8 10 12 : Women axis

1980 ■ 2000

Assuming fertility rates that provide for a constant population replacement, the younger population will not grow at a similar rate. In fact by the year 2000 the number of persons in their 20s will be less than in 1980. The age pyramid, as the traditional chart in Figures 1 and 2 show will become increasingly rectangular over time as the "baby boom bulge" in population ages. As shown in Figure 1, by 2000 the 35 to 55 population shows great gains over 1980. But by 2030, as shown in Figure 2, the major increases are in the population ages 65 and over.

Given estimated mortality trends, growth in the number of aged women will be especially marked. They will increase by 28 percent between 1980 and 2000, compared with 26 percent for men aged 65

Exhibit 2
Total Population (In Millions) By Age Group And Sex

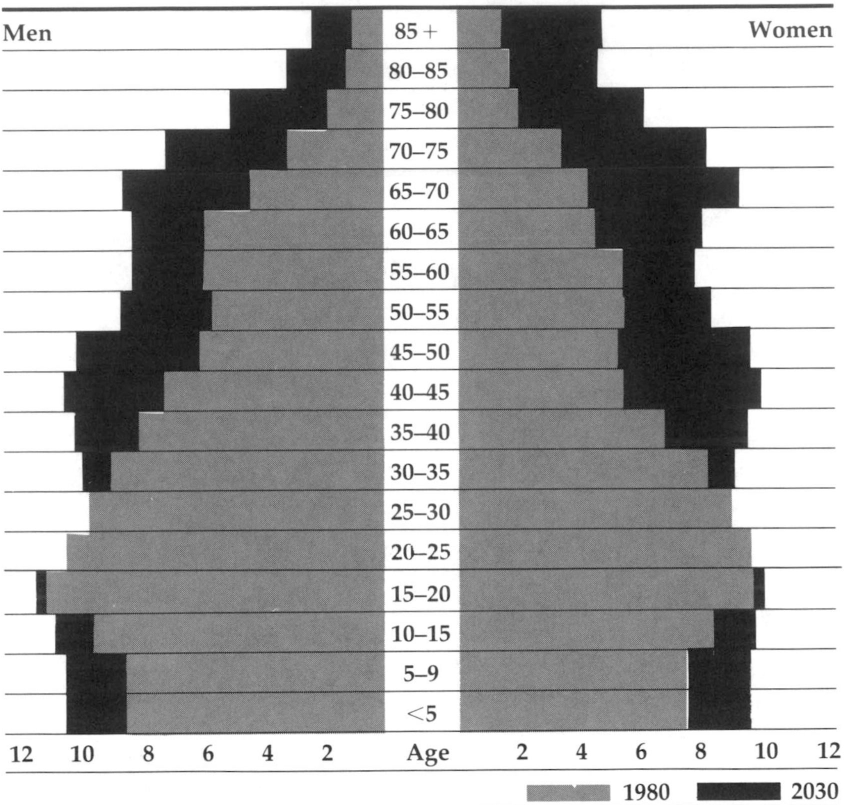

Men							Women

Population pyramid with age groups from <5 to 85+. Horizontal axis labeled "Age" with values 12, 10, 8, 6, 4, 2 on the Men side and 2, 4, 6, 8, 10, 12 on the Women side. Legend: 1980, 2030.

and older. Among those over age 85, women will increase by 81 percent between 1980 and 2000 and by 206 percent between 1980 and 2030, compared with 71 percent and 200 percent for men over the same periods.

Since people living alone or without a spouse are at greater risk of needing help and long-term care assistance, this change in demographic composition of the population has important implications for the health sector. The increase in the number of very old women by 2000 suggests that there will be many more women widowed and living alone. As shown in Figure 3, 77 percent of all men age 65 and over are married, while 60 percent of older women are widowed or single. (Among women 75 and older, this figure is 76 percent.) By

Exhibit 3
Demography, Marital Status, By Age and Sex, 1980

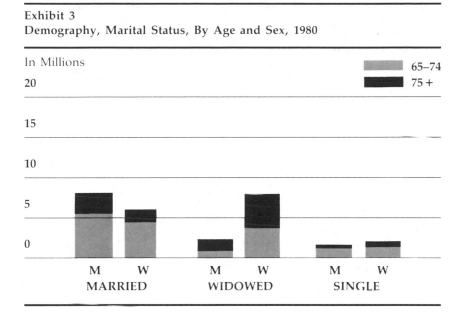

2000, 6.4 million women 75 and older will be widowed or single, up 56 percent over 1980; see Figure 4.

The dramatic growth in the overall size of the elderly population, of course, is testimony to the remarkable progress that has been made and seems likely to continue in extending life expectancy. In 1960, a woman reaching age 65 could expect to live to age 81. In 1980, she could expect to live until age 83, and by 2000 she can expect to live to age 86. Life expectancy for men upon reaching age 65 has increased from 78 years in 1960 to 79 years in 1980 and is expected to increase to 81 years in 2000.

As the number of old people and their survival rate from heart and cerebrovascular disease increases, so will the number of people with chronic conditions or limited functional ability. The growth in the aged population suggests that the number of arthritic people living outside of institutions will increase from 11 million in 1979 to 14 million in 2000, those with hypertension from 10 million to 13 million, and those with hearing impairments from 7 million to 9 million.

This means that more people will need assistance in functioning at home. For example, the number of aged people at home confined to bed is expected to increase from 458,000 in 1977 to 658,000 in 2000 (Figure 5). Those needing help getting around within their own home will increase from 1.9 million to 2.7 million, while those needing help

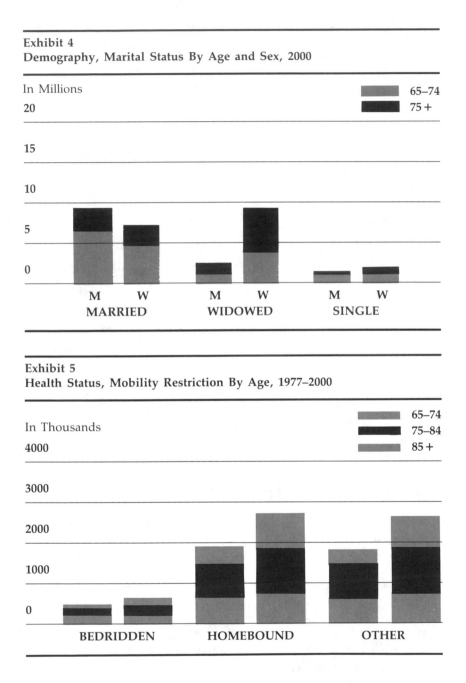

Exhibit 4
Demography, Marital Status By Age and Sex, 2000

In Millions

65–74
75 +

20

15

10

5

0

| M | W | M | W | M | W |
| MARRIED | | WIDOWED | | SINGLE | |

Exhibit 5
Health Status, Mobility Restriction By Age, 1977–2000

65–74
75–84
85 +

In Thousands

4000

3000

2000

1000

0

BEDRIDDEN   HOMEBOUND   OTHER

Exhibit 6
Health Utilization, Physician Visits, 1977–2000

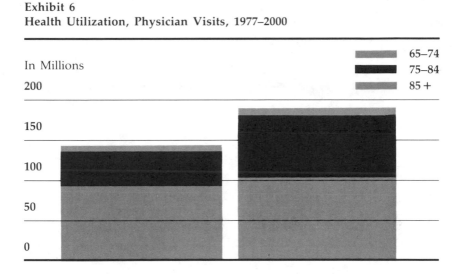

In Millions

200

150

100

50

0

▬	65–74
▬	75–84
▬	85 +

getting around in their own neighborhoods will increase from 1.9 million to 2.6 million. Those so severely limited as to need assistance carrying out some of the common activities of daily living also will increase substantially in the future. For example, those requiring assistance with bathing will increase from 0.85 million to 1.21 million between 1977 and 2000.

III. Health Services Utilization

In light of the serious health problems faced by many aged persons, heavy utilization of a range of health care services is not surprising. The elderly average 30 percent greater use of physician services than adults and about 40 percent more hospital days annually.

Growth in the size of the elderly population will bring with it greater demands on the health care system. It is estimated that total visits to physicians by all elderly will increase from 145 million in 1977 to 186 million in 2000 (Figure 6). Given the complexity of the health problems of the aged, demands for specialty care should grow at an even greater rate.

If past patterns continue, major increases can be expected in use of hospitals by the aged. Over the period from 1976 to 1980, hospital discharges per elderly person increased at an annual rate of 3.6 percent. For those over age 85, hospital discharges per capita in-

57

Exhibit 7
Health Utilization, Hospital Patient Days By Age, 1980–2000

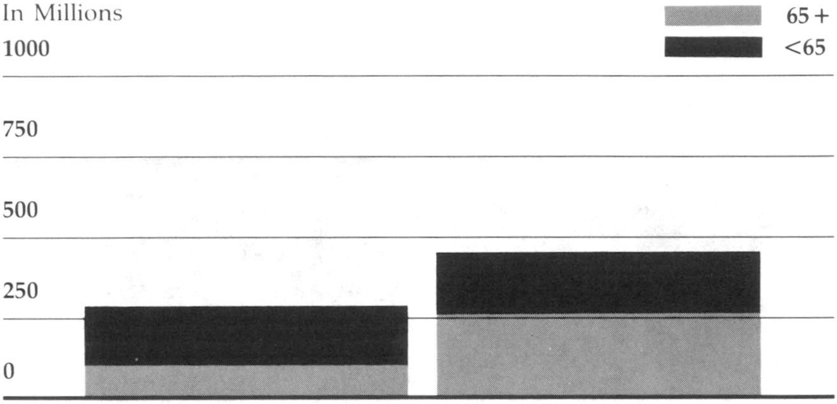

In Millions   ▨ 65+
1000   ■ <65

750

500

250

0

creased by 4.1 percent annually. Total hospital patient days of persons age 65 and over increased from 60 million in 1965, before the introduction of Medicare, to 105 million in 1980 and could reach 273 million days in 2000, almost tripling use of hospital care by the aged in a 20 year period (Figure 7). Total use of hospital services by those under age 65 has not increased in the last 15 years, by contrast.

Medicare has enabled vulnerable subgroups of the elderly population to receive hospital care (Davis, 1982). Studies have demonstrated that the initial impact on hospital use was greatest for individuals living alone, with low incomes, minorities, and residents of the South and nonmetropolitan areas (Lowenstein, 1971). Certain types of surgical procedures also increased dramatically with the introduction of the program. Cataract operations doubled between 1965 and 1975, and arthroplasty nearly tripled, leading some analysts to conclude that the quality of life for the aged improved as a result of Medicare.

Whatever the gains in health brought about by Medicare, and whatever the trends in hospitalization to the year 2000, a major expansion in hospital utilization will occur (simply because of the larger share of the elderly population), with important implications for staffing requirements, hospital capacity, and costs. Nursing homes will also experience an increase in the number of patients if current trends and policies continue. The number of aged in nursing homes should increase from 1.2 million in 1977 to 1.8 million by 2000.

These projections, based on historical experience, are not immuta-

58

ble. Greater efforts can be made to care for the aged at home or on an ambulatory basis, rather than relying as heavily on inpatient hospital and nursing home care as in the past. Technological advances to prevent or better control chronic conditions may markedly reduce reliance on high cost institutional care. But if no steps are taken, serious strains on the health care system could result.

IV. Health Expenditures

The aging of the U.S. population will further feed rising expenditures in the health sector. As shown in Figure 8, health expenditures as a percent of the Gross National Product have increased from 5.3 percent in 1960 to 9.8 percent in 1981. Econometric forecasts predict that this will increase further to almost 15 percent by 2000.

As suggested by the greater health care utilization of the aged, health expenditures per capita for the aged will exceed those for other age groups. Figure 9 indicates that in 1978 the average health expenditure per elderly person was $2,026 compared with $286 for children. By 2000 health expenditures per capita for the aged will reach $6,024 (in constant 1980 dollars) while expenditures for children will reach $627.

When the growth in the number of old people is included, total health expenditures on the aged are expected to increase from about $50 billion in 1978 to almost $200 billion in 2000, in constant 1980 dollars. Extended life expectancy and improved health of the elderly will bring with it a cost—one that is clearly affordable to a growing and prosperous society. But it does represent a challenge to develop innovative approaches to providing quality health care more economically.

A large portion of the increased health expenditures for the elderly will be borne by federal, state, and local governments. As shown in Figure 10, publicly financed expenditures for the aged will increase from $1,165 per person in 1978 to $3,464 per person in 2000. This represents an increase from approximately $29 billion in 1978 to $114 billion in 2000 (in constant 1980 dollars).

Medicare expenditures will increase from $893 per aged person in 1978 to $2,655 per aged person in 2000, or a total increase from $22 billion in 1978 to $88 billion in 2000. Medicaid expenditures per aged person will increase from $271 in 1978 to $806 in 2000, or an increase from $7 billion to $27 billion (see Figure 11). Total program expenditures will be even higher, since they include expenditures for the disabled and nonelderly poor.

Exhibit 8
GNP And Health Expenditures, 1960–2000

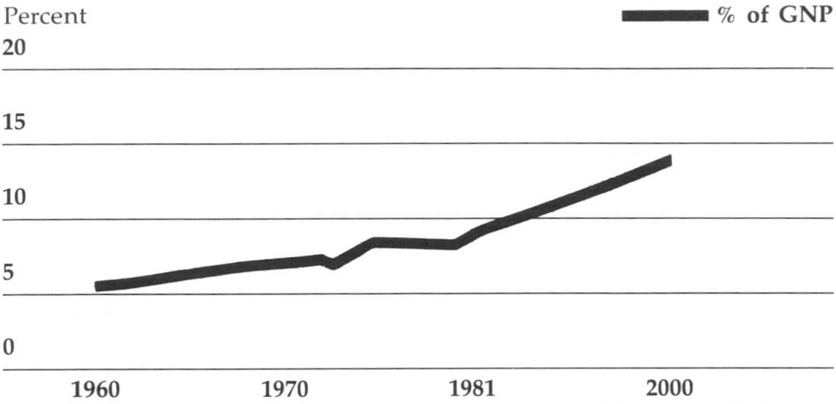

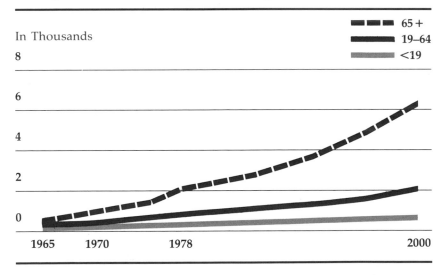

Percent   ▬▬▬ % of GNP
20

15

10

5

0

          1960   1970   1981   2000

Exhibit 9
Per Capita Personal Health Expenditures, Age Differences

                                                    ▬ ▬ ▬ 65 +
In Thousands   ▬▬▬ 19–64
8   ▬▬▬ <19

6

4

2

0

      1965   1970   1978   2000

V. Implications for Future Policy

The growth in the size of the elderly population will lead to a major increase in use of health resources in the coming decades. This is a policy issue that has received surprisingly little attention. Much has

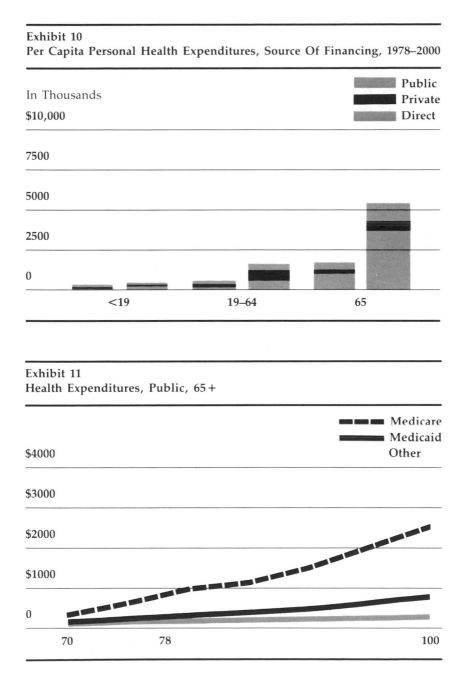

Exhibit 10
Per Capita Personal Health Expenditures, Source Of Financing, 1978–2000

In Thousands

$10,000

Public
Private
Direct

7500

5000

2500

0

<19   19–64   65

Exhibit 11
Health Expenditures, Public, 65 +

$4000

Medicare
Medicaid
Other

$3000

$2000

$1000

0

70   78   100

been made of the future implications of aging for the Social Security system in the U.S. But aging will also affect governmental health expenditures and real resource consumption.

It is important not to be alarmist about these trends. The economy will grow, real incomes will increase, and even in constant dollars an outlay of $6,000 per aged person for health care may not seem burdensome if the median family income in constant dollars is $40,000 to $50,000.

Further, much can change between now and the year 2000. Technological advances could cure cancer or reduce the prevalence of senility. Healthier lifestyles could reduce heart disease and a number of chronic conditions such as arthritis and hypertension.

A head-in-the-sand attitude, however, is just as inappropriate as an alarmist one. Cost-reducing and quality-of-life enhancing technological advance is more likely to occur if biomedical research aimed toward this objective is funded adequately. Greater emphasis needs to be placed upon prevention and those activities that will reduce the prevalence of chronic conditions or slow deterioration from such conditions.

One of the most important steps that could be taken, however, is to begin now to reverse the incentives toward excessive reliance on institutional care in hospitals and nursing homes. Lying behind the projected cost increases are major increases in both inpatient hospital care and nursing home care. Financial incentives encourage institutional care through inadequate coverage of noninstitutional care alternatives. Even more importantly, reimbursement methods make it financially attractive for physicians to place the aged in hospitals, even if quality care could be provided more cheaply on an ambulatory basis.

Policy prescriptions for reversing the bias toward institutional care are many. Some would propose substantial charges to the elderly for hospital care. But this would create serious financial burdens on those chronically ill elderly who have no choice but to make extensive use of hospital care. Further, it would penalize the aged for decisions made by physicians.

An alternative would be to change financial incentives for physicians and hospitals. The most promising of these is to change payment methods to discourage unnecessary care and to encourage lower cost methods of providing quality care. One approach would be to pay a greater array of health care providers on a capitation basis. For example, hospitals could be paid a flat annual rate per elderly person indicating that hospital as their preferred choice in the event of hospitalization. For such a payment system to be feasible, a substantial research effort needs to begin now to develop methodologies for setting such capitation payment rates in a fair way that will take into account differences in the health status and characteristics of different groups of elderly. This research would in all likelihood require a ten year effort—comparable to that devoted to development of the Diagnosis-Related Grouping (DRG) prospective payment system. But unlike the DRG approach, capitation payment systems would provide incentives to reduce, not increase hospitalization. Just as computer technology evolves over time, we must begin now to prepare for the generation of payment methods that lie beyond prospective DRG payment.

The current structure of long term care financing must also be reformed to reduce the institutional bias and provide improved protection for the frail elderly. Additional community services should be developed and financing provided for those without the ability to pay. The elderly who wish to remain at home ought to have assistance in their effort to live at home. Chore services and companion services as well as more traditional home health and nursing services should be available. Capitation payment for a full array of health and social services offers a financing alternative without the risk of open-ended financing.

These and other approaches must be tested and refined in the coming years to prepare for the 20th century. Truly far-sighted and visionary planning is required if our society is to meet the challenge posed by an aging population.

References

Davis, K. *Medicare Reconsidered*. Paper presented at the Duke University Medical Center Seventh Private Sector Conference on the Financial Support of Health Care of the Elderly and the Indigent, Durham, North Carolina, March 14-16, 1982.
Fries, J. F., Aging, natural death and the compression of morbidity. *The New England Journal of Medicine* 303:130-135, 1980.
Gruenberg, E. M., The failures of success. *Milbank Memorial Fund Quarterly— Health and Society*, 55:3-24, 1977.
Kramer, M., The rising pandemic of mental disorders and associated chronic diseases and disabilities. *Acta Psychiatrica Scandinavia Supplement* 285, 62:382-396, 1980.
Lowenstein, R., The effects of Medicare on the health care of the aged. Social Security Bulletin, No.(N):3-20, (April 1971, 34).
Manton, K., Changing concepts of morbidity and mortality in the elderly population. *Milbank Memorial Fund Quarterly— Health and Society* 60:183-245, Spring 1982.
Social Security Administration, Office of the Actuary. Published in Rice, D. P. and Feldman, J, *Tables and Charts for Demographic Changes and the Health Needs of the Elderly*, for the Institute of Medicine, Annual Meeting, Aging

and Health: New Perspectives in Science and Policy, Washington, D.C., October 20, 1982.

U.S. Department of Health and Human Services, Health Resources Administration. *Summary Report of the Graduate Medical Education National Advisory Committee to the Secretary of the Department of Health and Human Services*. Volume 1, September 30, 1980.

Unless otherwise cited, all figures quoted in this paper are generated from the CAPAS presentation.

5

Prevention: Can We Reduce the Demand for Long-Term Care?

Robert L. Berg

Prudent strategies for reducing morbidity and mortality in the aged should almost without exception begin in early life. These strategies relate partly to prevention or correction of physical abnormalities, and partly to a set of mind which is the result of deeply embedded social, cultural, and individual forces and idiosyncrasies. We manipulate these factors only with difficulty, but the components that lay the foundation for a high quality of life in later years include the following:

A commitment to a healthy life style from childhood which springs from a belief that it is worth maintaining oneself at a high level of mental and physical fitness. We know too little about instilling a sense of personal responsibility for one's own health, or about avoiding defense mechanisms such as denial ("it won't happen to me") to mount preventive programs aimed at restructuring deep-seated human motivations. We do know, however, that behavioral modification is not impossible (Maccoby, et al., 1977; McAlister, et al., 1982).

A respect for the value of life in later years. Closely tied to denial responses to the risk of injurious behavior is the notion of the "now generation," that life is worth living only at the exuberant peak of one's physical potential. Smoking cigarettes, it is argued, carries little immediate risk, and later years aren't worth much anyway (Berg, 1976). The decline in social and fiscal authority of the aged exacerbates the problem. Political, social, and administrative approaches to widening the role of aged persons deserve thoughtful consideration.

A process of long-range planning for the individual's life course. Old age

and death are almost unthinkable to many young adults, but optimistic plans for later years (including retirement planning) will enhance the importance of continuing physical fitness, the likelihood of
meaningful roles, and the full exploitation of an increasingly rectangular life expectancy (Fries, 1980). Preventive practices that can prevent disability in old age are rooted in this set of mind.

1. Resistance to Preventive Measures

Failure to avail oneself of interventions that will prevent disease,
either absolutely or secondarily, is perplexing and challenging to the
health care provider. A good deal of this failure is related to denial on
the part of the patient; they want to believe that they are not at risk
and will not be the victim of a disease or disorder. Partly this is related
to lack of information regarding effectiveness of treatment, side effects, and cost. A good deal relates to the lack of belief in the validity
of the information, and to the extent that it comes from a physician,
it is undoubtedly tied to questions about physician competence or
motives. Often the underlying issue is simple dissatisfaction with the
physician's care for whatever reason (Larson, Olsen, and Shortell,
1979), but often this is due to a lack of evident commitment or
emotional support. Other factors relate to irrational fears or religious
beliefs. These are often focused on objection to injections or the use
of "unnatural products."

Public or professional resistance to the use of interventions aimed
at prevention is related to poor reimbursement by third parties and to
lack of information. Much of this lack of information concerns effectiveness and particularly cost effectiveness. The whole field of cost
effectiveness analysis is beset by incomplete and irrational arguments
and misinformation. However, it is of great importance, since it will
generally be the principal focus of public policy decisions.

2. Costs of Preventive Interventions

The cost of a given intervention is often not accurately estimated,
sometimes being limited only to the cost of the product itself and
neglecting perhaps the personnel and other services needed. Typically, indirect or overhead expenses are underestimated; costs or
savings are not discounted to present values, and productivity losses
or gains are omitted. On the other hand, often the indirect savings
from an intervention, such as the avoidance of hospital care, is
neglected (see also the discussion concerning tetanus). Furthermore,
the savings may not accrue to the provider; indeed, the death of a

chronically ill patient may save the provider substantial resources. A further error in these estimates relates to the use of average cost instead of marginal cost. For example, if one is calculating the cost of a program of immunization, the cost estimates may be based on floating an independent large campaign, when, in fact, in most circumstances, particularly for institutionalized patients, the immunization program may be tied to health visits for other reasons where the marginal cost is small.

In considering the cost effectiveness of a program, the emphasis may be almost entirely on the saving of health care funds in return for an intervention. This is a useful analysis because if the program actually saves money for the provider or for society, it will presumably have merit on that account alone. On the other hand, many programs have no cost savings, or very few, and are overwhelmed by the actual net additional cost. In this circumstance, the argument as to whether or not the program saves the health care system money is not appropriate; rather, the question should be whether the cost of improvement in quality of life or the saving of life years (weighted for quality) is consistent with societal standards (Berg, 1973). In this respect, there are a few guidelines and there has been little public consensus. However, the existing examples of what society has been willing to expend to save a life year, as in the case of end stage renal disease, may provide a useful benchmark (Berg and Ornt, 1984).

3. Opportunities for Prevention

On the basis of this summary of factors which influence preventive behavior, the following will deal with selected disorders which are responsible for much disability in old age and for which substantial gains may be achieved with sound preventive practice.

I. Primary Prevention: The Avoidance of Disease

The absolute prevention of disease, or primary prevention as it is usually termed, is obviously the best strategy in health care. The rational appeal of this concept led to an oversell in the past, when health educators and public health officials pressed for expanded programs of prevention, even though some were not of established value. The situation today is almost the reverse, and health providers and patients alike are at fault in underestimating the opportunities for primary prevention.

Primary prevention can be divided into preventive measures involving procedures performed by physicians or other health professionals on patients (specifically and almost exclusively immunizations), and those approaches to prevention which involve behavioral modification.

Immunizations.

Among the immunizations which merit attention for the aged are influenza vaccination as well as vaccination for pneumococcal pneumonia and tetanus. In addition, vaccination against tuberculosis and diphtheria should probably be listed. BCG vaccination has been calculated (Waaler, 1968) to be more cost effective for vaccination of tuberculin sensitive persons than chemotherapy in tuberculin positive patients. Recent increases in reported cases of tuberculosis suggest that further attention should be paid to this disease in older patients. Although the number of diphtheria cases reported nationally have been less than 10 in each of the last several years, there is a potential for outbreaks of diphtheria if the antibody status of the aged persons is much diminished.

Immunizations in the elderly present a number of problems. In the first place, the immune response is depressed, related to the poor memory or recall function in previously exposed immune cells, both T and B cells. Not only are the immune globulins reduced, but there are also increased autoantibodies (Adler, Jones, and Nariuchi, 1977; Makinodan and Kay, 1980).

With the decrease in responsiveness of the immune system, there is also a more rapid falling off in antibody levels so that studies on younger age populations are not a sufficient guide for what is needed for the elderly.

1. Tetanus

Incidence. Although the incidence of tetanus has been sharply reduced in recent years, there are a lingering number of cases, between 70 and 100 in each of the last few years. More than half of these were in patients more than 60 years old, with a higher mortality than in younger ages (U.S. DHHS, 1981a). The actual mortality rate in a study in the mid 1960s (LaForce, Young, and Bennett, 1969) was 75 percent for persons over 50 years of age and 50 percent for younger ages.

Etiology. The higher mortality of aged persons has been shown to be associated with low antibody levels. In an urban population, adults over 60 years of age were poorly protected in this respect, with only 41 percent of men and 29 percent of women achieving protective levels (Crossley et al., 1979). The occupants of nursing homes have also been shown to have poor protective levels; only 59 percent of nursing home residents in one study achieved protective levels (Ruben, Nagel, and Fireman, 1978). Among the 507 cases reported in 1965 and 1966, 53 percent resulted from home injury, 17 percent on the farm, 10 percent in the garden, and 4 percent from chronic skin ulcerations. A few cases were related to amputations or abdominal surgery (LaForce, Young, and Bennett, 1969).

Interventions. Immunization has proven to be fully protective even in the aged after three doses (Solomonova and Vizev, 1973), and a full schedule is recommended for those with an uncertain history of adequate immunization, with booster doses every ten years and after injury and before surgery (Bentley, 1984).

Cost Effectiveness. There has been some discussion in the literature about the desirability of large-scale immunization programs for the aged, for example, in nursing homes. At the current rate of tetanus, there are only about 2 cases a year among nursing home residents, and it has been argued that a large scale immunization program cannot be justified on a cost-benefit basis (Sherman, 1980). Most preventive services, especially immunizations, will be unnecessarily costly when undertaken as isolated procedures and the arguments should avoid this assumption. When added to the cost of an ordinary office visit for other reasons, the marginal expense is small. Nevertheless, the total cost for the 2.2 million patients in nursing homes in the United States at a minimal charge of $5 for a single tetanus shot would amount to $11 million for this population. If only 2 deaths occur due to tetanus in the population in a year, and if life expectancy were estimated at 5 years for this population, with an average age of 82.5 (we have no good evidence about the life expectancy of persons admitted to nursing homes), then a saving of 10 life years might be expected, which would amount to more than a million dollars per life year saved. This is palpably far in excess of what we have been prepared to do in other circumstances, specifically for end stage renal disease, where we are currently spending approximately $25,000 for each patient on dialysis per year (Berg and Orut, 1984).

2. Influenza

Incidence. Although only about 10 percent of the aged contract flu during an epidemic, their illness accounts for 50 percent of hospitalizations for influenza and for 75-80 percent of the deaths (Schoenbaum, 1980). For the aged, mortality is higher than in younger persons and is highly correlated with the presence of complicating disease. In one study of a defined population, the mortality rate was 9/100,000 for those with no high risk conditions, 217/100,000 with one high risk condition, and 306/100,000 for two or more conditions, especially underlying cardiovascular disease in combination with either diabetes or chronic pulmonary disease (Barker and Mullooly, 1982).

Etiology. Epidemics of influenza have largely been due to A strains in recent years, although they have affected mostly younger patients. However, outbreaks have been described of influenza A strains in chronic disease hospitals (Mathur et al., 1981). In 1979-80 a new B variant (B Singapore) caused outbreaks among the aged in long-term care institutions and hospitals (Silverstone et al., 1980; van Voris, Belsche, and Shaffer, 1982).

Less than 20 percent of older persons were observed to have been vaccinated in 1976, though as a result of major publicity campaigns, the number was increased to 44 percent (Kavet, 1976; U.S. DHHS, 1977). This reluctance or failure to receive influenza vaccine may partly have been related to the anxieties regarding the swine influenza vaccine problem of the mid-seventies, but undoubtedly it is also related to a lack of conviction by both patients and physicians as to its efficacy.

Interventions. Currently available influenza vaccines are formalin inactivated viruses incubated on eggs, which have been shown to be highly effective. Vaccines aimed at specific strains current in a given epidemic have been shown to provide a 72 percent decrease in hospitalization and an 87 percent decrease in mortality among an elderly population in a prepaid group practice (Barker and Mullooly, 1980). The only contraindications to the use of influenza vaccine relate to anaphylactic sensitivity to eggs or a previous history of Guillian-Barre syndrome following previous flu vaccination. Studies of patients accepting influenza vaccination showed that the patients felt that they were more likely to be infected than others. They took the disease more seriously and felt they were more likely to have a serious attack and that the vaccine was safe and effective (Rundall and Wheeler, 1979). The Advisory Committee for Immunization Practices recommends annual vaccination for all persons 65 years of age and older, especially those with chronic cardiovascular, pulmonary, or renal disease, diabetes, or compromise in their immune system.

In addition to influenza virus vaccines, more recent approaches include the use of chemoprophylaxis with amantadine hydrochloride. This agent, which is effective in preventing influenza caused by A virus, has proved effective in older persons (O'Donoghue, Ray, and Terry, 1973) and is especially recommended (1) in the unvaccinated person at high risk for pulmonary complications when inactivated influenza A virus vaccines are unavailable or contraindicated; (2) in conjunction with influenza immunization in the high risk person (Bentley, 1984). The toxic effects of amantadine are troublesome, however, and a new antiviral compound, rimantadine hydrochloride, is as effective with fewer side effects (Dolin et al., 1981).

Cost Effectiveness. The regular use of influenza vaccine for the aged achieves substantial savings in the cost of hospitalization for this group (Barker and Mullooly, 1980). Analyses by the Office of Technology Assessment indicate that the vaccination saves money in "base care." However, comprehensive analysis, including medical care costs in extended years of life, indicates during the period 1971-78 a cost of $1,782 per year of healthy life gained for those over 65 years. If the analysis is limited to Medicare costs (omitting out-of-pocket and other payments), the Medicare cost would have been $791 per healthy life year gained. These costs include costs of original vaccination, treatment for cases of Guillain-Barre Syndrome, reduced influenza treatment costs, and medical care costs in extended years of life. It omits increased payments to Social Security from older individuals remaining in the work force, and increased payments to beneficiaries because of longer life expectancy. Since 1976, there have been no cases of Guillain-Barre associated with the use of influenza vaccine (Douglas and Betts, 1979), so that that risk balanced against the substantial mortality for those contracting the infection is trivial.

3. Pneumococcal Pneumonia

Incidence. The mortal effects of pneumonia in the aged are well known, particularly in those who have underlying chronic disease. Studies of pneumococcal pneumonia in a community found about 3 cases per thousand annually in aged persons (Fried, 1973); in institutions, an incidence of 1316 per thousand annually has been observed (Bentley, 1984). Mortality rates are much higher in the aged than among younger patients, and while the mortality rate prior to penicillin was in excess of 90 percent, after the introduction of penicillin, rates of 28 percent were reported (Austrian and Gold, 1964).

71

Intervention. The development of an effective vaccine for pneumo-coccal pneumonia has proceeded slowly without conclusive proof so far as to its effectiveness. Trials in an ambulatory, prepaid practice population of generally healthy persons suggest no difference between vaccinated and unvaccinated controls. In one chronic disease institution, there was some reduction in the vaccine susceptible sero-types in cases of pneumonia, although there was no overall difference between vaccinated and unvaccinated groups (Bentley, 1984). Nevertheless, the Food and Drug Administration recommends pneumo-coccal vaccination for patients entering chronic care institutions who are over 50 years of age (FDA, 1978). The vaccine can be given at the same time as influenza vaccine. When given, a twofold increase has been noted in types of specific antibodies after two to three weeks persisting at the 30-50 percent level for five to eight years. Antibody levels probably decline faster in older patients than at younger ages (Bentley, 1984), but this precaution is prudent at the present time.

Cost Effectiveness. On the assumption that the vaccine would be 80 percent effective against type-specific pneumococcal pneumonia, it has been estimated that it would cost approximately $1,000 per year of healthy life gained for those 65 years of age or older (Willems and Sanders, 1981). At a 60 percent efficacy rate, the cost per life year gained for aged patients increases to $3,700, a figure well within the guidelines presented by end stage renal disease. It is, however, substantially more expensive than the use of influenza vaccine, which has been estimated by the same authors to cost approximately $500 to $800 per life year gained.

Falls and Accidents.

Much attention has been focused on falls by aged persons and on their serious consequences, particularly fractured hips, which are often sentinel events in a rapid decline in mobility and longevity.

Incidence. As the major predisposing factor to fractured hips, any fall in an aged person is risky. Hip fractures in the elderly have been reported to achieve a rate of 7/10,000 elderly (higher in women), with a mean age of falls of 73 years for women and 69 years for men (Sabin, 1982). Falls are especially common in institutions. A history of frequent falls or a fall leading to a major fracture is a common reason for admission. In one Veterans Administration Hospital, patients averaged more than one fall per patient year (Krishna and VanCleave, 1983). In three intermediate care facilities in Rochester, New York, newly admitted patients averaged more than five falls per year (Tinetti, Williams, and Mayewski, 1984). Of all falls in one study of several British general practices, by contrast, 95 percent occurred at home and only 5 percent in residential accommodations (Wild, Nayak, and Isaacs, 1981). Among disabled patients in long-term institutions, falls are one of the most serious sources of disability (Krishna and VanCleave, 1983).

Etiology. Falls may be due to tripping on rugs or other impediments, or slipping on the ice or wet linoleum. Even such falls may be associated with disturbances of balance, which in turn may arise from visual, vestibular, or proprioceptive disorders. Ordinary control mechanisms may be deranged due to circulatory or neurologic problems or the effect of drugs (Wild, Nayak, and Isaacs, 1981). In senile dementia, for example, a reversal to certain motor reflexes otherwise found only in infancy may be seen. In addition, some signs and physiological changes are seen as common in aging: reduced deep tendon reflexes at the ankle, distal symmetrical loss of vibration sense and equivocal responses to plantar stimulation (Sabin, 1982). Deficits in balance may be evaluated by measuring sway in a standing position. Abnormal sway is highly correlated with falls, tripping, giddiness, loss of balance, and a history of fractures. A drop in blood pressure on standing is also associated with sway, but both seem related to some underlying common cause rather than the hypotension causing sway (Overstall, Johnson, and Exton-Smith, 1978).

A variety of factors have been found to be associated with falls. Among these are excessive use of sleeping medications and other drug interactions; deficits in vision and hearing; limitations in activities of daily living; mental status; and difficulties of ambulation. These disorders are additive, so that the presence of several is almost inevitably associated with falls (Tinetti, Williams, and Mayewski, 1984; Krishna and VanCleave, 1983). The concomitant presence of osteoporosis makes fracture of the hip more likely with falls (Perry, 1982). Bed rest itself aggravates the problem, for there is weakness and difficulty with mobility after even a few days of bed rest (Sabin, 1982). Other forms of trauma, particularly those sustained in automobile crashes, are an important issue for aged persons since one-fourth of fatal injuries for the aged are the result of automobile accidents.

Diagnosis. Some 32 disorders involve gait disorder and falling. Often one finds the term "senile gait disorder" used as an umbrella term to cover this array of disorders including parkinsonism, cervical spondylosis, some tumors, toxic and metabolic disorders, myasthenia gravis, polymyositis, episodic disorders including seizures, infectious disease, and normal pressure hydrocephalus. Often, the gait is abnormal, and careful analysis may provide opportunities for focused therapy. The analysis includes the examination of the position of the feet while walking, evaluation of balance, and the study of sway and reaction time. Often there is excessive weight bearing on the heels with the head tilted forward, leading to curvature in the upper spine (Nayak et al., 1982; Overstall, Johnson, and Exton-Smith, 1978; Tinetti, Williams, and Mayewski, 1984).

Interventions. For those disorders which arise from gait disorders, vigorous physical therapy can remedy much of the disability and is especially important after short-term bed rest. The reduction or elimination of bedtime hypnotics and the prudent use of neuroleptics and antihypertensive agents is important. In many cases, the total load of drugs can be substantially reduced without injury to the patient. A combination of physical therapy, attention to the use of drugs, and staff education reduced the falls in one Veterans Administration hospital from 32 falls per 10,000 patient days to 20 falls per 10,000 patient days (Krishna and VanCleave, 1983).

Sensible management of living arrangements to avoid unnecessary obstacles such as tripping over rugs and thresholds may avoid serious problems. Instruction for the patients on the use of bi- and trifocal glasses is important in using stairs and walking on irregular surfaces. Grab bars for an aged person with poor balance or with physical or neurological deficits may be useful in avoiding the most serious difficulties (Wild, Nayak, and Isaacs, 1981).

The issue of driving licenses to aged persons may present a serious problem. There is a great reluctance to withhold the privilege of driving, especially when it is a necessary condition of independent living. Nevertheless, more thoughtful monitoring of driving skills by families and physicians is undoubtedly needed.

Atherosclerosis.

Atherosclerosis is a process affecting the walls of arteries and is thought to have its origin in some injury to the arterial wall from circulating toxic materials. The development of atherosclerosis is significantly affected by a high level of the circulating fats in the blood, by high blood pressure, and by diabetes. These factors are further modified by smoking and dietary habits. Thus, the major cause of atherosclerosis is related to lifestyle and dietary and smoking behavior.

a. Coronary artery disease

Incidence. Mortality rates for coronary heart disease (CHD) in the general population have dropped sharply from a rate of 308/100,000 in 1950 to 210/100,000 in 1977. Similarly, in the elderly, mortality rates due to coronary artery disease dropped conspicuously during the 1970s after a twenty year period of relatively unchanging mortality. However, the mortality rate for women has declined more or less continuously since 1950. For those over 85 years of age, there was a peak mortality rate in the early 1960s with subsequent declines.

For the total population 65 years and older, the death rate due to heart disease (almost entirely ischemic) dropped from a rate of 3,314/100,000 in 1960 to 2,813/100,000 by 1978 (U.S. DHEW Annual, 1978). For those 65-69 years of age, the rate was 975.7/100,000, while for those 80 years and older, the rate was 7,084.3/100,000. Female rates were conspicuously lower than male rates, and black rates were conspicuously higher than white rates. While it is difficult to draw valid conclusions from the available data, this set of events is consistent with the changes in the pattern of cigarette smoking and of dietary changes. The rapid increase in cigarette smoking from the 1920s to the 1950s and 1960s leveled off and has been declining since that time, with a drop in the proportion of adult males smoking from 53 percent in 1955 to 39 percent in 1978. Adult women showed an increase to 33 percent in 1965 that decreased to 30 percent by 1978. The percentage of all adults who smoked was the lowest in 1978 in over 30 years. Mortality rates are considerably higher in men than in women in all developed countries, particularly in countries such as Finland and the United States, which have a high intake of saturated fats (Keys, 1970). In developing countries, the rates are much lower.

Etiology. In the evolution of atherosclerosis, the underlying lesion begins as a fatty streak, consisting mostly of macrophages containing much fatty material. These cells become localized within the intima of the artery and subsequently give rise to an overlying fibrous plaque. This is the major lesion in atherosclerosis and is modified by calcification, ulceration, and ultimately thrombosis. A number of factors play important roles: nutrition, smoking, hypertension and diabetes.

Diet. A diet high in saturated fat has a profound effect on the circulating blood lipids. The evidence is particularly strong for a link between the nature of the circulating blood lipids and resulting CHD incidence. Low density lipoproteins are associated with increased incidence of coronary heart disease, while increased high density

75

lipoproteins appear to protect against it. The effects of high density lipoproteins are greater at older ages. Polyunsaturated fatty acids may protect against CHD (Blackburn and Gillum, 1980). While excess weight does not emerge as a major contributor to excessive risk of coronary heart disease, it is highly correlated with factors that are related and may play a larger role than has yet been established. Alcohol up to two drinks a day actually appears to protect against CHD, while larger amounts may predispose to it. Coffee does not appear to be an independent risk factor for CHD.

Smoking has a large effect on premature coronary heart disease. It increases the relative risk by 1.5 to 2 times and is comparable for men and women. Thus, although the relative risk is not as large as for cancer of the lung, the number of people affected by the relationship is larger than for lung cancer. It also exacerbates the degree of hypertension (Izzo, 1982).

Hypertension contributes to the risk of a coronary event, but data from trials have not been sufficient as yet to reveal a significant increase in mortality from coronary heart disease. The amount of salt intake has an effect on the level of the blood pressure but shares with hypertension data the lack of conclusive evidence on coronary disease mortality (Blackburn and Gillum, 1980).

Interventions. Coronary heart disease represents a disorder whose prevention lies almost exclusively in the domain of a healthy lifestyle. Such a style must be pursued over a lifetime to realize its full potential. Cessation of *smoking* is of crucial importance to reduce the likelihood of coronary artery disease. The life expectancy of smokers who give up cigarette smoking is prolonged beyond that of continuing smokers. As with any addiction, giving up smoking is difficult, and temporary abstinence is too often followed by a return to the status of an addict. Nevertheless, fewer people smoke in the United States today than in many years.

The approach to smoking cessation through behavioral modification has made use of negative conditioning, patient education, and social pressure. Patient education has been provided by physicians, nurses, and public health educators, face-to-face in organized groups or through media. There is never complete success, but significant success can be achieved by persistent follow-up and continuing concern by health care providers.

Healthier *diets* play a significant role. Industrialized societies need to adjust diets to preindustrial components. Indeed, the recent decline in CHD mortality is presumably related to such dietary changes and to reduction in smoking. A diet restricted in total calories and animal and other saturated fats is the principal goal. Salt intake should be reduced because of its relationship to high blood pressure. Alcohol is apparently protective in moderation, damaging in excess.

Exercise has a beneficial effect on life expectancy. Furthermore, fewer cardiac illnesses are found in adults who regularly and frequently engage in vigorous exercise. This protective effect is related to the degree and extent of exercise and is not tied to other risk factors. The effect is related to current levels of activity and is not much influenced by previous activity (Blackburn and Gillum, 1980).

b. Hypertension and stroke

Most strokes are related to atherosclerosis in blood vessels of the brain. The discussion of strokes thus belongs as a subset of atherosclerosis. However, high blood pressure greatly increases the likelihood of stroke so that they are discussed together. Indeed, the control of blood pressure has such a marked effect on the likelihood of stroke that reduction of hypertension deserves attention as a primary preventive measure.

Incidence. Persons with high blood pressure cannot be identified as a unique subset of the general population. They are simply those with higher blood pressure than some defined normal limit. But if hypertension is defined as systolic readings in excess of 160mm Hg or diastolic readings in excess of 95mm, then the following proportions of the population are hypertensive: 7.5 percent of white men between 25 and 34 years; 2.2 percent of white women of that age; 16.4 percent of black men and 12.4 percent of black women of that age. For those 65-74 years, the incidence increases sharply: 30.8 percent of white men, 34.9 percent of white women, 43.3 percent of black men, and 46.3 percent of black women. The increase with age is gradually progressive, except for black men, who actually hit a peak of 58.6 percent in the 55-64 age group and decline thereafter (U.S. DHHS, 1981b). Since the risk of stroke is directly related to the level of blood pressure, this increase with age carries a much increased risk of stroke.

As with coronary heart disease, the incidence of stroke has decreased in recent years. In 1950, there were 89 strokes/100,000 population. In 1977, the rate had dropped to 48/100,000, perhaps related to changes in diet and smoking habits, but also and undoubtedly to medical control of hypertension. For those 65-69 years of age, the incidence was 171/100,000 while for those 85 years and older, the rate was 2,282/100,000. As with CHD, the rates are higher for older men than for older women, and higher for blacks than whites. After 80 years of age, the incidence rate is higher for whites than blacks.

Etiology. The pathologic lesions of most strokes are atherosclerotic. Hypertension appears to aggravate the underlying disorder, and in the brain more than in the heart, for the relationship is not clearly established in regard to CHD but is predominant for strokes. Hypertension is well documented to be associated with stress, body weight, salt and glucose intake, and oral contraceptives (Borhani, 1981).

Some strokes are related to the rupture of a congenital weakness in the arterial wall. Others result from emboli from a diseased heart. Most are the result of local atherosclerotic lesions with subsequent thrombosis and/or hemorrhage. Thus, prevention of strokes is tied to the prevention of atherosclerosis and hypertension.

Interventions. The prevention of hypertension is aimed at control of all known risk factors, particularly obesity, stress, and intake of salt. These will reduce the likelihood of hypertension. However, when it is found, effective drugs are available for its control and, with control, the prevention of stroke. Useful drugs include thiazide diuretics, vasodilators such as hydralazine, and adrenergic blockers such as reserpine. With appropriate pharmacologic regimens, most hypertension can be controlled, with sharp reductions in the incidence of stroke.

Stroke control programs have frequently been mounted as hypertension detection stations set up in supermarkets or airports. Such screening activities may do more harm than good unless case detection is tied to responsible medical care on a continuous basis. Effective control of hypertension requires good patient compliance with an optimal regimen, and that is unlikely without a trusting doctor-patient relationship and intensive follow-up (Borhani, 1981).

Dental Health.

Incidence. The poor dental health of the aged population is indicated by the fact that in 1971, 46 percent of persons between 65 and 75 were edentulous. Fifty-five percent had periodontal disease in remaining teeth. Although the edentulous proportion was reduced by 10 percent in the period between 1965 and 1975, it is still a substantial and unnecessary disorder (U.S. DHEW, 1979a). In nursing homes, some two thirds of patients have been found to need dental care (Silverman, 1984).

Etiology. Caries is the underlying disorder which led to most dental defects now seen in the elderly. It is an infectious disease in which bacteria, bedded down in a matrix of plaque developing in the absence of adequate tooth cleansing, generate acids. These demineralize the enamel, the denture, and the cementum, leaving a residual organic matrix vulnerable to digestion. This ultimately leads to the loosening of the tooth in the bony socket and its loss. The process of developing caries is now believed to be related invariably to plaque. In addition to production of acid, the degraded products of bacteria are thought to irritate the gum margin, leading to periodontal disease (gingivitis in the gums) which encourages the development of caries (Silverman, 1984). Perhaps much of the poor quality of dental care in the population, especially in the aged, is related to a low perception of the need for dental care.

Interventions. The efficacy of adequate levels of fluoride in the drinking water has long been known. There also is substantial evidence that a careful cleansing of the teeth, including brushing and flossing from childhood, will prevent caries entirely. The reduction of sugar in the diet is helpful.

Senile Dementia.

The inclusion of a not yet preventable disease in a background document for planning preventive health services for the elderly may appear foolishly optimistic. After all, forgetfulness and confusion in old age have been viewed traditionally as untreatable and unpreventable; they are the curse of old age. But it does not affect all aged persons, and recent developments in pathophysiology and in research on experimental models in animals suggests that we should aim for prevention.

Incidence. Senile dementia imposes an enormous health care burden. In nursing homes more than half of all patients are diagnosed as suffering from senility or chronic brain syndrome (U.S. DHEW, 1979b). In the total population, 40 percent of persons over 85 years of age require supervision for mental problems (Berg, 1980).

Etiology. Traditionally viewed as an inevitable consequence of cerebral arteriosclerosis, the recognition that it was essentially a parenchymal brain disease (in spite of the 15 percent of dementia related to multiple brain infarcts) offered small promise of effective interventions or prevention. Recently there is increasing agreement that most senile dementia is the result of similar pathologic processes as those associated with presenile dementia (Alzheimer's Disease; Mortimer and Schuman, 1981). There are the same amyloid deposits and neurofibrillary tangles. Indeed, the presence of amyloid suggests an immunologic or infectious process (Nandy, 1978). The pathology, and to some extent the symptomatology, resembles scrapie, a brain disease found in sheep and experimentally in mice. Similar lesions are also found in certain viral disorders such as Semliki Forest virus disease (McDermott, Fraser, and Dickinson, 1978). In addition to multiple infarcts and Alzheimer's Disease, a number of other disorders may present with a picture of dementia, so that demented patients need careful evaluation (Small and Jarvik, 1982). Primary dementia includes not only Alzheimer's disease, but Pick's disease, Huntington's chorea and progressive supranuclear palsy. Secondary causes in addition to multiple infarct dementia include hydrocephalus, Korsakoff's psychosis, trauma, space-occupying lesions, metabolic and infectious disorders, and side effects of medication (Gershon and Herman, 1982).

Interventions. The finding by Gibbs et al. (1968) that Creutzfeld-Jakob disease could be transmitted to the chimpanzee lends further credibility to the notion that Alzheimer's Disease may be the result of an infection with a slow virus. The isolation of an agent responsible for dementia would have profound effects on the management of the disease and immediately raises the possibility of the development of a vaccine that would prevent the disease entirely.

Many health problems in the elderly might have been entirely prevented with a healthy life style or with prudent interventions. Whether the disease is preventable or not, much of the consequent disability is preventable. Incontinence, visual disorders, and dental disease are of special significance in this regard.

II. Secondary and Tertiary Prevention: Detection, Treatment, and Rehabilitation

Psychological Health

A life of high quality is dependent on several factors: psychological and physical health, and the ability to be independent, among others. Of these, psychological health rates the highest. Adults generally rate the ability to think clearly and to love and be loved as the most valuable of all functional capacities (Berg, Hallauer, and Berk, 1976).

80

Dementia, depression, and anxiety states are principal threats to good psychological health.

1. Dementia

Incidence. Dementia, seen in old age and referred to as senile dementia in that case, has been discussed in terms of possible primary prevention in the future. It is a common disorder in old age, particularly in nursing homes, where more than half of all patients suffer from substantial forgetfulness and confusion. The affective disorders (depression and anxiety states) are the most prevalent in the general population (Rothblum, et al., 1982; Berg, 1980). Psychotic depression associated with the risk of suicide is common in the aged, particularly among men. When older men talk about possible suicide, it is not to be taken lightly, for they are in the high risk category. Depression is common in the elderly with some rates reported as high as 26 percent (Kay, Beamish, and Roth, 1964).

Forgetfulness and confusion so severe as to require supervision increase with age; in the population over 90 years of age, some supervision because of mental health problems is needed for 75 percent of the population (until the age of 80, the situation is reversed, with only a quarter of the population needing such supervision; Berg, 1980).

Etiology. Presenile dementia appears to be related to the pathophysiologic changes described above. In older patients, where the onset may be gradual, increasing isolation and loss of a functional role in society may play a major role in precipitating increased confusion and forgetfulness. Depression is often precipitated by some major event, usually the death or other loss of a spouse or child. It may be related to the loss of home or possessions or of a cherished role in life. Such patients have often had a history of other mental illness (Rothblum et al., 1982). Anxiety states tend to be ongoing and often represent only an exaggeration of ordinary concerns such as for safety in terms of fire, accidents, or theft; financial worries, especially lack of resources in case of long-term institutionalization; or the impending loss of loved ones or one's home or possessions. Fear of illness and disability is a major concern.

Interventions. Counseling and psychotherapy have an important place in the management of these mental health problems. For the demented person, especially early in the course of forgetfulness and confusion, attention to simple mnemonic devices may be very helpful. Such patients are particularly likely to develop confusion in strange surroundings, as during hospitalization. At such times, easily read descriptions as to where the patient is located, and why they are there, help to maintain their equanimity. At some point the family and physician may have to consider the need to recommend withholding of driving privileges or independent financial management. In this case, the recommendation for an adequate financial counselor and the assignment of powers of attorney to a responsible person may be necessary. Often the physician must initiate such sensitive discussions with the family.

Lacking a fully preventive measure (such as vaccination) for dementia, considerable work has been done on the use of acetylcholine potentiating medications, including choline or lethicin (Wurtman, Hefti, and Melamed, 1981). The results thus far are not particularly encouraging, but combined therapy, such as the use of choline together with a choline esterase inhibitor, may be more effective.

2. Depression

For the depressed patient, much can be achieved with effective psychotherapy. It is something of a puzzle as to why the medical profession has shown such sense of therapeutic nihilism and futility when dealing with aged, depressed patients (Butler, 1975). They tend to regard such patients as a poor investment and untreatable. Open discussion in regard to fears of death and dying can permit more balance in the approach to these issues. Often a meaningful role can be found for the older patient who might volunteer in community activities. The patients treated with such counseling and the appropriate psychotropic drugs (such as alprazolam or imipramine) generally show favorable responses in depression (Rothblum et al., 1982).

Interventions. Cognitive rehabilitation utilizing reality orientation classes has been found to have beneficial effects on improving forgetfulness and confusion (Hanley, McGuire, and Boyd, 1981); the use of cognitively demanding efforts, such as electronic games, requiring coordination, timely response, and good spatial and visual judgment has been described by Reinke, Holmes, and Denney (1981) and Gummow, Miller, and Dustman (1983). Such "tuning up" is in an early stage of development, and it is not yet clear how enduring improvements may be. On the other hand, improvement appears to represent a response to a challenge, a social involvement as well as specific cognitive practice.

Physical Health and Function.

Of all physical disorders in the aged, the most troublesome and most significant to the aged person are those which reduce functional status. The particular diagnosis is of little importance; its impact is of great significance. The crippling physical problems described have been selected because of major and often similar impacts on functional status, especially mobility and the activities of daily living.

1. *Musculoskeletal and Neurologic Disease*

a. *Arthritis*

Incidence. Arthritis may be due to a variety of degenerative and inflammatory diseases of the joints, but the common problems are related to osteoarthritis and rheumatoid arthritis. *Osteoarthritis* is more common with advancing age. In a British general practice (Eade, Morris, and Nicol, 1979) some 5 percent of all patients were seen for rheumatic disorders. Of these, ten times as many are related to osteoarthritis as the rheumatoid arthritis. Data from the National Health Survey (U.S. DHEW, 1979c) indicate that regardless of source, 9 percent of persons between the age of 65 and 74 are "quite a bit restricted" due to arthritis. Osteoarthritis affects substantial numbers of aged persons, particularly in the knees, where three times as many men as women are affected, and to a lesser extent in the hips and the sacroiliac joints, where men again are almost twice as likely to be affected as women (U.S. DHEW, 1979c). The most commonly involved joint in rheumatoid arthritis is the wrist. In persons between 65 and 75 years, almost 1 percent are affected, so that is a much less common disorder in the aged than osteoarthritis.

While not primarily arthritic in origin, misshapen feet and painful bunions and calluses account for much discomfort and difficulty in ambulation. They are largely the result of mismanagement in early life, including poorly fitting shoes and delayed attention to abnormalities. It has been estimated that 85 million persons in the United States have foot problems, 90 percent of which are due to ill-fitting shoes, and high heels in women (du Vries, 1965). Foot problems are one of the main sources of disability and immobility on the part of older people.

Etiology. Osteoarthritis is a degenerative disease, often of traumatic origin. The wear and tear of the joint leads to mechanical and biochemical breakdowns of the joint cartilage with some resulting inflammation. The radiologic changes evident in osteoarthritis are often not associated with severe symptoms. The involvement of the knee is felt to be related to increased body weight and angulation of the knee joint, which may account for its greater frequency in women. Hip involvement is more common in men, perhaps as a result of early activity in sports or other marked use of joints. It is quite possible that knee involvement will become more common in men as a result of current jogging practice.

In rheumatoid arthritis, the underlying lesion is an inflammatory process in the synovia or lining of the joint with an ultimate destruction of joint surfaces. Osteoarthritis and rheumatoid arthritis are sometimes confused but generally may be differentiated on the basis of the greater likelihood of osteoarthritis to affect the knees, hips, and sacroiliac joints and the small finger joints, often in single joints, whereas rheumatoid arthritis is more likely to affect the wrists and shoulders. Furthermore, rheumatoid arthritis is much more of a systemic or constitutional disease, often with associated weight loss or fever. Other diseases of the joint which must be taken into consideration in establishing a diagnosis are gout, systemic lupus erythematosis, multiple myeloma, polymyalgia rheumatica, fibrocytis, and bursitis (Baum, 1984).

Interventions. For all arthritic disorders, salicylates are effective agents in reducing both pain and the inflammatory response. A number of other anti-inflammatory agents have been used as well, especially steroids. Gold salts have been increasingly used in the treatment of rheumatoid arthritis with good effect, inducing a remission in some 60 percent of cases, although toxic effects on the bone marrow and kidney need to be monitored.

For the osteoarthritic patient with severe involvement in the hip, total hip replacement may be indicated. Some 60 percent of the 75,000 hip replacements that have been done in the United States have been for patients over 65 years of age. For arthritic patients, appropriate exercises are of great importance. This is important not only to improve general physical fitness but also as a means of strengthening the muscles around the joint which act as a protective mechanism, so as to avoid further injury to the joint and to improve the likelihood of maintaining a full range of motion and strength for effective mobility. In addition, walking aides such as canes or walkers may be of substantial help in relieving the burden to the joint. In all programs of promoting better mobility, a major obstacle that must be overcome is the patient's fear that further harm will be done. In fact, unless good mobility is maintained, particularly of full motion in the joints, the opportunities to help patients to regain maximal physical activity may be sharply impaired.

Timely foot care which might avoid or reduce the troublesomeness of painful feet is often neglected. Podiatric advice and care is of great importance to the elderly. Surgical intervention may be necessary for disorders of the nails, bony malformations or excrescences. Careful attention to appropriate footwear will reduce the frequency of calluses and corns (Helfand, 1984).

b. *Stroke*

While stroke has been discussed under atherosclerosis together with coronary artery disease, many strokes occur in spite of, or in the absence of, preventive measures. Much can be done for victims of stroke by rehabilitation programs which help the stroke patients to regain maximal function in spite of residential neurologic problems.

Incidence. Stroke is a major cause of death and disability in the aged and responsible for much institutionalization. In 1979, there were 747,000 hospital admissions for stroke in the United States, of which 554,000 were in persons 65 years of age and older. This amounted to a rate of 721 admissions/10,000 elderly persons. The average stay was 10.5 days. There were 139,400 admissions to nursing homes for stroke, where the average stay was 709 days. About 30 percent of these patients died in the nursing home (U.S. DHEW, 1981c; U.S. DHHS, 1981d).

Etiology. The disability occasioned by strokes is due to interruption of nerve pathways in the brain substance. Much of the injury is reversible, but some is permanent. The goal of rehabilitation is to achieve the maximal recovery of physical, psychological and social function possible with residual deficits. Weeks or months may pass before the extent of this residual deficit can be evaluated.

These deficits involve loss of muscle control with consequent loss of mobility to perform tasks involved in the activities of daily living. Additionally, there often is loss of speech when the right arm and leg are paralyzed, and inability to understand the speech of others. Control of urination and defecation is frequently disturbed or lost. Pressure sores often develop if patients are not moved every two hours when they exhibit little spontaneous movement. Joints may become stiff or "stuck" (ankylosed) without passive or active movement. Much anxiety and depression will be experienced by patients following strokes, particularly when speech is affected.

Interventions. The possibility of maximal functional recovery after a stroke depends on the success of rehabilitative efforts to counter the immediate complications (stiffening of the joints and development of bed sores) and to retain the patient's use of muscles and joints in ambulation and in the activities of daily living. All stroke patients must have their joints passively moved daily through a full range of motion or until their neurological recovery allows them to exercise the joints themselves. Without such exercise, the joints may lose motion by ankylosis.

Physical therapy for maintaining joint motion and recovering muscular strength, and occupational therapy for regaining use of the upper extremities in activities of daily living, are essential. Retraining for bladder and rectum control are often necessary. Speech therapy is often indicated. All patients and their families require counseling, reassurance, and assistance in managing the return to the home environment (Gibson and Caplan, 1984). Many families will be reluctant to take on this burden, but in most communities, home care organizations can provide supplementary services. Supported by such home services, a willing family or spouse can often manage the care of post-stroke patients at home, a major achievement in the prevention of disability. When this proves impossible, long-term institutionalization may be inevitable.

2. Incontinence

a. Urinary incontinence

Urinary incontinence is an important precipitating cause for burnout of families caring for aged persons in their home. Much incontinence is not amenable to therapy, but too often there is a neglect of careful diagnostic evaluation of such patients.

Incidence. Urinary incontinence is the second most common cause of admission to long-term care facilities after a physical disability. More nursing home residents are incontinent than are cognitively impaired. More than half of all nursing home residents are troubled by urinary incontinence. In the total population, about 7 percent of males over the age of 64 are incontinent (Ehrman, 1983; Ouslander, Kane, and Abrass, 1982; Marron et al., 1983). The impact on families and on the patients is enormous: incontinence reduces social contacts and it leads to anger and guilt and almost always to increased isolation.

Etiology. The principal causes of urinary incontinence have been reviewed by Williams and Pannill (1982) and relate to the following disorders:

1. Detrusor instability related to defects in central nervous system inhibition, hyper-excitability of afferent pathways, and deconditioned micturition reflexes.
2. Overflow incontinence, arising from bladder outlet obstruction, detrusor inadequacy, or impaired sensation.
3. Sphincter insufficiency often related to inadequate estrogen to maintain urethral mucosa in women, weakness of pelvic and urethral muscles, urologic surgery, severe neuropathy, and urinary infections.
4. Functional incontinence related to psychologic factors, impaired mobility, inconvenient facilities, and inflexible schedules of staff and family.
5. Iatrogenic incontinence arising from inappropriate use of drugs, especially diuretics and sedatives and autonomic nervous system agents as well as physical restraints.

Intervention. This varied and complex array of factors does not imply that the situation is by any means hopeless; many of the underlying disorders will yield to careful diagnosis and therapy. Indeed, by minimizing the use of medications, approximately one-third of incontinent patients may spontaneously recover in a few weeks. Overall, with the use of different medications, most ambulatory elderly patients may be cured of incontinence (Williams and Pannill, 1982). For those not responding, various training techniques may be effective. These include exercises in actively stopping urinary flow (Mohr et al., 1983), or more extensive biofeedback exercises including control of urinary flow after injecting fluid into the bladder retrogradely. About 80 percent of patients have a marked reduction in incontinence after such exercises (Ehrman, 1983). These approaches to resistance problems of incontinence can usually be resolved without the use of catheters (Marron et al., 1983).

No carefully controlled studies have been reported in which the cost of such interventions has been weighed against the benefits achieved. Nevertheless, it is almost a foregone conclusion that these relatively modest approaches to supporting a major problem in long-term care are bound to be cost effective. The ability to retain elderly persons in their own home and the avoidance of catheterization and the subsequent almost inevitable urinary tract infections represent a large potential saving in the cost of care.

b. *Fecal incontinence*

Incidence. Fecal incontinence represents a much more challenging problem in patient care than urinary incontinence and often represents the final factor in a family's decision that an aged relative must be institutionalized. In hospitals, different studies have shown the proportion of aged persons who have fecal incontinence may rise as high as 65 percent, while in residential homes, it has been noted as between 10 and 14 percent. In one geriatric unit, more than half the patients were discovered to be incontinent at least once a week and 14 percent were persistently incontinent, with episodes occurring more than 3 times a week. In nursing homes (Smith, 1983), fecal incontinence has been reported as high as 25 percent (Ehrman, 1983).

Etiology. Fecal incontinence is generally related to some underlying disease process, to fecal stasis, or to a neurologic disorder (Smith, 1983). Underlying disease is usually of colonic origin but may be associated with drugs with specific irritant effects on the colon. Fecal stasis generally results in impaction as a result of constipation. This may be of two types, one related to a prolonged transit time through the colon which leads to excessive water absorption with resultant hard fecal accretions in all parts of the colon and rectum. The other type is related to a delayed movement only through the sigmoid colon, which results in the collection of a large amount of soft fecal material. Neurologic disorders may be either central or peripheral in origin. The peripheral problems may arise as secondary changes to prolonged straining at stool or damage to the mesenteric plexus as a result of prolonged abuse of laxatives as well as damage from other drugs, particularly anticholinergics and phenothiazines.

Central neurologic deficits are commonly related to severe dementia and the loss of ability to inhibit rectal contractions, resulting from distension. This leads to an incontinence of formed stools often following the ingestion of food. This differs from other forms of fecal incontinence in which there is more or less continuous loss of fluid and fecal material. Fecal incontinence is often associated with urinary incontinence and both commonly with severe dementia (Smith, 1983). As with urinary incontinence, careful diagnostic evaluation is indicated. A review of all current drugs will often reveal excessive use of one or more agents. In those cases where no obvious cause is found, a regimen of appropriate bowel management should be instituted, including adequate fiber and fluid. Physical exercise should be increased, as immobility is a major cause of incontinence (Smith, 1983). A surprising number of patients, regardless of mental status, will respond to a regimen in which all cathartics are eliminated and a regular use of suppositories every two days or twice a week initiated. Some chronic disease institutions have been successful in almost eliminating fecal incontinence with such a program, in spite of varying mental and physical status (Brocklehurst and Khan, 1969).

3. Visual Disorders: Blindness and Refractive Error

Blindness is a major cause of disability and dependence because of the limitation it imposes on both mobility and visual communication. Much blindness is preventable or treatable, and yet many persons do not receive the full benefits of modern technology. Unnecessary dependence and disability is the result. The chief causes of blindness in the aged are senile cataracts, senile macular degeneration (SMD), open angle glaucoma, and diabetic retinopathy. In addition, a number of aged persons have faint or almost no vision in one eye (amblyopia), and many others have correctible refractive errors.

Incidence. Blindness (visual acuity of less than 20/200) increases markedly in old age. In the Framingham eye study, 2.7 percent of those under 65 years of age were blind; between 65 and 74 years, the blind increased to 5.2 percent; and over 74 years, blindness affected 13.6 percent. Most of this was due to cataracts or SMD, although open angle glaucoma, diabetic retinopathy, and amblyopia accounted for significant amounts of blindness. With or without blindness, these disorders are widespread and increase with age. SMD affected 1.2 percent before age 65, 6.4 percent between 65 and 74, and 19.7 percent for those over 74. Senile cataracts were even more widespread: 3.5 percent in those under 65, 13.0 percent in those between 65 and 74, and 41.4 percent in those over 74. Open angle glaucoma and diabetic retinopathy each affected more than 2.0 percent between 65 and 74 years, and 3.5 percent for those over 74 years.

These studies, based on one middle class community, probably underestimate the national incidence of these visual disorders. Such underestimation, indeed, was evident in the Framingham results, which found substantially fewer refractive errors (visual acuity) than that found in the National Health Survey (U.S. DHEW, 1978). Both studies were done in the early 1970s. For aged persons between 65 and 74 years, the Framingham study found 91.9 percent with visual acuity between 20/10 and 20/25, while the national data found only 62.1 percent at that ("normal") level. For those elderly persons with refractive deficits, many did not have optimal correction from their current glasses, a deficit found in 5.2 percent of white persons between 65 and 74 years and in 10.2 percent of black persons.

Etiology. The development of a cataract in the lens of the eye represents a degenerative biochemical process which leads to clouding of the lens and a lack of clarity of transmission of visual images. Over time, vision is severely impaired and ultimately the process proceeds to a point of blindness. *Glaucoma* is characterized by an impairment of the outflow of fluid from the anterior chamber of the eye. This leads to an increase in intraocular pressure with peripheral visual loss. Patients may disregard the earliest evidence of this loss such as the appearance of halos around lights. The diagnosis of increased pressure can conveniently be done with a tonometer, which may be used in evaluating patient complaints or in widespread screening programs. *Senile macular degeneration* of the neovascular type is a process in which there is a growth under the retina of abnormal new blood vessels leading to damage of the macula and impairing central vision. This neovascular type is the most serious form of the disease. Provisional evidence of the problem may be determined in a simple home test by noticing that a vertical line, such as a door jamb appears bent or wavy.

Interventions. The traditional treatment for *cataracts* has been to remove them and substitute eyeglasses or contact lenses for the loss of the lens. Recently, progress has been made with insertion of plastic lenses, although too little time has elapsed to evaluate possible late side effects. *Glaucoma* may be preventable in most cases with early detection, and the closed angle type may be controlled surgically. The open angle type may require systemic or oral medication. Glaucoma leads to substantial use of medical care and hospitalization. It is the third most common reason for visits to ophthalmologists, and in 1980 accounted for 3.25 million patient visits or 8.5 percent of all visits to ophthalmologists. It also accounts for about 5 percent of all hospital admissions for eye complaints (Leske, 1983). For *senile macular degeneration*, the recent development of laser therapy has proved effective. The laser treatment does not restore sight but prevents further visual deterioration. It acts by sealing off vessels, avoiding bleeding and fluid leakage, and is not associated with scar tissue formation (National Eye Institute, 1983). The treatment reduces or delays blindness in some 90 percent of those so treated.

For patients with deteriorating vision for which therapy is ineffective, a number of aids are available. These include large print newspapers and books, closed circuit television, and radio reading services. Furthermore, a remarkable number of correctable but neglected visual deficits are present in older patients. There is probably no deficit in aged persons that will so easily yield to intervention as correctable visual problems (Kivett, 1979).

Refractive errors. As indicated above, a considerable number of readily correctable refractive deficits are present in older patients. Additional refractive screening is undoubtedly warranted, especially if it were to be done at the time of regular medical check-ups. Even so, refractive errors were found to be the commonest cause for patient visits to ophthalmologists in 1976. Elderly patients in long-term care institutions are particularly likely to be neglected in regard to visual deficits.

4. Independent Living

The prevention of untimely death and disability and dependence is the ultimate purpose of primary, secondary, and tertiary prevention. With advancing age, an independent lifestyle becomes increasingly difficult, but a remarkable proportion of aged persons do remain independent.

Incidence. In Rochester, the Health Care of Aged Study, based on a sample of all aged, found that 92 percent of persons 65-69 years could live independently. This dropped off to 77 percent for aged 75-79, to 44 percent for those 85-89, and to 17 percent for those 90 and over. Overall, 75 percent of all aged persons could live independently without additional services or supervision. An additional 5 percent could manage almost independently at home with occasional public health nursing services. A further 12 percent could live at home with supervision for mental health reasons. Some of these would also require public health nursing services (Berg et al., 1970).

Etiology. The inability to live independently, requiring a *dependent* life style, is related to physical or psychological disabilities. Social deficits are also responsible, at least for partially independent living such as living with a relative or friend who can provide needed assistance.

The *quality of life* becomes a major issue for aged persons. The environmental features of one's place of residence which are viewed as important by elderly persons include living in a neighborhood with friendly people, good walking conditions, nearby bus stops and food

91

stores, and esthetic features including general attractiveness, cleanliness and lack of litter, quiet, nice landscaping, and minimal air pollution (Carp and Carp, 1982).

Psychological deficits are often related to dementia or depression as discussed above. These in turn are closely allied to social shortcomings. Old age tends to lead to social isolation, and loneliness is one of the most common complaints of the elderly. While loneliness may be dealt with in the context of the optimal living environment discussed above, a pervasive problem is the death of a spouse or the lack of housing with one's children. Indeed, the increasing proportion of women in the work force is significantly correlated with institutionalization of aged persons and an increase in the number of aged hospitalized patients waiting for admission to nursing homes (Berg, Rice, and Varricchio, 1981).

The reluctance of families to accommodate an elderly relative in their homes is especially related to dementia. Confused and forgetful old folks present an added burden of supervision, a limitation on leisure and recreation, and often a loss of sleep. When abusive language and behavior occur, the load my be intolerable.

Anxiety increases with advancing age in regard to fiscal support and management of fiscal resources. Fear of fire, sudden illness, robbery, and accidents may make living alone undesirable in spite of an independent spirit.

Physical deficits may be based on any medical problem interfering with function, but in practical terms, the major disabilities interfering with independent living are problems with walking and the activities of daily living: dressing, feeding, bathing, toileting, and grooming. Urinary incontinence poses additional burdens, but fecal incontinence of any frequency is as poorly tolerated as abusive behavior. Visual and hearing deficits aggravate any other limitation and reduce the quality of life. Television viewing (the outside world for many aged persons), reading, or handiwork become impossible. Painful feet, neurologic deficits from stroke, and shortness of breath from cardiac disorders make ambulation difficult. When a previously independent person can no longer drive a car or walk to a nearby store, only an extraordinarily committed support can allow that now dependent person to live in their own home.

Interventions. Most of the problems limiting independent living can be alleviated with the help of prudent planning and a committed advocate for the aged person. This usually is a family member with support from a health professional. The *living environment* can be

92

developed for its contribution to the quality of life. The client should be helped to set priorities and make choices accordingly. A regular schedule of visiting and reviewing medical regimens should be set up when the client is housebound or almost so. The burden on a spouse or family can be reduced with sitters to free the caretaker for independent activities. For the same purpose, respite care can often be found for weekends or holidays. Instruction in bladder and bowel control can reduce the impact of incontinence. Proper foot care will increase comfort and the ease and likelihood of walking about indoors and out. Specific assistive aids for walking, toileting, and bathing are available (Friedman and Capulong, 1984). Ingenious self-help devices have been developed for extending the reach and assisting in fine hand movements (Itoh, Lee, and Shapiro, 1984).

Communications. The evolution of convenient two-way radio communication has not been well adapted to the needs of older persons. Tape recorded health and medical advice for cassette recorders are one example of an underused technology that is readily available. Two-way radios might be appropriately adapted for emergency and other communication as well as special telephone extensions.

Safety Measures. Specific safety evaluation of the residences of aged persons in much the same way as a review of energy loss can avoid serious problems. Fire hazards can be eliminated, fire extinguishers of a kind that can be readily handled by even infirm persons need to be in place, and safety arrangements around gas and electrical appliances may be necessary. Grab bars, ramps, and stair rails may be helpful. Alarm systems for fire, assault, or sudden illness must be developed.

Independent Living Arrangements. While separate apartments within residences occupied by other members of the family is a well-established approach to caring for an elderly person in one's home, the British have developed so-called "granny flats," mobile homes which are brought on wheels and attached to another residence where additional space is needed. Other housing arrangements may make substantial improvements (Carp, 1977), and an emphasis on general services to the homebound and special socialization programs enhance the potential of independent living (Leviton and Santa Maria, 1979).

IV. *Conclusions*

Much disability in old age is preventable, either primarily or with secondary interventions or rehabilitative efforts. These potential remedies are often neglected, adding greatly to dependence of aged persons and consequent societal costs. Improved education of health professionals is often identified as the solution to the problem. Education, however, is not a sufficient solution; incentives for prevention and coordination of health care need to be woven into the health care system. These issues are discussed elsewhere in this volume.

ROBERT L. BERG

References

Adler, W. H., Jones, K. H., and Nariuchi, H., "Ageing and Immune Function," in *Recent Advances in Clinical Immunology*, vol. 1, R. A. Thompson, ed. (New York: Churchill Livingstone Press, 1977).

Advisory Committee for Immunization Practices, "Influenza Vaccine 1980-81," "*Morbidity and Mortality Weekly Report* 29(19):225, May 16, 1980.

Aloia, J. A., "Exercise and Skeletal Health," *Journal of the American Geriatrics Society* 24(3):104, March, 1981.

Austrian, R., and Gold, J., "Pneumonoccal Bacteremia with Especial Reference to Bacteremic Pneumococcal Pneumonia," *Annals of Internal Medicine* 60:759, 1964.

Barker, W. H., and Mullooly, J. P., "Influenza Vaccination of Elderly Persons," *Journal of the American Medical Association* 244(22):2547, 1980.

Baum, John, "Rehabilitation Aspects of Arthritis in the Elderly," in *Rehabilitation in the Aging*, T. F. Williams, ed. (New York: Raven, 1984).

Bentley, D. W., "Immunization for the Elderly," in *Medicine and Old Age: Immunology and Infection*, R. A. Fox, ed. (London: Churchville Livingston, 1984).

Berg, R. L., "Weighted Life Expectancy as a Health Status Index," *Health Services Research* 8:153, 1973.

Berg, R. L., "The High Cost of Self-Deception," *Preventive Medicine* 5:483, 1976.

Berg, R. L., Hallauer, D. S., and Berk, S. N., "Neglected Aspects of the Quality of Life," *Health Services Research* 11:391, 1976.

Berg, R. L., "Prevention of Disability in the Aged," in *Public Health and Preventive Medicine*, J. M. Last, ed. (New York: Appleton-Century Crofts, 1980).

Berg, R. L., Browning, F. E., Hill, J. G., et al, "Assessing the Health Care Needs of the Aged," *Health Services Research* 5:36, 1970.

Berg, R. L., and Ornt, D. B., "End Stage Renal Disease: How Many, How Much?," *American Journal of Public Health* 74:4, 1984.

Blackburn, H. and Gillum, R. F., "Heart Disease," in *Public Health and Preventive Medicine*, J. M. Last, ed. (New York: Appleton-Century Crofts, 1980).

Borhani, N. O., "Hypertension," in *Advances in Disease Prevention*, C. B. Arnold, ed. (New York: Springer, 1981).

Brocklehurts, J. C., and Khan, M.Y., "A Study of Faecal Stasis in Old Age and the Use of 'Dorbanex' in its Prevention," *Gerontologia Clinica* 11:293, 1969.

Butler, R. N., "Psychiatry and the Elderly: An Overview," *American Journal Psychiatry* 132(9):893, 1975.

Carp, F. M., "Impact of Improved Living Environment on Health and Life Expectancy," *The Gerontologist* 17(3):242, 1977.

Carp, F. M., and Carp, A., "The Ideal Residential Area," *Research on Aging* 4:411, 1982.

Crossley, K., Irvine, P., Warren, J. B., et al, "Tetanus and Diptheria Immunity in Urban Minnesota Adults," *Journal of the American Medical Association* 242(21):2298, 1979.

Dolin, R., Reichman, R. C., Madore, H. P., et al, "Comparison of Amantadine and Rimantadine in the Prophylaxis of Influenza A Infection," Twenty first Interscience Conference on Antimicrobial Agents and Chemotherapy Abstract No. 245 (Chicago, 1981).

Douglas, R. G., Jr., and Betts, R. F., "Influenza Virus," in *Principles and Practice of Infectious Diseases*, G. L. Mandell, R. G. Douglas, Jr., and J. E. Bennett, eds. (New York: John Wiley & Sons, 1979).

Du Vries, H. L., *Surgery of the Foot*, 2nd ed. (St. Louis, Mo,: C. V. Mosby, 1965).

Eade, A. W. T., Morris, I. M., and Nicol, C. G., "A Health Centre Survey of Rheumatism," *Rheumatological Rehabilitation* 18:148, 1979.

Ehrman, J. S., "Use of Biofeedback to Treat Incontinence," *Journal of the American Geriatrics Society*31(3):182, March 1983.

Food and Drug Administration, *Drug Bulletin* 8(1):5, 1978.

Fried, M. A., "Epidemiological Study of Pneuymococcal Disease," Annual Contract of Progress Report, NIAID, Contract No. NIAID 72-25103, Kaiser Permanente Medical Center, San Francisco, California 1983.

Friedman, L. W. and Capulong, E. S., "Specific Assistive Aids," in *Rehabilitation in the Aging*, T. F. Williams, ed., (New York: Raven, 1984).

Fries, J. F., "Aging, Natural Death, and the Compression of Morbidity," *New England Journal of Medicine* 303(3):130, 1980.

Gershon, S. and Herman, S. P., "The Differential Diagnosis of Dementia," *Journal of the American Geriatrics Society* 30(11):S58, November, 1982.

Gibbs, C. J., Gasusek, D. C., Asher, D. M., et al., "Creutzfeld-Jakob Disease Transmission to the Chimpanzee," *Science* 161:388, 1968.

Gibson, C. J. and Caplan, B. M., "Rehabilitation of the Patient with Stroke," in *Rehabilitation in the Aging*, T. F. Williams, ed. (New York: Raven, 1984).

Greenland, P., "Cardiac Fitness and Rehabilitation in the Elderly," *Journal of the American Geriatrics Society* 30(9):607, September 1982.

Gummow, L. J., Miller, P., and Dustman, R. E., "Attention and Brain Injury: A Case for Cognitive Rehabilitation of Attentional Deficits," *Clinical Psychology Review* 3:1983.

Hale, W. E., Stewart, R. B., Cerda, J. J. et al, "Use of Nutritional Supplements in an Ambulatory Elderly Population," *Journal of the American Geriatrics Society* 30(6):401, June, 1982.

Hanley, E. G., McGuire, R. J., and Boyd, W. D., "Reality Orientation and Dementia: A Controlled Trial of Two Approaches," *British Journal of Psychology* 138:10, 1981.

Helfand, A. E., "Common Foot Problems in the Aged and Rehabilitative Management," in *Rehabilitation in the Aging*, T. F. Williams, ed., (New York: Raven, 1984).

Hogue, C. C., "Injury in Late Life: Part I. Epidemiology," *Journal of the American Geriatrics Society* 30(3):183, March, 1982.

Hypertension Detection and Follow-up Program Cooperative Group, "The Effect of Treatment of Mortality in "Mild" Hypertension," *New England Journal of Medicine* 307(16):976, Oct. 14, 1982.

Itoh, M, Lee, M., and Shapiro, J., "Self-Help Devices for the Elderly Population Living in the Community," in *Rehabilitation in the Aging*, T. F. Williams, ed., (New York: Raven, 1984).

Izzo, J. L., "Hypertension in the Elderly: A Pathophysiologic Approach to Therapy," *Journal of the American Geriatric Society* 30(5):352, 1982.

Kavet, J., "Trends in the Utilization of Influenza Vaccine: An Examination of the Implementation of Public Policy in the United States," on *Influenza: Virus, Vaccines, Strategy*, P. Selby, ed. (New York: Academic Press, 1976).

Kay, D. W. K., Beamish, P., and Roth, M., "Old Age Mental Disorders in Newcastle upon Tyne," *British Journal of Psychiatry* 110:146, 1964.

Keys, A., ed., *Coronary Heart Disease in Seven Countries* (New York: The American Heart Association, 1970).

Kivett, V. R., "Discriminators of Loneliness Among the Rural Elderly: Implications for Intervention," *The Gerontologist* 19(1):108, 1979.

Krishna, K. M. and VanCleave, R. J., "Decrease in the Incidence of Patient Falls in a Geriatric Hospital after Educational Programs," *Journal of the American Geriatrics Society* 31(3):187, 1983.

LaForce, F. M., Young, L. S., and Bennett, J. V., "Tetanus in the United States 1965-1966," *The New England Journal of Medicine* 280(11):569, 1969.

Larson, E. B., Olsen, W. C., and Shortell, S., "The Relationship of Health Beliefs and a Postcard Reminder to Influenza Vaccination," *The Journal of Family Practice* 8(6):1207, 1979.

Leske, M. C. and Hawkins, B. S., "Screening: Relationship to Diagnosis and Therapy," in *Duane's Clinical Opthalmology* (Philadelphia: J. B. Lippincott, 1983).

Leviton, D., and Santa Maria, L., "The Adults Health & Developmental Program: Descriptive and Evaluative Data," *The Gerontologist* 19(6):534, 1979.

Maccoby, N., Farquhar, J. W., Wood, P. D., et al., "Reducing the Risk of Cardiovascular Disease: Effects of a Community-Based Campaign on Knowledge and Behavior," *Journal of Community Health* 3(2):100, Winter, 1977.

Makinodan, T., and Kay, M. M. B., "Age Influence on the Immune System," *Advances in Immunology* 29:278, 1980.

Marron, K. R., Fillit, H., Peskowitz, M., et al, "The Nonuse of Urethral Cathertization in the Management of Urinary Incontinence in the Teaching Nursing Home," *Journal of the American Geriatrics Society* 31(5):278, May 1983.

Mathur, W., Bentley, D. W., Hall, D. C. et al, "Influenza A/Brazil/78/(HINI) Infection in the Elderly," *American Review of Respiratory Disease* 123:633, 1981.

McAlister, A., Pusk, P., Salonen, J.T., et al, "Theory and Action for Health Promotion: Illustrations from the North Karelia Project," *American Journal of Public Health* 72(1):43, January, 1982.

McDermott, J. R., Fraser, H., and Dickinson, A. G., "Reduced Choline Acetyltransferase Activity in Scrapie Mouse Brain," *The Lancet* ii:318, 1978.

Mitenki, P. A., Comfort, A., and Crooks, J., eds., *Journal of Chronic Diseases: Drugs and the Elderly—Proceedings of a Symposium held at Tornoto, May 4-5, 1981*, 36(1), 1983.

Mohr, J. A., Roger, J., Brown, T. N., et al., "Stress Urinary Incontinence: A Simple and Practical Approach to Diagnostic Treatment," *Journal of the American Geriatrics Society* 31(8):476, August 1983.

Mortimer, J. A. and Schuman, L. M., eds. *The Epidemiology of Dementia* (New York: Oxford University Press, 1981).

Moss, A. J., "Diagnosis and Management of Heart Disease in the Elderly," in *Clinical Aspects of Aging, Second Edition*, W. Reichel, ed. (Baltimore: Williams and Wilkins, 1982).

Nandy, K., ed., *Senile Dementia: A Biomedical Approach* (New York: Elsevier/North Holland, 1978).

National Eye Institute, "Laser Treatment Found Effective in Preventing Blindness from Senile Macular Degeneration," *Journal of the American Geriatrics Society* 31(4):238, 1983.

Nayak, U. S. L., Gabell, A., Simons, M. A., et al, "Measurement of Gait and Balance in the Elderly," *Journal of the American Geriatrics Society* 30(8):516, 1982.

O'Donoghue, J. M., Ray, C. G., and Terry, D. W., Jr., "Prevention of Nosocomial Influenza Infection with Amantadine," *American Journal of Epidemiology* 97(4):276, 1973.

Ouslander, J. G., Kane, R. L., and Abrass, I. B., "Urinary Incontinence in Elderly Nursing Home Patients," *Journal of the American Medical Association* 248(10):1194, September 10, 1982.

Overstall, P. W., Johnson, A. I., and Exton-Smith, A. N., "Instability and Falls in the Elderly," *Age and Ageing* 7(supplement):92, 1978.

Perry, B. C., "Falls among the Elderly: A Review of the Methods and Conclusions of Epidemiologic Studies," *Journal of the American Geriatrics Society* 30(6):367, June, 1982.

Ross, R., "Recent Progress in Understanding Atherosclerosis," *Journal of the American Geriatrics Society* 31(4):231, 1983.

Reinke, B. J., Holmes, D. C., and Denney, N. W., "Influence of a Friendly Visitor Program on the Cognitive Functioning and Morale of Elderly Persons," *American Journal of Community Psychology* 9:491, 1981.

Rothblum, E. D., Sholomskas, A. J., Berry, C., et al, "Issues in Clinical Trials with the Depressed Elderly," *Journal of the American Geriatrics Society* 30(11):694, November 1982.

Ruben, F. L., Nagel, J., and Fireman, P., "Antitoxin Responses in the Elderly to Tetanus-Diphtheria (td) Immunization," *American Journal of Epidemiology* 108(2):145, 1978.

Sholomskas, A. J., Berry, C., et al, "Issues in Clinical Trials with the Depressed Elderly," *Journal of the American Geriatrics Society* 30(11):694, November 1982.

Sabin, T. D., Biologic Aspects of Falls and Mobility Limitations in the Elderly," *Journal of the American Geriatrics Society* 30(1):51, 1982.

Schoenbaum, S. C., "A Perspective on the Benefits, Costs, and Risks of Immunization," in *Seminars in Infectious Disease*, vol. 3, L. Weinstein, and B. N. Fields, eds. (New York: Thieme-Stratton, Inc., 1980).

Sherman, F. T., "Tetanus and the Institutionalized Elderly," *Journal of the American Medical Association* 244(19):2159, 1980.

Silverman, S. I., "Dental Care for Rehabilitation of the Aging," *Rehabilitation in the Aging*, T. F. Williams, ed. (New York: Raven Press, 1984).

Silverstone, F. A., Libow, L. S., Duthie, E., et al, "Outbreak of Influenza B, 1980, in a Geriatric Long-term Care Facility," *Gerontologist* 20(3)Part III:200, 1980.

Small, G. W., and Jarvik, L. F., "The Dementia Syndrome," *The Lancet* ii:1443, 1982.

Smith, C. M., Swase, M., Exton-Smith, A. N., et al, "Choline Therapy in Alzheimer's Disease," *The Lancet* ii:318, 1982.

Smith, R. G., "Fecal Incontinence," *Journal of the American Geriatrics Society* 31(11):694, November 1983.

Solomonova, K., and Vizev, S., "Immunological Reactivity of Senescent and Old People Actively Immunized with Tetanus Toxoid," *Zeitschrift fur Immunitaetsforschung, Experimentelle und Klinische Immunologie* 146:81, 1973.

Stafford, J. L., and Bringle, R. G., "The Influence of Task Success on Women's Interest in New Activities," *The Gerontologist* 20(6):642, 1980.

Thompson, T. L., Moran, M. C., and Nies, A. S., "Psychotropic Drug Use in the Elderly," *New England Journal of Medicine* 308(3):134, January 20, 1983.

Tinetti, M. E., Williams, T. F., and Mayewski, R., "A Fall Risk Index in an Ambulatory Geriatric Population," working paper, 1984.

U.S. Congress, Office of Technology Assessment, *Cost Effectiveness of Influenza Vaccination*, GPO Stock No. OTA-H-152 (Washington, D.C.: U.S. Government Printing Office, December 1981).

U.S. Department of Health, Education, and Welfare, National Center for Health Statistics, "Refraction Status and Motility Defects of Persons 4-74 Years, United States, 1971-1972," *Vital and Health Statistics*, series 11, no. 206, DHEW publication no. (PHS) 78-1654, 1978.

U.S. Department of Health, Education, and Welfare, National Center for Health Statistics, *Vital Statistics of the United States*, Annual, 1978.

U.S. Department of Health, Education, and Welfare, National Center for Health Statistics, "Basic Data on Arthritis Knee, Hip, and Sacroiliac Joints in Adults Ages 25-75 United States, 1971-1975," *Vital and Health Statistics*, series 11, no. 213, DHEW publication no. (PHS) 79-1661, 1979 c.

U.S. Department of Health, Education, and Welfare, National Center for Health Statistics, "Basic Data on Dental Examination Findings of Persons 1-74 Years United States, 1971-1974, *Vital and Health Statistics*, series 11, no. 214, DHEW publication no. (PHS) 79-1662, 1979 a.

U.S. Department of Health, Education, and Welfare, National Center for Health Statistics, "The National Nursing Home Survey: 1977 Summary for the United States," *Vital and Health Statistics*, series 13, no. 43, DHEW publication no. (PHS) 79-1794, 1979 b.

U.S. Department of Health and Human Services, Public Health Service, Center for Disease Control, *National Survey of Public Attitudes Toward A/New Jersey/76 Influenza Vaccination*, report no. 8, table 3, 1977.

U.S. Department of Health and Human Services, National Center for Health Statistics, "Hypertension in Adults 25-74 Years of Age United States, 1971-1975," *Vital and Health Statistics*, series 11, no. 221, DHEW publication no. (PHS) 81-1671, 1981 b.

U.S. Department of Health and Human Services, National Center for Health Statistics, "Discharges from Nursing Homes: 1977 National Nursing Home Survey," *Vital and Health Statistics*, series 13, no. 54, DHHS publication no. (PHS) 81-1715, 1981 c.

U.S. Department of Health and Human Services, National Center for Health Statistics, "Utilization of Short-Stay Hospitals: Annual Summary for the United States, 1979," *Vital and Health Statistics*, series 13, no. 60, DHHS publication no. (PHS) 82-1721, 1981 d.

U.S. Department of Health and Human Services, Public Health Service, Morbidity and Mortality Weekly Report Annual Summary 1980, volume 29, no. 54, HHS publication no. (CDC) 81-8241, 1981.

U.S. Department of Health and Human Services, Public Health Service, Morbidity and Mortality Weekly Report Annual Summary 1981, volume 30, no 54, HHS publication no. (CDC) 82-8241, 1982.

van Voris, L. P., Belsche, R. B., and Shaffer, J. L., "Nosocomial Influenza B Virus Infection in the Elderly," *Annals of Internal Medicine* 96(2):153, 1982.

Waaler, H. T., "Cost-Benefit Analysis of BCG-Vaccination under Various Epidemiological Situations," *Bulletin of the International Union Against Tuberculosis* 41:42, 1968.

Wild, D., Nayak, U. S. L., and Isaacs, B., "Description, Classification, and

Prevention of Falls in Old People at Home," *Rheumatology and Rehabilitation* 20:153, 1981.

Shaffer, J. L., "Nosocomial Influenza B Virus Infection in the Elderly," *Annals of Internal Medicine* 96(2):153, 1982.

Waaler, H. T., "Cost-Benefit Analysis of BCG-Vaccination under Various Benefit Analyses of Vaccines," *The Journal of Infectious Diseases* 144(5):486, November 1981.

Williams, M. E., personal communication, 1983.

Williams, M. E., "A Critical Evaluation of the Assessment Technology for Urinary Continence in Older Persons," *Journal of the American Geriatrics Society* 31(11):657, November 1983.

Williams, M. E., and Pannill, F. C., "Urinary Incontinence in the Elderly," *Annals of Internal Medicine* 97(6):895, December 1982.

6

Assessment of the Elderly in Relation to Needs for Long-Term Care: An Emerging Technology

T. Franklin Williams

Aging itself is a relatively benign process with some, relatively modest, loss of maximum functional abilities. When no or little chronic disease has been acquired, it is compatible with maintaining an active and varied life of independence. Unfortunately, most persons as they grow older acquire chronic diseases and resulting disabilities which do limit their independence and increase in frequency with very old age, resulting in the need for continuing assistance and care. Beyond age 65, 80 percent of persons have at least one chronic condition; among the most common are arthritis (44 percent), hearing impairment (29 percent), and one or another chronic cardiac condition (20 percent).

These chronic conditions become reflected in limitations in activity: most recent surveys of the National Center for Health Statistics show that 45 percent of persons age 65 and older not living in institutions were found to have some degree of limitation of daily activities; this rises to 60 percent of those aged 85 and older. Among this very old age group (not in institutions) 18 percent were found to need help with dressing, 11 percent with bathing, 7 percent with toileting, and 4 percent with eating (Rice, 1981, Rice and Feldman, 1982).

These chronic disabilities in turn call for supportive long term care. In a careful assessment of the needs for care of a complete random sample of all persons age 65 older (in the community and in institutions) conducted in Monroe County, New York, in the 1960s, approximately 17 percent were found to need some form of long term care (University of Rochester, 1968). This was one of the few truly population based studies of extent of need for care; other studies in Western societies have also rather consistently found that approximately 15 percent of elderly need some form of long term care: approximately 5 percent are judged to need care in institutions, and 10 percent need various home support services. With the increasing numbers of very old persons, we can expect the total numbers (and percent of those over age 65) needing institutional and home support services to increase. Continuously updated information on the extent and types of long term care services needed is essential for adequate health care planning. This point is addressed further below in relation to the roles that assessment technologies should serve.

In light of the extensive and growing need for long term care services, it is generally agreed that approaches and procedures are necessary which will help assure that each person in need of such services will have specific needs identified in order that services appropriate to those needs can be provided. This in turn, calls for adequate planning, administration, and financing of services. The process of identification of needs, addressed here as the "assessment process", can then lead to decisions on long term care services.

It is worth emphasis that such assessment is important both for good care decisions for the individual person and for sound public policy in the provision of this large segment of health and social services. The public policy issue has been addressed by a number of bodies in essentially the same way; an example is the first recommendation of the policy statement on the elderly and functional dependency of the Institute of Medicine:

> The federal government should reimburse for long term care provided to the functionally dependent elderly. Long term care should include both health and social services and should provide for choices between institutional and home-based care. Eligibility for federal reimbursement of long term care should be based on a comprehensive assessment process. (Institute of Medicine, 1977)

Assessment thus is recommended to serve a "gate keeper" function for long term care services as well as to assure appropriateness of care for the individual patient.

It is clear that efforts including sound assessment are needed to achieve appropriate long term care. Considerable inappropriateness of use of services, particularly skilled nursing services, has been documented in a number of studies. In two studies, teams consisting

102

of a physician (internist) and public health nurse, who had received special preparation for assessment of need for long term care, made clinical evaluations of random samples, first of the population age 65 and over in Monroe County, New York (Table 1), and in the second study of all patients in acute hospitals, long term care institutions, and persons at home for whom long term care had been suggested (Table 2; University of Rochester, 1968; Williams, 1981; Williams and Williams, 1982). In both studies, 50 percent or more of persons needing some form of long term care were not receiving what was judged to be the appropriate type or level of care.

Findings such as these have led to efforts involving more adequate assessment, of two general types: (1) efforts to achieve more appropriate long term care services for individual patients through comprehensive assessments of need and assistance in arranging for appropriate services (i.e., case management); and (2) efforts to identify inappropriate use of services as well as unmet needs, through population based assessments, and to improve use through management steps and planning decisions. The following are examples of such efforts.

I. An Overview of Selected Demonstration Projects

1. *Evaluation and Placement.* A subsequent project, (Williams et al., 1973; Williams and Williams, 1982) attempted to determine whether appropriate care based on comprehensive multidisciplinary assessments could achieve better arrangements, as judged by an independent professional team similar to that used in the studies cited above. In a series of patients referred to this new service and already on the waiting list for nursing home admission, two-thirds were recommended for and assisted in receiving long term care in settings other than nursing homes after this assessment; 23 percent were assisted in remaining at home with support services (Table 3). Independent review of the appropriateness of the long term care arrangements for these patients showed that 85 to 90 percent were judged to be appropriate in each care setting.

2. *ACCESS Program.* The ACCESS program was developed as a county-wide demonstration project to determine whether a system providing assessment of long term care needs, case management in obtaining the identified needed services, and authorization for payment of these services for Medicaid-eligible (and, since 1982, Medicare-eligible) persons would be effective for an entire community.

Table 1
Persons 65 and over needing or receiving some form of care; Monroe County, 1964

Type of Institution	Number Needing or Receiving Care	Misplaced	
		Number	Percent
General Hospitals	484	34	7.0
State Mental Hospitals	890	840	94.4
Chronic Hospitals	379	140	36.9
Nursing Homes	1,118	216	19.9
Homes for Aged	550	183	33.0

Source: University of Rochester, 1968.

Table 2
Appropriateness of current setting for sampled elderly patients in long-term care facilities

Level of Care	Number Evaluated	Percent Appropriate
Supervised boarding home	226	47
Health-related facility		26
Nursing home	305	52
Psychiatric hospital	53	17

[a]Based on independent evaluations by a physician-nurse team, as described by Williams, et al. 1973, 1977.

Objectives were to encourage more care at home and minimize the pressure for more use of expensive skilled nursing beds, leading to greater cost-effectiveness as compared to communities not using such a system (Eggert, Bowylow, and Nichols, 1980; Eggert and Brodows, 1982).

A standard Patient Assessment Form was developed which is used by the ACCESS case manager in collaboration with the patient, his family, and involved health professionals to arrange for long term care services from a wide variety of community sources and for authorizing payment for Medicaid or Medicare-eligible clients.

This program is now serving approximately 5,000 new clients per year; approximately half are Medicaid recipients and half are self-pay or Medicare patients. A few of the results obtained to date may illustrate the potential of such an assessment plus case management system (Table 4). Compared to self-pay clients, who predominantly continued to enter skilled nursing facilities, a much higher proportion of Medicare clients who had been assessed as needing skilled nursing

Table 3
Results of assessments by evaluation-placement unit for frail elderly persons living at home, most of whom were already on waiting lists for nursing home admission, 1973

Setting for Long-term Care Determined by E-P Unit	Number	Percent
At home with support service	72	23
Supervised boarding home	96	30
Health-related facility	26	8
Skilled nursing facility	110	35
Psychiatric hospital	11	4
Total	315	100

Table 4
Disposition of hospital clients needing a skilled nursing level of care

Year	Medicaid Clients			Other Clients		
	No.	Home Care (%)	SNF (%)	No.	Home Care (%)	SNF (%)
1978	295	35	65	480	19	81
1979	403	57	43	412	20	80
1980	469	57	43	501	27	73
1981	540	68	32	559	26	74

care after hospital discharge received this care through home care services rather than entering skilled nursing facilities. Payment for the home care services was arranged through ACCESS, and the total Medicaid cost for these services on average amounted to approximately 60 percent of the average Medicaid cost for skilled nursing facility beds in this county. Table 5 shows the impact of the ACCESS program on overall Medicaid expenditures for persons age 65 and older (who constitute over 80 percent of ACCESS clients) in Monroe County compared to six similar counties in New York State. Although average expenditures for home care services increased at twice the rate in Monroe County as in the other counties, nursing home and health related (intermediate care) facility increases were considerably less, the average total increase in expenditures was slightly more than half as much as that in the other counties.

Preliminary data on the effect of including Medicare in this system suggest that hospitalizations and hospital stays are being reduced for elderly patients who require most extensive long-term care and who were thus contributing most to "back up."

Table 5
Percent change in Medicaid expenditures for clients aged 65+

	Monroe County	Six Comparison Counties
Inpatient Hospital	+ 36.9%	+37.0%
Nursing Homes	+ 5.7%	+23.1%
Health-related Facilities	+ 22.3%	+48.2%
Home Health Care	+131.0%	+57.2%
Total	+ 18.9%	+32.7%

Comparable demonstrations in other settings, such as TRIAGE in Connecticut, and projects in Georgia and Wisconsin, have also demonstrated some favorable outcomes through use of an assessment and case management approach to community-wide needs for long term care services. These efforts in turn have led to other "channeling" demonstration programs supported by the Health Care Financing Administration and by The Robert Wood Johnson Foundation. The ACCESS and similar programs illustrate the applicability and value of assessment procedures in determining and planning for long term care.

3. *The Geriatric Consultative Team Project.* Another use of the assessment approach is illustrated by the Geriatric Consultative Team Project, conducted in 1982 in seven of the eight hospitals in Monroe County. This project was developed in response to the increasing numbers of patients "backed up" in acute hospital beds awaiting admission to long term skilled nursing care facilities despite the efforts of ACCESS and other community efforts. The problem in Monroe County has perhaps been more critical than in other areas because of a long-standing restraint on construction of acute hospital beds (with a current ratio of 3.6 hospital beds per 1,000 population, Monroe County has one of the lowest ratios in the nation), and an enforced cap on addition of skilled nursing beds.

With temporary funds from the Rochester Area Hospitals Corporation, geriatric consultative teams were established in each of the seven participating hospitals, consisting of a physician (internist), nurse clinician, and social worker. In the six months from January through June 1982, these teams screened all newly admitted patients aged 70 and older and attempted to identify those at high risk of eventually being "backed up" for admission to skilled nursing facil-

106

ities. For the approximately 7 percent of patients so identified, the teams carried out full consultative evaluations and made recommendations aimed at maintaining or restoring function and independence of living practices from the earliest possible hospital day and at using all possible community resources for care other than in skilled nursing beds (Williams et al., 1982).

During the six months of full team activities, the numbers of "backed up" patients in participating hospitals were reduced by 35 percent, compared to consistent rises over the previous two years. The recommendations made by the teams were carried out in 50 percent to 70 percent of cases. The teams identified a number of issues and problems which the hospitals have been encouraged to address in order to assist these elderly patients in maintaining function and ability to return home or to a less than a skilled nursing level of care.

4. *Assessment of Long Term Care Patients in Institutions.* Examples of standardized assessment of patients in long term care institutions for patient care planning and evaluation and for program review include the studies of the Harvard Center for Community Health and Medical Care using the "Patient Classification for Long Term Care" (Harvard Center, 1977), and the study of Kane and collaborators at Rand (Kane et al., 1982) of the Rand Corporation. In the Harvard study, the patient classification system was tested in seven nursing homes and found to be feasible in repeated administrations. The resulting data indicated changes in patient care plans and also illustrated the predictive applicability of the measures of function in terms of likely survival in the nursing home and duration of stay.

The Kane study is devoted to the development of a comprehensive assessment instrument covering a number of dimensions or domains (activities of daily living, affect, cognition, social activity, pain/discomfort, and satisfaction). Its protocols have established a relatively high interrater reliability and can be used for predicting the outcomes for nursing home patients. They thus can be used for comparing different treatment efforts and possibly as the basis for incentive reimbursement for more effective treatment approaches.

In summary, the examples presented illustrate the development of assessment approaches and their application to arranging appropriate long term care services for individual patients and to institutional and community program evaluation and planning. Two types of assessment technology have been developed: clinical assessment and judgment, and the use of standardized assessment protocols. A series of basic questions arise in this context:

1. What are common and different characteristics of various assess-

ment protocols, for different domains of information? How thoroughly have these protocols been tested for reliability, validity, and comparative usefulness?

2. In what ways can assessment protocols assist in clinical management decisions in long term care screening, diagnosis, monitoring, and prognosis? Are different types of protocols needed for different purposes?

3. What is the role of standardized assessment protocols in the long term care of individual patients? Are assessment instruments to be viewed in the same sense as other diagnostic technologies such as laboratory tests, i.e., as adjuvants to clinical decision-making?

4. Is there a tendency to substitute the use of protocol results for clinical judgment? When, if ever, is this justified?

5. What are the potential advantages and disadvantages of scoring systems for assessment protocol data?

6. To what extent can standardized protocols instead of clinical judgment be used for aggregate data in management and planning decisions about long term care? What are the potential hazards of such use?

These questions are addressed in the following.

II. Characteristics of Assessment Protocols for Different Domains of Information

Attention is focused on protocols or portions of protocols which address assessment as it applies to decisions about long term care. There are conceptual models which consider the assessment of all types of human behavior (see for example, Lawton 1972). The domains or areas of interest relevant to long term care have been delimited somewhat differently by various investigators and users; the following encompasses those domains which are most important for decisions about long term care.

Assessment of Needs for Chronic Medical Treatment. This need is listed first simply because certain requirements for chronic medical treatment may override all other features in determining the extent of services a patient requires and where these services may be obtained. These include needs for tracheostomy or other ostomy care, oxygen or other forms of respiratory therapy, intravenous fluids or medications, daily or very frequent services of physicians, physical, occupational, and speech therapist, or specialized nursing treatments such as care of a major skin ulcer or complicated traction or casts. Most assessment protocols addressing needs for long term care provide this type of information; there is usually no problem with reliability or face validity (although documentation justifying the medical treatment may be deficient, as well as consideration of alternative modes of treatment which might simplify the delivery of services).

Assessment of Physical Functioning. In attempting to make decisions about appropriate long term care, it is clear that the characteristics of personal *functioning*, physical and mental, are the determinant factors for choice of services, and that medical diagnoses or underlying diseases and conditions contribute only in how they affect function. The development of more precise and useful definitions of the important physical functioning elements has been led by the work of Katz, in defining activities of daily living (ADL; Katz et al., 1963), and of Lawton in emphasizing also "instrumental" activities of daily living (IADL; Lawton, 1972). Over the past twenty years, numerous assessment protocols have been developed which are intended to measure these and closely related aspects of physical functioning. These various assessment guides or protocols have much in common but vary considerably in the way individual items are rated or scored. Interrater reliability has been determined for a number of the instruments and found to be reasonably high, with correlation coefficients of the order of .80 to .90; validity has been judged in relation to clinical decisions made for the same person.

The content of various assessment instruments for physical functioning have been compared and analyzed in several careful studies, including those of Kane and Kane (1981), Hedrick, Katz and Stroud (1980/1981), and Lawton and Klaven (1979). Kane and Kane's analyses of ADL and IADL instruments include available information about reliability and validity. Hendrick, Katz, and Shroud compare the compatibility or consistency of ADL items in a number of assessment instruments with two major patient classification systems, i.e. the Long Term Care Minimum Data Set developed by the National Center of Health Statistics (Technical Consultant Panel 1979) and the Patient Classification Manual (Jones 1973).

The choice of format may depend on its usefulness for particular purposes. For example, it has been suggested that the Katz ADL scale may be as useful as any for initial screening by physicians and emphasizing or identifying areas where further diagnostic investigation is needed, as well as serving as a guide to planning for services for the individual patient. On the other hand, the Barthel index has found much more extensive use in rehabilitative settings for monitoring and predicting progress.

IMPACT OF TECHNOLOGY

Assessment of Mental Functioning. Assessment of mental functioning in relation to long term care needs presents considerably more difficulty than assessment of physical functioning. As discussed by Kane and Kane (1981) the entire realm of measurement of mental status is fraught with definitional problems as to what is being measured, reproducibility or reliability, and validity in relation to the patient's behavior and overall functional status. The aim of a number of efforts has nevertheless been to develop a relatively short assessment guide to cognitive functioning and to the affective state of the patient, as important aids in making decisions about extent and types of needed long term care. Problems in mental functioning and resultant behavior are present in over half the patients in nursing homes, and, in my experience, over half the patients referred to a general geriatric consultative clinic. Thus this domain needs much attention.

Current approaches, as summarized in Kane and Kane (1981), use tests of orientation and cognitive functioning and of affective functioning. In my experience with a number of these tests, they are of value only as gross screening instruments: if the patient performs perfectly, then there probably is no major mental or affective problem that will be a factor in determining long term care; anything less than perfect suggests potential or likely problems. But it is impossible to rely on any of these tests as quantitative predictors of the impact of mental problems on the extent of supportive services needed. For example, many older persons will score at the very bottom of any of the short mental status questionnaires, i.e., they may be oriented only to their own person and not be able to answer correctly any of the other questions, and yet may be able to function adequately and safely in a familiar home environment, often for long periods of time and by themselves. Other patients may be able to perform perfectly on some portions of these tests, such as the numerical or visual-space tests or memory, and yet be subject to episodic or continuous problems with confusion or agitation. The agitation may represent subtle paranoid or delusional problems which are not a part of these assessment protocols.

Moreover, thus far we have only minimal knowledge of what must be some form of relationship between the various types or elements of mental functioning assessed in these tests and areas or organizational features of central nervous system anatomy and function, and in turn relationships to overall functional capabilities. It has been suggested, for example, that patients with dementia of the Alzheimer type may be differentiated in part into those who have disorders of visual-space functioning and those who have disorders of memory,

110

with some overlap, and that the prognosis for these two groups is somewhat different.

Tests of affective status may be helpful in providing some indication of depressive features in the patient, but again current tests cannot be quantitatively related to the support services that may be needed. In addition to tests which emphasize evidence of depression, other tests have been devised aimed at measuring morale (which is, of course, closely related to sense of depression versus sense of well-being), and degree of social interaction and social functioning (which again is dependent upon affective status as well as life-long habits and life events). Determination of stressful events and coping response have also been developed into test scales and protocols. Assessments of these types are discussed thoroughly in Kane and Kane (1981). In general they have been used for research including population surveys and psychosocial research; their usefulness in decisions about long term care and in long term care quality review and planning has received little attention.

Attempts have been made to develop markers or indicators of overall function (physical and mental) which would reflect overall degree of dependency or need for supportive services. One promising example is the measure of manual ability developed by Mark Williams (Williams, Hadler, and Earp, 1982) as a set of simple tests in performing common hand tasks. The time required to perform these tasks was measured in three groups of age-matched elderly women—one group living independently, one "intermediate" group living at home but using a nutritional assistance program, and a "dependent" group living in nursing homes but still ambulatory and carrying out some activities of daily living. The results showed high discriminant value (Table 6); a manual skills index (the product of the three best manual skill times) accounted for more of the variance in the actual levels of dependency (as identified by their living settings) than any other measure (Table 7).

Assessment of Social Support and Environment Characteristics. Assessment instruments which have been designed to assist with decision making for the individual patient about possible settings for long term care include items which describe the degree and type of social support available and characteristics of the home environment (both internal and external, e.g., neighborhood). Good examples are the PAF form of ACCESS and the assessment instrument of TRIAGE (now the Connecticut Community Care, Inc.). Multidimensional assessment instruments which obtain such information include the CARE instrument (Comprehensive Assessment and Referral and

Table 6
Time in Seconds (Mean ± One Standard Deviation) to Open the
Compartments of the Hand Skill Panel

Compartment Fastner	Group		
	Independent (N = 20)	Intermediate (N = 16)	Dependent (N = 20)
Bolt	3.2 ± 1.2	6.1 ± 2.2	12.4 ± 7.5
Cupboard latch	1.3 ± 0.3	2.9 ± 1.5	4.1 ± 2.3
Screen latch	3.4 ± 0.8	4.7 ± 3.4	9.3 ± 5.0
Door knob	1.3 ± 0.4	2.1 ± 0.7	2.9 ± 1.0
Round knob	1.7 ± 0.5	1.7 ± 0.5	4.5 ± 2.9
Padlock	12.3 ± 2.2	20.6 ± 9.9	50.9 ± 29.7
Nightlatch	3.5 ± 1.4	5.9 ± 3.9	10.8 ± 6.8
Drawer lock	8.2 ± 3.3	13.7 ± 8.9	31.3 ± 19.7
Turnbuckle	2.4 ± 0.9	5.8 ± 4.9	8.8 ± 4.0

Table 7
The Contribution of Individual Variables as Markers of Dependency

Independent variables	F Value	P Value	R^{2**}
Manual skill index	143.86	<0.0001	0.86
Mental status score	16.87	<0.0001	0.39
Total number of drugs	14.08	<0.0001	0.34
Number of medical problems	8.9	<0.0005	0.25
Level of education	8.7	<0.0005	0.25
Morale score	4.07	0.022	0.13
Abnormalities on physical exam	1.30	NS*	0.05
Age	1.19	NS*	0.04
Social network strength	0.90	NS*	0.03
Past medical problems	0.15	NS*	0.01

*NS = not significant (P >0.05).
**R^2 is reported for each variable, taking into account the influence of all variables below it in the table.

Evaluation, Gurland et al., 1977), the OARS instrument (Older American Resources and Services; Duke University, 1978), and the Philadelphia Geriatric Center Multilevel Assessment Instrument (MAI, Lawton et al., 1982).

On the other hand, the multidimensional PACE instrument (Patient Classification for Long Term Care, Jones et al., 1973), which is designed primarily for use in long term care institutions, does not contain specific information about social supports or environmental features.

The questionnaire items on social support and environmental characteristics obtain objective information which has face validity in relation to making decisions about whether, and under what circumstances of outside support, long term care may be maintained at home. Other efforts, which have thus far been largely confined to psychosocial research and population surveys, have attempted to measure the extent and quality of intergenerational support and social networks. These are discussed in Kane and Kane (1981).

To summarize, all of the aspects or domains of assessment discussed must be considered in determining what long term care support services are needed by a frail elderly person, and in deciding what options of settings for care, home or institutional, may be most appropriate and feasible. (The financial aspects, i.e., what the costs will be for services and who will pay, are not addressed in this paper; they represent another, obviously important domain affecting decision making.)

The major factors from each of the domains described may be brought together in an algorithmic form or decision sequence which proceeds from the most severe to lesser disabilities. An example is illustrated in Figure 1 from Williams and Williams, (1982). Another approach to a decision sequence, which includes delineation of the health and support services required, (Williams, 1983), proceeds from the fully functional, independent status to progressively more severe degrees of disability. It would be helpful to determine which approach is preferable.

III. Other Questions Concerning The Uses of Assessment Methodologies

Assessment Protocols and Clinical Management Decisions in Long Term Care. In the design of assessment instruments too little attention has thus far been given to the specific use or uses for which the instrument might serve. If the purpose is to screen elderly persons for potential or existing functional or social problems which will then be investigated in depth, as is the approach in comprehensive geriatric evaluation clinics or hospital units, then relatively simple screening tests should suffice. As commented earlier regarding the short mental status tests, anything less than a perfect score should call for thorough investigation; screening tests cannot serve as quantitative measures of disability. There is often the temptation to use more elaborate assessment instruments than are needed or are appropriate for the purpose

113

Figure 1
Decision Sequence

I. 1. Is the patient medically unstable?
   2. Is the patient mentally unstable to the extent of being a danger to himself/herself or others?

   <u>NO</u>   <u>YES</u> → <u>ACUTE HOSPITAL</u>
   ↓

II. 1. Is the patient totally disoriented chronically?
    2. Is the patient immobile, i.e., always requires human assistance in locomotion?
    3. Does the patient have need of special therapy—IV, tracheostomy, O₂, ostomy, etc.?
    4. Does the patient require total supervision?
    5. Does the patient require total ADL* care?

   <u>NO</u>   <u>YES</u> → <u>SNF†</u> or
   ↓   <u>HOME IF APPROPRIATE SUPPORT AVAILABLE</u>

III. 1. Does the patient have intermittent disorientation or wandering?
     2. Does the patient fluctuate in ADL ability?
     3. Does the patient require a structured environment—some supervision?
     4. Does the patient require special therapeutics—complex diet, complex medication schedule, close monitoring?

   <u>NO</u>   <u>YES</u> → <u>HRF‡</u> or
   ↓   <u>HOME IF APPROPRIATE SUPPORT AVAILABLE</u>

IV. Can the patient do all the following:

   1. Feed self   6. Shop
   2. Bathe   7. Plan meals
   3. Dress   8. Use transportation
   4. Use the toilet without help 9. Use telephone
   5. Change position   10. Handle finances
                                  11. Manage medications

   <u>NO</u>   <u>YES</u> → <u>HOME</u>
   ↓

V. Are resources available to meet these needs at home?

   <u>NO</u>   <u>YES</u> → <u>HOME WITH SUPPORT</u>
   ↓
   <u>DOMICILIARY CARE</u>

*ADL = activities of daily living.
†SNF = skilled nursing facility.
‡HRF = health-related or intermediate-level care.

114

of screening and detection of disabilities in individual patients. For such screening purposes, the Katz ADL questions (or any of several modifications of them), one of the short mental status questionnaires, and the short list of questions on the availability of social supports and environmental setting included in the PAF or TRIAGE protocols should suffice.

For *diagnostic* purposes, considerably more information is needed, as is true of any problem requiring a thorough diagnosis as a basis for treatment plans. The finding of urinary incontinence on a screening assessment, for example, should lead to a complete evaluation of the possible causes and ways to manage this problem as a part of decision making about long term care. Similarly, the finding of any suggestion of dementia or of depression on screening tests should lead to a thorough work-up, including more detailed neuropsychological tests than any assessment instrument contains. The disabling conditions discovered on functional and social screening have long term implications, including associated treatment costs, which warrant the same fairness of evaluation that would be applied to any potentially life threatening acute medical condition.

For *monitoring* and *prognostic* purposes, some of the existing assessment instruments are useful. Reference has already been made to the usefulness of the Barthel Index in following rehabilitative efforts. Kane and Kane (1981) discuss and tabulate their judgments about the usefulness of various physical and mental assessment instruments for these purposes.

Standardized Assessment Protocols in the Long Term Care of Individual Patients. The information from assessment protocols should be treated and used in the same manner as any other objective information, such as laboratory tests, in clinical decision making for the individual patient. That is, they can serve a screening function and a monitoring function, but they cannot by themselves establish a diagnosis or a final decision about care plans. A laboratory example is the blood glucose level: it serves as a screening assessment measure for abnormalities in glucose metabolism including, most commonly, diabetes mellitus, and as a monitor of progress in treatment, but by itself it does not establish a diagnosis. Yet there is the common but unfortunate tendency to accept and use a functional assessment finding as a diagnosis and to proceed with decisions about long term care without investigating the real differential diagnosis of the functional disability, or its reversibility with treatment. Part of the explanation for this tendency rests with the still common but erroneous view both among professionals and the public that aging itself inevitably produces these disabilities, and that no efforts at further diagnosis or treatment are worthwhile. This nihilistic attitude was well illustrated in the evaluation-placement unit project referred to earlier (Williams et al, 1973); it was found that among the first 315 patients seen by the unit, almost all of whom had applications for nursing home admission, over half had not actually been examined by a physician in the previous year, and over half also had potentially remediable problems which, when addressed, resulted in the patient continuing to live at home or in some less intensive care setting than a nursing home. It is hard to think of any situation in which assessment findings alone should substitute for more thorough evaluation and overall clinical judgment in decision making for the individual patient. Such decision making for ill or disabled older persons requires the team work of physicians, nurses, and social workers and often of psychiatrists, occupational and physical therapists, and dieticians.

The Advantages and Disadvantages of Scoring for Assessment Protocol Data. There seems to be an almost irresistible urge to assign scores to items in assessment protocols and then add them up. The general assumption underlying such an urge is *that the items being scored consist of a systematic, ordinal set of characteristics of a single phenomenon* (e.g., total physical functional disability, total mental disability, total physical plus mental disability). A single score could then represent the overall status of the patient regarding this disability and might be used to describe and define the quantitative degree of disability, to determine the extent of services required, and in turn the setting in which services might be rendered, to monitor improvement or regression, and/or to serve as an index for utilization review purposes.

In a few instances scoring systems or scaling systems have been developed through the use of accepted scaling/scoring techniques. Examples of this are the Guttman scaling of the Katz ADL measures (Katz et al., 1970), and the Guttman scales for IADL of Lawton and Brody (1969). Kane et al. (1982) have recently used factor analysis to establish some internal coherence within the assessment domains for which they have developed sets of questions. However, it may be noted that they put arbitrary scale values on the responses to individual questions. Many other scaled or scored assessment instruments have arbitrary or "best judgment" values.

There are, in my view, several serious flaws in virtually all of the scoring systems in relation to their use in decision making about an individual patient. First, they obscure information about individual disabilities a given patient may have, which should be addressed

116

specifically in terms of potential reversibility and/or type of service supports needed. One person may have severe urinary incontinence but be able to walk well and be mentally clear; another may be severely demented but able to walk and be continent; another may have moderate degrees of disability in all three realms, but all might have the same total score on a test. Yet the approach to management and the setting in which the person might be best cared for would probably be quite different.

Second, the items being scored are rarely if ever of an ordinal nature. This is true within functional disability areas as well as across functional disability areas. For example, within the short mental status test commonly used, there is, as noted, no consistent hierarchy or qualitative relationship between the questions: one person may do well on the arithmetic questions but poorly on memory or orientation, another may have a different pattern. These different patterns probably reflect different types and degrees of neuropathology. There is no basis for assuming an ordinal relationship in which a given score would represent a given degree of total mental function and a higher score would represent a predictably proportional better level of total mental functioning.

The theoretical and practical inadequacies and disutilities of scores which involve multiple systems of physical and mental functioning are even more apparent. It is hard to see how most of the scoring systems could have any use in addressing the long term care needs of individual patients. In fact, they offer much potential for inadequate and misguided decision making. The DMS-1 scoring system of New York State, described below in another context, has encouraged decisions about the extent of need for various elements of care more on the basis of fitting the patient to newly defined levels of care, rather than on the basis of individual needs.

Use of Standardized Protocols for Aggregated Data in Management and Planning. Numerous assessment approaches have been developed and used in making planning decisions about need for long term care institutional beds and services, and in such critical management functions as utilization review, i.e., determining whether patients using long term institutional beds are at the appropriate level of care. A number of the assessment instruments already referred to have been used in these ways . One of the earliest approaches was that in Monroe County, New York, where the Patient Care Planning Council (the predecessor to and model for the Health Systems Agency National Program) used expert assessments of the type described earlier in this paper as a basis for planning decisions about nursing home and other beds.

Many states have developed profiling or algorithmic or numerical scoring approaches to utilization review of patients in long term care facilities and as a basis for determining appropriateness of admission and thus appropriateness of reimbursement by Medicaid or Medicare. Foley and Schneider (1980) and Schneider (1980) have analyzed and compiled a number of these programs and illustrated the widely divergent decisions that would be made about level of care, depending upon which state's criteria were used for the same case information.

One of the most ambitious of such assessment programs is that of New York State, which illustrates one of the more sophisticated approaches and also some of the implicit hazards. In the mid-1970s, New York State began requiring all skilled nursing and intermediate care facilities to provide information on a prescribed form, their DMS-1, which includes information on physical and mental functioning as well as need for special procedures or treatments. With the data from a large number of these forms, statisticians conducted a series of discriminant analyses to determine the numerical weights they might apply to the assessment items which would, when added up, yield the best prediction of whether a patient was in a skilled nursing facility or an intermediate care facility. For the purposes of this analysis the assumption was made that the patients, or at least most of them, were at the appropriate level of care (even though other studies, as described above, had shown otherwise).

With the numerical weights ultimately chosen, a total score for the DMS-1 of 180 or higher (with a possible top score of over 1100) predicted that a person was (and presumably should be) in a skilled nursing facility in over 90 percent of instances. Similarly, scores between 60 and 179 predicted that a patient was (and should be) in an intermediate care facility in over 90 percent of instances.

With this statistical background, these scores have been used as the determinant of level of care for admissions to long term care facilities of Medicaid eligible patients in New York State, and in utilization review to identify patients at presumptively inappropriate levels of care. Used as a management tool applicable to over 80 percent of skilled nursing facility patients in New York City and over 60 percent elsewhere in the state (i.e., Medicaid recipients), this assessment system has had a powerful influence on long term health care practices and in turn has brought to light a number of problems with such an approach.

The DMS-1 system has influenced decisions about long term care because there has been an overwhelming tendency to accept weighted scores as being the *only* determinant of appropriate level of care, even though the State's instructions stated that the scores should be used only as guides and that professional judgment should be exercised, with documentation of justification for decisions other than the one indicated by the scores. The result has been a neglect of using professional judgment in making such decisions.

Weighted scores of the DMS-1 type might be used with statistical appropriateness for such purposes as comparisons between institutions or comparisons of institutions and others groups of patients over time. But where the data have been used for such purposes, the results have been misleading because they were based on the use of mean (average) scores for patients within one institution compared with the mean of another, and conclusions were drawn about apparent differences in extent of services needed based on differences in the means of these scores. No attention has been given to the distribution of the scores for various patients within each institution. For example, an institution with some patients with relatively low scores plus other patients with quite high scores (i.e., needing extensive or total care) might still have a mean score value similar to or lower than another institution whose patients all had scored close to the mean and had no or few patients with high intensity needs. An examination of the actual distribution of such scores within institutions has shown very broad and flat distributions that do not remotely resemble a normal distribution (Williams, unpublished data). Thus, use of these scores even for comparison of grouped data, as by institutions, would require more careful attention to statistical principles than indicated by present attempts.

In at least one setting (Carl Adams, Murfreesboro, Tennessee), the assessment findings for functional disability in nursing homes have been scored such as to translate into numbers of nursing care hours per day needed to respond to the disability state. The results, repeated monthly, have been used to guide nursing staffing assignments and to generate differential bills for care based on varying degrees of intensity of care identified.

IV. Summary

This paper has described, illustrated, and discussed the development and use of assessment methodologies for decision making, management and planning in long term care. Certain conclusions seem warranted:

1. A number of assessment instruments have been developed which have many items in common, in particular the items which are likely to have the most usefulness as data to be incorporated into

clinical decision making. It should be possible with modest adjustments to use such instruments interchangeably and/or to develop a few more generally accepted instruments.

2. Different uses for assessment information may call for different assessment methodologies.

3. Assessment information when used in relation to making decisions about long term care for an individual patient must be incorporated as any other objective data, as adjuvants to and not as a substitute for clinical judgment. If this purpose and the restricted scope of the assessment role is recognized, then it will be much easier to define and develop generally agreed assessment methodology.

4. Scoring or scaling of assessment findings, if developed carefully according to generally accepted principles, may have some value in monitoring changes in functional status and in grouped data for management and planning purposes. On the other hand, such scoring or scaling has little if any place in the clinical decisions and management for an individual patient, where efforts to add up disparate elements will only obscure the specific details which should be addressed in the clinical care process.

5. The efforts of governmental regulatory and reimbursement bodies to use assessment methodologies for such purposes as control of utilization of long term care services has further highlighted the difficulties inherent in attempting to use grouped data for decisions about individual patients. Clinical epidemiological and statistical methods exist which might, if applied as carefully as they have been to other clinical data sources, lead to more valid applications of assessment information in long term care.

6. The costs of comprehensive assessment are probably modest compared to the benefits to be obtained in quality of life and in lesser overall costs of long term care. They should be reimbursed in the same ways as other diagnostic and treatment services.

References

Duke University Center for the Study of Aging and Human Development, Multi Dimensional Functional Assessment: The OARS Methodology. Durham, N.C.: Duke University, 1978.

Eggert, G.M., Bowlyow, J.E. and Nichols, C.W., Gaining control of the long term care system: First returns from the ACCESS experiment. The Gerontologist, 20(3):356-363, 1980.

Eggert, G.M. and Brodows, B.S., The ACCESS Program: Assuring Quality in Long Term Care. Quality Review Bulletin: 9, 10-15, February 1982.

Foley, W.J., and Schneider, D.P., A Comparison of the Level of Care Predictions of Six Long Term Care Patient Assessment Systems, American Journal Public Health, (11): 1152-1161, 1980.

Gurland, G., Kuriansky, J., Sharpe, L., Simon, R., Stiller, P. and Birkett, P., The Comprehensive Assessment and Referral Evaluation (CARE): Rationale, development and reliability. Part II: A factor analysis. International Journal of Aging and Human Development, 8:9-42, 1977.

Harvard Center for Community Health and Medical Care, An Approach to the Assessment of Long Term Care. Final report and executive summary to the National Center for Health Services Research, Boston, Massachusetts, 1977.

Hedrick, S.C., Katz, S. and Stroud, M.W., Patient assessment in long term Care: Is there a common language? Aged Care and Services Review, 2(4):1, 3-19, 1980/81.

Institute of Medicine, National Academy of Sciences, A Policy Statement: The Elderly and Functional Dependency. Washington, D.C.: National Academy of Sciences, June 1977.

Jones, E. W., Patient Classification for Long Term Care: User Manual. DHEW Publication No. HRA 74-3107, DHEW, Health Resources Administration, Bureau of Health Services Research and Evaluation, 1973.

Kane, R.A. and Kane, R.L., Assessing the Elderly: A Practical Guide to Measurement. Lexington, Mass.: Lexington Books/D.C. Heath, 1981.

Kane, R., Riegler, S., Bell, R., Potter, R., and Koshland, G., Predicting the Course of Nursing Home Patients: A Progress Report. Prepared for National Center for Health Services, Rand Corporation, Santa Monica, California, 1982.

Katz, S., Ford, A.F., Moskowitz, R.W., Jackson, B.A. and Jaffee, M.W., Studies of illness in the aged, the index of ADL: A standardized measure of biological and psychosicial function. Journal of the American Medical Association, 185:94, 1963.

Katz, S., Downs, T.D., Cash, H.R., and Gratz, R.C., Progress in Development of the Index ADL. The Gerontologist, 10:20-30, 1970.

Lawton, M.P. and Brody, E., Assessment of older people: Self-maintaining and instrumental activities of daily living. The Gerontologist, 9:179 188, 1969.

Lawton, M.P., Assessing the competence of older people. In D. Kent, R. Kastenbaum and J. Sherwood (eds.), Research, Planning and Action for the Elderly, New York: Behavioral Publications, 1972.

Lawton, M.P. and Kleban, M.H., Assessment: The Concept and Prospects. Written for the National Institute of Mental Health, March 1979.

Lawton, M.P., Moss, M., Fulcomer, M., and Kleban, M.H., A research and service oriented multi-level assessment instrument. Journal of Gerontology, 37:91-99, 1982.

Rice, D.P., Morbidity, Mortality and Population Trends in the United States. Presented at the Annual Spring Meeting, Council of Teaching Hospitals, Atlanta, Georgia, May 7, 1981.

Rice, D.P. and Feldman, J.J., Demographic Changes and Health Needs of the Elderly. Presented at the Annual Meeting, Institute of Medicine, National Academy of Sciences, October 20, 1982.

Schneider, D. Patient/Client Assessment in New York State, Vol. I: Historical Review, Purposes/Uses, Framework/Recommendations. Troy, NY: Rensselaer Polytechnic Institute, May 1980.

Technical Consultant Panel on the Long Term Care Health Data Set, U.S. National Committee on Vital and Health Statistics, Long Term Health Care: Minimum Data Set, Final Report. Hyattsville, Md.: National Center for Health Statistics, 1979.

University of Rochester School of Medicine and Dentistry, Health Planning Council of Monroe County, and Council of Social Agencies of Rochester and Monroe County, Inc. Health Care of the Aged Study, Part I, 1968; Williams, T.F. Clinical and service aspects of geriatric teaching programs, Somers and Fabian, editors, The Geriatric Imperative: An Introduction to Gerontology and Clinical Geriatrics, New York: Appleton-Century-Crofts, 1981.

Williams, T.F., Hill, J.G., Fairbank, M.F., and Knox K.G., Appropriate Placement of the Chronically Ill and Aged: A Successful Approach by Evaluation. Journal of the American Medical Association, 226:1332, 1973.

Williams, T.F., Hill, J.G., Fairbank, M.E. and Knox, K.G., Evaluation Placement of the Chronically Ill and Aged. Final Report to National Center for Health Services Research, Rochester, New York: Monroe Community Hospital, 1977.

Williams, M.E. and Williams, T.F., Clinical conference: Assessment of the elderly for long term care. Journal of the American Geriatrics Society, 30(1):70-75, 1982.

Williams, T.F., Zimmer, J.G., Barker, W.H. and Vincent, S., Geriatric Consultative Team Project: Interim Report. Rochester, NY: Rochester Area Hospitals Corporation, October 1982.

Williams, M.E., Hadler, N.M., and Earp, J.A.L., Manual ability as a marker of dependency in geriatric women. Journal Chronic Diseases, 35:115 122, 1982.

Williams, T.F., Assessment of the Geriatric Patient in Relation to Needs for Services and Facilities. In W. Reichel (ed.), Clinical Aspects of Aging (2nd ed.), Baltimore, Md.: Williams and Wilkins, 1983.

7

Interactions Among Citizens, Providers, and Technologies in Various Settings

Ruth Bennett

There are at least two groups of elderly in need: one group residing in the community (95 percent) and one residing in institutions (5 percent). This paper explores needs in the community-based elderly and some techniques, programmatic as well as technological, used to fulfill their needs; it also explores needs among the institution-based elderly and some techniques, programmatic as well as technological, used to fulfill their needs. Since more information about the community-based elderly is presented in other papers in this collection, this paper was focused more on the institutionalized elderly. Central to this presentation is the concept of need. For purposes of this presentation, need is viewed rather crudely as follows:

1. For community-residing elderly, bottom line needs are those which must be met to keep them out of an institution; at a higher level, meeting needs may mean providing that which improves (or maintains) their quality of life.
2. For the institutionalized elderly, needs are defined quite differently. Bottom line needs are those which must be met to improve (or maintain) the quality of life; at a higher level, meeting needs may mean providing that which facilitates discharge from the institution.

I. Status and Needs of the Community-Based Elderly

A number of papers in this volume, especially that by Weissert, seem to be addressing the community-based elderly; so this paper will not go into too much detail on this subject. However, something should be said about this group only because the approach taken in this paper is a bit different from Weissert's and by others, though we may end up in the same place. For the community-based elderly, bottom-line needs, that is, needs which should be met in order to keep them out of institutions, center on a few risk factors, age, living arrangements, and health status. Weissert cites several other risk factors, including climate and bed supply.

Age. The elderly population in general is growing (*U.S. Bureau of the Census*). The population at risk in terms of age also is growing and at a faster rate. By the year 2000, the group 85 and older is expected to double while those in the 75-84 year old group will increase by 57 percent (Brotman, 1982). Most of the elderly in institutions are very old; it is estimated that by 2030, three million rather than one million long-term care beds will be needed.

Living Arrangements. Between 1960 and 1979, there was an increase in the proportion of older persons, male and female, living in households; during this time, the proportion of older persons living alone also increased. Also, the proportion in institutions increased. The proportion of older males living in families *dropped* from 67.7 in 1960 to 56.5 percent in 1979. A major reason for institutionalization seems to be living alone and/or lack of spouse. (See Davis, in this volume.)

Health Status. A great deal has been said and remains to be said about how to assess health needs and methods for meeting these needs. However they are assessed, health needs are great among the community-based elderly. The 1975 National Council of Aging (NCOA) report based on a random sample of over 2,000 persons in the U.S. 65 and older asked: "What is the worst thing about being over 65?" About two-thirds considered failing health a major problem and ranked it first among the worst aspects of aging. Loneliness was the second problem, though only 20 percent of the elderly mentioned it. Financial problems were identified as the third ranking problem, with 17 percent listing it as the worst thing about aging. (It may well be that relatively few considered finances a problem because until recently Social Security and other financial support pro-

Table 1
Limitations in mobility and activity in the elderly

Mobility
80% of older people are mobile
Of the 20% who are not:

2% are bedfast
5% are housebound
7% can move about with assistance
6% can move about with difficulty

Activity
Functional limitations:

57% are free of limitations
17% are unable to carry out their major activity
21% are limited
5% are limited, but *not* in major activity

(U.S., DHEW, PHS, 1978), cited by Brody and Brody (1980).

grams have been highly effective in meeting financial needs. Projected reductions in financial assistance may lead to finances becoming a greater problem for more of the aged than has been the case in the recent past.)

Older people have more hospital episodes and have longer hospital stays, more physician visits, and more days of disability. Among the community-residing elderly, 20 percent need assistance for mobility, and 43 percent need at least some assistance in order to function (Table 1). According to Brody and Brody (1980) "estimates of the proportion of elderly in need and those requiring any assistance range from 17 percent to 40 percent of the elderly, with a clustering of opinions around 30 percent." In a U.S.-U.K. random sample survey of 500 over 65, about 20 percent of the community-residing elderly in New York City were called personal care dependents in the sense that they were receiving extensive personal care from families (Gurland, et al., 1978). Weissert (in this volume) indicates that those who are personal care dependent are at greatest risk for institutionalization. Most of those unable to carry out a major activity of daily living are among the poor, live with others, and live outside a Standard Metropolitan Statistical Area (National Center of Health Statistics, 1978).

Numerous studies have found that family and friends actually provide about 70 percent of the value of services received by older people who are physically impaired, and that those living with a spouse or child have a much lower probability of institutionalization than those living alone (GAO, 1977; Cantor, 1979, 1981; *Sussman*, 1980; Callahan et al., 1980). In most instances the supportive relative

125

is a spouse who is also elderly and possibly stressed. Weissert's paper goes into much greater detail on health needs of the community residing aged and gives exact numbers of persons who need help with certain tasks. His paper also extends the concept of need to the caretakers of the elderly. Mental illness should also be mentioned, though it is often hard to differentiate those who need assistance because of mental illness from those who need it because of physical illness or because of a combination of both mental and physical illness. Certainly, those elderly who are mentally ill are at risk of institutionalization and, worse, death. The NCOA *Fact Book on Aging* (1978) estimates that

— One of four suicides in the United States is committed by persons 65 and over.
— Three million older persons, 13-15 percent of the older population, are in immediate need of mental health services.
— Seven million elderly live in conditions conducive to the development of mental illness. Many suffer from depression. About 5 percent suffer from dementia, some of which is treatable (p. 143).

These items are quoted verbatim because their wording illustrates how difficult it is to get an exact description as well as an estimate of mental health needs among the elderly. If the criterion of risk for institutionalization is applied, the estimate of mental health needs among the aged would probably be quite low; if the criterion of improved quality of life is applied, the estimate would probably be as high as the highest estimate quoted above.

1. Programs

Many existing programs (coordinated community care, channeling demonstrations, home care programs, senior centers, day care programs) contain mixtures of the following elements, which are usually coordinated by case managers: day care and day hospitals, home care and homemakers, respite care, hospice care, congregate housing, enriched housing and other housing types, surrogate families, friendly visitors, Meals on Wheels, and transportation services. There are a variety of organizations to assist families caring for the elderly in the community, such as national organizations for Alzheimer's disease, Parkinson's disease, and other specific disease entities.

Dunlop (1980) noted that services in the community are brokered by the families of the elderly. This may mean that programs may not be getting delivered to many who are without families. For those with families, services possibly as costly as institutional care seem to be needed, e.g., transportation.

Services are also being delivered to the elderly by church and other groups which are not funded as demonstrations. It is important to know how many elderly are receiving services and to learn about the array, allocation, and distribution of all services in communities. At this point it seems virtually impossible to get a comprehensive view of what is going on in the community to meet both bottom line and higher level long-term care needs. A survey seems essential to determine which communities are doing what and with what degree of success. Surely such information would be useful for policy and planning purposes.

2. Technology

While we can cite examples of technological innovations, we cannot tie them to specific community programs, e.g., coordinated care demonstrations and channeling demonstrations, because of the lack of comprehensive data. Examples of technological innovations are:

- Alarm systems—an example is the Lifeline System being marketed in Watertown, Mass. The elderly person wears a transmitter at all times. To call for help, the elderly person would press a button on the transmitter which sends a signal to a receiving station via telephone lines. (There are variants of this system.)
- Shelf-stable meals—which can be mailed and stored in quantity without spoilage. Most can be reconstituted with water (freeze dried process), steam, or are packaged in boilable pouches.
- Interactive T.V.—a two-way T.V. transmitter-receiver with a small pickup T.V. camera. It can be used for communication, care, and emergencies.

These three technological developments in combination might meet the bottom line needs of some community residing elderly; that is, they might prevent institutionalization. Obviously, other technological innovations, some of which are listed below, might meet the higher level need of improving (or maintaining) the quality of life.

- Artherapedic chairs, a seating and positioning device for people with musculo-skeletal limitations due to arthritis, hip surgery, stroke, multiple sclerosis, or Parkinson's disease.
- Raised toilet seats—which enable patients to rotate the seat from front to side and have a special tilting feature which reduces the amount of hip flexion needed for sitting. The soft raised toilet seat has extra thick 4 inch foam padding (for patients with spinal cord injuries).
- Adaptive eating utensils—for example knives with a bicycle-type

handle with ridges to assure a secure grip while slicing. Spoons and forks have built-up handles and rings that slide along the handle to provide additional support. There are also one-handed cutlery sets and bottle openers.

- Dressing aids include stocking aids for use with surgical or regular hose; these come equipped with pull-up cloth tapes which are attached to a plastic sheet. When foot is inserted into stocking, tapes may be pulled up to withdraw sheet and hosiery is in place.
- Cooking and household cleaning aids which can be programmed for use, e.g., ovens, toasters, vacuum cleaners. Also, there are specially designed cleaning devices, such as long handled dustpans.
- Clocks with voice reminders.
- Telephone ring indicators and telephone amplifiers for the hard-of hearing. For the visually impaired, there are large-numbered phones.
- "Electronic shoppers" which are computerized terminals connected to supermarkets.
- Crutch clutches which fold for carrying things on crutches or walkers.

II. Status and Needs of Institutionalized Elderly

About 4.2 percent of people over age 65 and 9.2 percent of those over age 74 are housed in about 20,000 long-term care institutions. If higher level needs were to be met, some of the institutionalized elderly probably could be discharged.

In at least half of all cases of severely incapacitated institutionalized elderly, nursing homes or other formal service programs seem necessary because families are not available (U.S. Bureau of the Census, 1978). Could the other half of nursing home residents who presumably have families conceivably be discharged to their own homes? According to the 1977 National Nursing Home Survey (1979) one-third of all nursing home residents are dependent in six activities of daily living. In other words, they probably need nursing home care. But of the 1,303,100 residents surveyed, there were no discharge plans for 1,254,100. (There were discharge plans for only 49,000 residents or about 5 percent.) Thus, assuming that 50 percent of nursing home residents have families, very few were viewed as candidates for discharge. Presumably, this is because most are so debilitated that they could not be cared for by their families even if their families were ready and able to do so. However, this cannot be asserted with any degree of certainty without trying to meet their

128

needs with the aid of programs and/or technology. That such programs do make a difference may be inferred from figures taken from the National Health Survey of October 1980, which shows that nursing home discharge patterns vary from state to state. For the U.S. as a whole, 73.9 percent are discharged alive, mostly to other health facilities. Only 37.2 percent are discharged to private or semi-private residences, while 25.9 percent die in the nursing home.

It is interesting to note the contrast in these figures by the states for which comparative data are available. In California, 44.4 percent of nursing home residents are discharged to private residences, in Illinois, only 31.4 percent, in Texas, 30.2 percent, in Massachusetts 23.7 percent, and in New York only 19.1 percent. Several factors may contribute to these highly variable rates, assuming that nursing home residents are similar in all five states (which may be an erroneous assumption). Among these possible factors are:

- Availability of single level dwellings in some states but not in others;
- Intact and caring families in some states but not in others;
- The problem of paying rents for unoccupied apartments in states where home ownership is not very common, e.g., Massachusetts and New York;
- Availability of more home care and other community based services in some states as compared to others;
- More favorable weather conditions in California as compared to the other four states.

Apparently because of soaring costs of nursing home care (Pollak, in this volume) and projected future increases in such costs, there has been a great drive to return the care of the aged to families and communities. However, as was noted earlier, about 50 percent of the elderly in institutions have no families and, for unknown reasons, of those with families few are viewed as candidates for discharge. Thus, the mere presence of families is not sufficient for keeping or getting people out of institutions.

Despite their cost, therefore, the case for nursing homes or similar settings cannot be stated strongly enough, at least at this time. Most of those who are in them undoubtedly need to be there.

Let us now turn to bottom line needs, that is those which must be met in order to preserve or improve the quality of life for residents of institutions. Very little research has been done on this subject. Obviously, food, clothing, shelter and some sort of nursing or health care is required and, as is well known, even the provision of these varies from state to state. As for improving the quality of life, these needs seem to be met by a large number and a wide variety of programs in different homes in different states.

1. *Programs* As a result of our recent survey of innovative programs in long-term care institutions funded by the Administration on Aging (Bennett et al., 1982) we have a somewhat clearer picture of programming for the elderly in long-term care institutions in contrast to programming available in the community.

For this survey, a random sample of 1,058 long-term care facilities for the elderly stratified by size (60 beds; 60-149 beds; 149 + beds) and ownership (public, non-profit, for-profit) was studied to determine the extent to which 90 specific programs in three categories (physical activity, rehabilitation, community linkage) exist and endure in such institutions. A checklist format enabled respondents to indicate programs which were provided at any time in the past 10 years and those still being provided.

Responding institutions provided descriptions of selected innovative programs as well as total number of programs. Religious services and crafts programs were most frequent and outreach programs of all kinds least frequent. The mean number of programs provided was 32.

Of course, there is the possibility that the respondents were a self-selected sample of only the "best" facilities. The original sample was distributed evenly over nine cells representing size and ownership categories. There were a few deletions of duplicates and non-geriatric facilities, for a net sample of 1058 institutions. The response total was 302 (29 percent), including 28 refusals and 274 usable questionnaires. Public facilities such as county homes, not usually thought of as the best homes, accounted for about 38 percent of total usable questionnaires. Proprietary facilities had a lower response rate than public and voluntary facilities. Of the 274 homes for which questionnaires were tabulated, some reported very few programs while others reported about 60. Thus, there was a wide range of total number of programs, possibly indicating the responding homes varied in quality. We are currently in the process of checking some characteristics of responding homes against other data sets available on them. However, this analysis has not been completed. At this point, we view these findings as exploratory and suggestive only.

Respondents also provided basic descriptive data (e.g., level of institutional care, staffing patterns, information about in-service education), patient demographic data (age, sex, ethnicity, disability levels), and information on administrator education and training. These administrative and organizational variables were used to determine characteristics of institutions successful in promoting innovative programs for the elderly when correlated with overall and categorical innovative program scores. A major finding was that the number of programs was correlated with institutional size. While not all findings from this survey can be discussed here, the program findings (*Handbook of Institutional Innovative Programs*, Bennett et al., 1982) are summarized in the following.

Ten focused questions were asked about program structure, content, staffing, and goals. We also asked respondents to select one currently provided program about which they were particularly enthusiastic from each of three major categories (physical activity, rehabilitation, and community linkage), and to answer 10 questions about each (30 in all). Not surprisingly, the response rate dropped somewhat for this section of the questionnaire; just over 75 percent of respondents filling in the checklist described in further detail any programs at all, but about 60 percent of this group did describe three programs, one in each category. We knew that this part of the questionnaire would be quite time-consuming and were gratified that so many respondents were cooperative. We have received a rich supply of program information which we believe will be very useful to other program directors. We did not ask respondents if these programs were geared to meeting bottom line needs, e.g., improving residents' quality of life, or higher level needs, e.g., preparing them for discharge. Perhaps we might ask these questions in the future. A brief description of a program in each program category follows.

Rehabilitation. One example of a rehabilitation program was offered by a 60-bed (20 SNF, 50 ICF) proprietary facility in New England. For many years, this institution had been providing movies for the residents— the typical old, grainy 16mm variety which are actually quite expensive to rent-and resident interest was waning visibly. Solution? Purchase of a VHS video unit for which cassettes of the latest Hollywood productions can be rented at minimal cost. It comes as no real surprise that R-rated movies were the best attended. A compatible movie camera was also purchased so that movies of special events in the institution could be made and shown for all residents, even the bedfast. This camera is also used extensively for the home's in-service education program as an instructional tool. Other examples of more usual types of rehabilitation programs are restorative and physical therapy, whirlpool bath programs, and speech therapy.

Physical Activity. Exercise programs were most frequent, both on the checklist and on the program description pages. Using music and props of various kinds to make repetitive motions less monotonous is the rule rather than the exception. Several facilities wrote about "slimnastics" programs specifically aimed at combating the "middle-third spread" which almost invariably accompanies the sedentary lifestyle common in most long-term care facilities. Of particular interest among the programs described are competitive team sports, with bowling being the most frequent (basketball, archery, and swimming were also written about). What makes the bowling programs of special interest is that most were designed to resemble as closely as possible the recreational bowling programs existing in almost every community. Thus, despite modifications required to accommodate physical limitations (such as lighter balls, shorter alleys, even table-top set-ups for residents in wheelchairs), most of the bowling programs involved teams who bowled against each other on a regular basis and had tournaments and even awards-night banquets. These programs were reported with much enthusiasm: basically, they are low-cost with great benefits to residents in the maintenance of physical, mental and social skills and in the enhancement of self-image and self-worth that comes with public recognition of being part of a team. Other examples of physical activity programs are physical excercises accompanied by music or concentrating on specific muscle movements, and dance programs.

Community Linkage. In the area of community linkage, several facilities reported fundraising activities to benefit groups and organizations outside the institutions. This is a refreshing counterpoint to the commonly held view of long term care facilities as closed entities that are preoccupied with their own concerns. One such fundraiser, reported by four skilled nursing institutions in disparate parts of the country (Alaska, New York, Pennsylvania and Wisconsin) was the Heart Association "Rock and Roll Jamboree", in which residents met the pledges of staff, family, and others by rocking in rocking chairs and wheeling (or rolling, if you will) in wheelchairs. In all cases, respondents reported that residents derived immense satisfaction from knowing that they were making contributions to the welfare of others. This particular activity is by definition episodic, but it certainly has potential for continuing at least on an annual basis and more often than that if other equally worthy causes were to be identified.

2. Technology

Some forms of technology are used to meet higher level needs of the institutionalized elderly, that is, they are imbedded in programs to prepare patients for discharge.
- Tilt tables are used in restorative therapy in conjunction with parallel bars and other restorative equipment.
- Hydraulic bathlifts allow patients to adjust a lever to be lowered into

or raised out of a bath. They operate on normal water pressure from the tub faucet with no electrical parts. A special faucet replaces the existing tub faucet.

- Cooking and cleaning utensils as mentioned above for the community based elderly. A discharge-oriented nursing home might emphasize programs of activities of daily living skills retraining which utilize some of the equipment listed above.

Some forms of technology are used in institutions to meet lower level needs; that is, simply to maintain skills or to improve the quality of life. For the most frail elderly, the following technologies are available:

- Bedsore devices, e.g., whirlpool baths, lambswool fittings and water and air mattresses.
- Urinary incontinence devices, e.g., adult diapers.
- Trapeze lift to help transfer patients from reclining to prone position or for getting them up from bed, bath, or toilet. One type of lift is attached to the ceiling; hence a builder must be consulted to determine if the ceiling is strong enough to bear weight.

Whether institutional programs are more effective with or without technological components remains to be determined. The needed experiments have yet to be conducted. An example of such an experiment could be contrasting two programs to prevent bedsores, one using turning and one using whirlpool baths. One can easily think of other experiments using current technology. Little of this type of research has been published. Moreover, very few homes learn from each other or from the literature about these types of innovations, as we found in the survey. Only 7 percent of the rehabilitation programs and 7 percent of the physical activity programs were conducted because staff had attended lectures or read papers. Two-thirds reported that such programs were started because of patient needs, whatever that means. One thing it does mean is a lot of expensive trial and error must be occurring.

III. Summary, Conclusions, Recommendations

Clearly there are many needs both among the community-based aged and their families and among the institutionalized elderly. It is hard to tell how long-term care needs are being met in the community. We have some idea of how some are being met in some institutions. But much more descriptive and evaluative research remains to be done.

An important issue seems to be the definition of need. I have suggested distinguishing bottom line and higher level needs both in the community and among the institutionalized aged. Others have suggested other needs or conceptualizations of need. Probably one task that remains is to try to reconcile different points of view.

Weissert and others have described programs in the community trying to meet some bottom line needs, e.g., trying to keep older people out of institutions, and it seems that some of these programs are not doing that. However, they, or other programs like them, might be meeting higher level needs, i.e., improving the quality of life of community residing elderly or that of their families.

Thus, it seems premature to suggest that these programs be discontinued. It would help if a survey were conducted to determine the array, distribution, and allocation of service programs throughout the country, which may or may not be federally funded. Some communities may be doing an excellent job of keeping old people out of institutions in ways that have not yet been described.

We have no idea of how many community programs make use of, or would be improved if they were to make use of, technological innovations. Seemingly, the marriage of social programs to technology has yet to be performed, at least in the community. It was noted above that some combinations of technology could be considered as substitutes for social programs. For example, in rural areas, a combination of mailed meals, interactive T.V., and electronic alarm systems might be viable substitutes for service delivery programs.

Institutions for the elderly seem to make greater use of technology, particularly for rehabilitation purposes. It is necessary to repeat at this point that it is difficult to determine objectively what is and what is not meeting the needs of the aged either in or out of institutions. We have described some needs and a wide variety of responses to these needs. But it is not obvious as yet what are the best responses for meeting the needs described above. In order to get more information, the following is suggested:

Descriptive Studies. Surveys of what programs exist in the community to meet long-term care needs as well as more direct surveys of programs in institutions (ours was a mail survey and suffers from some obvious limitations inherent in mail surveys) should be mounted.

Experimental Evaluation of Programs. Candidates for a given program could be assigned to such program alternatives, e.g., candidates for a social program might be offered interactive T.V. instead and outcomes of both alternatives could be assessed using similar outcome measures; some candidates for meals on wheels could receive them by mail; some fearful elderly could be provided with an alert system while others get companions, etc.

Systematic Addition of Technology. At this point it appears that little new technology is being used to facilitate the delivery of programs in or out of institutions. Research is needed on how to best fit such items as lifeline alarm systems into service program delivery in the community, to give but one example. At some point, funding of social programs could be made contingent on use of appropriate technology.

The results of the types of research listed above could result in:

Better Targeting. Few if any programs seem to be targeted to specific types of persons or problems. The "kitchen sink" approach seems to be taken: if there is a problem, give them everything or, conversely, if there is a program, give it to everyone. Obviously, under these conditions, it is hard to tell what works for whom.

Standardization of Programs. Probably this should await the outcome of research. To explain what is meant by standardization, let us take as an example exercise programs in institutions. Few institutions offer these programs in the same way using standardized equipment. Such variety might be appropriate because no two institutions may have the same patient mix. But, to date, it is hard to tell why the variations occur and which of them are the most useful. Certainly, standardization is a desirable goal but we probably know too little to set such a goal at this time.

Finally, it would be helpful to consumers, providers, and taxpayers if knowledge about successful programs and technology were better diffused, if only to keep from continually reinventing the wheel. Therefore, more efficient ways of diffusing knowledge about long-term care are needed.

Probably more in the way of technology could be used to meet the needs of the elderly both in and out of institutions. Of course, many practitioners will not stop conducting their programs just because an evaluation experiment shows they do not work. Too many secondary gains are derived from using tried and true programs, that is, many diverse community needs are satisfied by delivering a specific program in a predetermined way. Careers, jobs and money are at stake. There seems to be much resistance to change in the long-term care field. However, taxpayers may refuse to pay for programs that they believe have outlived their usefulness to consumers. Thus, it would be in their best interest to learn about the effectiveness of current programs as well as alternative service delivery systems.

References

Brody, E.M. and Brody, S.J., New Directions in Health and Social Supports for the Aging. M.A. Lewis (ed.) The Aging: Medical and Social Supports in the Decade of the 80's (Viewpoints of Distinguished American and British Authorities). Proceedings of the Anglo-American Conference on New Patterns of Medical and Social Supports for the Aging, held at Fordham University, May 12-13, 1980.

Brotman, H.B., Every Ninth American. In U.S. Senate Special Committee on Aging, Developments in Aging, 1979, Part I (Washington, D.C.: Government Printing Office, 1980), XB-XXXVII.

Callahan, J.J., Jr., Diamond, L.D., Giele, J.Z., and Morris, R., Responsibility of Families for Their Severely Disabled Elders. Health Care Financing Review, pp. 29-48, Winter, 1980.

Cantor, M., Neighbors and Friends. Research on Aging, Vol. 1, December, 1979.

Cantor, M., Factors Associated with Strain Among Family, Friends and Neighbors Caring for the Frail Elderly. Paper presented at 34th Annual Meeting of Gerontological Society of America, Toronto, 1981.

Dunlop, B., Expanded home-based care for the impaired elderly: Solution or pipe dream? American Journal of Public Health, 70:514-519, 1980.

General Accounting Office, Comptroller General of the U.S., The Well-Being of Older People in Cleveland, Ohio: Report to the Congress. GAO-13 HRD-77-70, April 1977.

Gurland, B., Dean, L., Gurland, R., and Cook, D., Personal Time Dependency in the Elderly of New York City: Findings from the U.S.-U.K. Cross National Geriatric Community Study. In Dependency in the Elderly of New York City. New York Community Council of Greater New York, October 1978.

Killeffer, E.H.P., Bennett, R. and Gruen, G. Handbook of Innovative Programs for the Impaired Elderly, Haworth Press, New York, 1984.

National Center for Health Statistics, unpublished data from 1978 Health Interview Survey.

National Council on the Aging, Fact Book on Aging. 1978.

National Council on the Aging, Myth and Reality of Aging. 1975.

National Health Survey, DHHS Publication No. (PHS) 9 October 1980.

The National Nursing Home Survey: 1977. Summary for the U.S. Dept. HEW, PHS, Office of Health Research, Statistics and Technology. National Center for Health Statistics, Vital and Health Statistics, Series 13, No. 43. DHEW Publication No. (PHS)79-1794, Hyattsville, MD, July 1979.

National Nursing Home Survey, Nursing Home Utilization in California, Illinois, Massachusetts, New York and Texas. Office of Health Research, Statistics and Technology, NCHS. DHHS Publication No. (PHS) 81-1977, October 1980.

Sussman, M. Social and Economic Supports and Family Environment for the Elderly. Final Report to the Administration on Aging, AoA Grant No. 90 A-316, Jan. 1980.

Technology Adaptation and the Elderly. Background Technology Papers. AoA Grant No. 13.637. Population Resource Center, N.Y. 1980.

U.S. Bureau of the Census, 1976 Survey of Institutionalized Persons: A

Study of Persons Receiving Long-Term Care. U.S. Department of Commerce, Washington, D.C.: U.S. Government Printing Office, 1978.

U.S. Bureau of the Census, Current Population Reports. Series P-20, No. 338 and earlier reports; Series P-23, Nos. 57 and 59; Series P-25, No. 800; and Series P-60, Nos. 118, 119.

8

Innovative Approaches to Long-Term Care and Their Evaluation

William G. Weissert

In the past, Medicaid policy has done little to encourage development of noninstitutional forms of long-term care, with two limited exceptions. State Medicaid programs are required to offer home health care services, and they are permitted at their option to offer what are called "personal care" services. But home health care under Medicaid has been very limited, typically provided only to post-hospital patients suffering acute problems. Even though new federal action was taken in 1976 to discourage these limits, most states continue to spend little for home health care.

The personal care option, while generally unregulated, nonetheless requires physician authorization and nursing supervision and prohibits coverage of homemaker (as opposed to personal care) services. While a few states have circumvented these restrictions, in general, long-term care under Medicaid has had little opportunity to encompass home and community based care settings.

This is no longer the case. In Section 2176 of the otherwise budget-cutting and program-reducing Omnibus Budget Reconciliation Act of 1981, Congress amended the Social Security Act to permit states to freely experiment much more with home and community based long-term care. Section 2176 added a new provision to the Social Security Act, Section 1915(c)(1), authorizing the Secretary of the Department of Health and Human Services to waive most or all statutory provisions of Medicaid law which discourage or restrict coverage of home and community based long-term care.

States may offer services on a less than a statewide basis—meaning that they are free to offer them only where providers are available. They can pick and choose among groups who are otherwise eligible for Medicaid—offering one or more services to some groups but not to others. This is because the legislation permits waiver of the "comparability" rule requiring that beneficiaries must be eligible to receive the same type of services.

States can now cover a wide array of services previously ineligible for Medicaid support. In the 42 applications submitted by the end of 1982, case management, homemaker, home health aide, personal care, adult day health, habilitation and respite care were the most frequently offered services (Krieger, Weissert, and Cohen, 1982).

The law permits states to waive statutory requirements to test a program for up to three years and to extend the waiver for an additional three years. The Secretary of the Department of Health and Human Services must approve each waiver and has the authority to terminate it at any time. Consequently, annual reviews of each state's operations are conducted to assure that certain regulatory requirements are being met.

Perhaps the most important of these regulatory requirements is that the services offered under the waiver program must result in Medicaid expenditures which are no higher than they would have been without the waiver. While the legislation speaks in terms of both spending "per capita" and "aggregate spending," the regulations make it clear that the emphasis is on aggregate spending, regardless of how many beneficiaries are served. In other words, states may choose to serve more people, but their total expenditures may not exceed what they would have been had they not chosen to expand their beneficiary pool. This provision reflects the view that when home and community based care are provided, nursing home use will go down. This leads to the hope that more people can be served at lower total costs because home and community based care is expected to be cheaper than nursing home care.

Congress is one of the few places where this view is still held, however, and even there doubters can be found. The problem lies in the assumption that provision of home and community based long-term care will result in reduced nursing home use. In point of fact, results are now available from a large number of studies to show that there is little or no evidence that nursing home use is reduced by home and community based care. Quite the contrary, study after study has shown that when these noninstitutional services are offered, the great majority of those who use them are at little or no risk of nursing home entry. Consequently, nursing home use does not decline. Meanwhile, total use of health care services, and therefore total expenditures, rise.

The first study to show this lack of nursing home substitution (Weissert et al, 1980a, b) indicated that when geriatric day care or homemaker services were offered to a random half of 1,872 Medicare-eligible aged persons, nursing home admission rates among the control groups were only 18 percent for the day care control group and 21 percent for the homemaker control group. In other words, 80 percent of those who used the experimental services were not at risk of nursing home admission. Consequently, their use of the experimental services was merely added to the expenses they would have incurred anyway. This produced costs 60 to 70 percent higher in the groups which got the experimental services over their control groups.

Part of the problem was that even among the group which did go into a nursing home, there were no statistically significant differences between the experimental and control groups in institutionalization. In other words, even among those who were at risk, the treatment was not effective.

Worse, perhaps, is the likelihood that savings would have been trivial even if there had been an effect on admission rates. This is because the small group which did go into nursing homes had very short stays. Contrary to popular belief, most patients who enter nursing homes are not destined to stay there forever. More than half are gone within three months and nearly two-thirds within six months, many within the first few days following admission (National Center for Health Statistics, 1979; National Nursing Home Survey, 1977). To be sure, no small portion of those discharges are deaths or transfers in anticipation of death. But analysis of the 1977 National Nursing Home Survey shows that one-fourth of nursing home admissions go back to their private residences, and another 3 percent go to other community care settings such as retirement homes (Weissert, Scanlon, and O'Loughlin, 1982). These tend to be younger, those suffering fractures rather than cancer, and those who have a spouse.

This evidently is the subgroup of the day care or homemaker services population which experienced a nursing home stay—those destined to be short stayers in nursing homes. The total bill for nursing home use in the day care control group, for example, was just $37,397. To prevent this expenditure, $637,631—nearly 20 times that figure—was spent on day care services.

It must be added that this expenditure difference was not typical of later studies, in which treatment and control group expenditures were generally much closer. But it remains true that only one study thus far

141

has reported statistically significantly lower rates of nursing home use as a result of the treatment. That study reported only 10 percent lower rates among a tiny "at risk" population: 16 treatment-group and 28 control-group admissions (Hughes et al, 1982). And no study has been successful in identifying and serving a patient population generally at high risk of institutionalization. Nursing home use rates have ranged from a high of 22 percent in the control group of one large study (Skellie, Mobley and Coan, 1982) to a low of just 2.5 percent in the control group of another (Papsidero et al, 1979). And lengths of stay have been short.

While critics have charged that individual studies may have been flawed in one way or another, the simple fact that so few users of community care had any potential to benefit through reduced nursing home use makes the conclusion unavoidable that most patients use it as an add-on rather than as a substitute for community care. This fact alone dashes the hope of any substantial cost savings through home and community care unless a much better job can be done in targeting those at risk of institutionalization.

Congress acknowledged this problem in the new community-care legislation. Forced by the terms of the Congressional Budget Act of 1974 to refrain from even bringing to the floor any legislation which would raise expenditures, those who wanted to expand home and community based care coverage acceded to those who wanted to cut Medicaid expenditures by adding a specific proviso, in a sense making it illegal to use the service as a complement without offsetting any added expenses by also using it as a substitute. That is, not only does the legislation require that expenditures under the waiver must be no higher than they would have been without the waiver, but another provision requires that those served by the waiver authority must be persons who "but for the waivered services" would be in nursing homes (Section 1915(c)(1) of the Social Security Act).

While this provision is taken seriously by the Health Care Financing Administration (HCFA), which reviews waiver applications and annual reports, there is no denying that it is easier to call for than to implement for both technical and political reasons. Recent research on the determinants of institutionalization (Weissert and Scanlon, 1982) illuminates some of these difficulties. Data from the 1977 National Nursing Home Survey were merged with data from the 1977 National Health Interview Survey to provide a study sample representative of most of the national aged population. Logistical analysis was run to identify the factors which were associated with living in a nursing home rather than in the community. By focusing on those living in nursing homes rather than those merely admitted, the study was able to describe characteristics of a population comprised largely of those who are or will be long stayers. While most admissions are short stayers, most beds are filled by long stayers (Keller, Kane, and Solomon, 1981).

The study showed that a relatively small number of health status, demographic, and nursing home market characteristics predict nursing home residency. These are dependency in activities of daily living, especially toileting and/or eating, although eating, bathing, and/or dressing dependency is also very important; diagnosis, especially presence of a mental disorder as a primary or secondary diagnosis; poverty; lack of a spouse (usually through widowhood); climate; and size of the nursing home bed supply relative to the number of poor aged in the market area.

Together, these and a few other variables permit quite accurate classification of those in nursing homes versus those in the community: 99 percent of cases were correctly classified in a logit analysis containing 20 variables.

Examining the populations which have been served by the various community care demonstrations, it is clear that, even though many demonstrations have served some patients who met some of these characteristics, few patients have manifested the combination of variables associated with institutional residency. For example, in most studies, about half of the population was married, a trait which alone reduces the probability of institutional residency by nearly 9 percent. More importantly, while some demonstration patients suffered dependency in toileting or eating, most suffered lesser dependencies, thereby further distinguishing them from institutional residents.

In other words, although the studies to date have served populations comprised of persons who few would quarrel are seriously in need of help, they have not typically served that desperately dependent population with long nursing home stays.

Consequently, unless the states choose to define their eligibility rules for home and community based care services in such a way as to limit use to those who fit this "desperate need" model, they are not likely to meet the legislative goal of serving exclusively those who but for the waivered services would be in nursing homes.

Unfortunately, there are also rather strong incentives for states to do just the opposite in some cases. That is, some states may take the opportunity made possible by the waiver authority to shift some of their block grant and state-funded community care recipients onto the Medicaid rolls. Since the federal government pays a half to four-fifths of Medicaid expenditures, this is strongly in their interest, given the cutbacks in the Title XX social services block grant program. A comparison of services now offered under the Title XX block grant with those to be offered by the waiver program shows that the potential for making such shifts is quite strong (Krieger, Weissert, and Cohen, 1982; Cohen, 1982).

Of course, unless the states are able to actually reduce nursing home expenditures to offset such shifts, they will be in violation of the provision that expenditures must be no higher under the waiver than without it. They must then reckon with the Health Care Financing Administration over whether or not their waiver is to be renewed. But what that reckoning will mean is yet to be determined, for two reasons. First, there is considerable evidence that the task of comparing what expenditures are with what they would have been may prove difficult (Weissert, 1983). Because the waiver frees them of statewide application, states are likely to put the waiver program into effect in areas where services are available. This vitiates many opportunities for comparison group designs. Consequently, analyses may be forced to rely in part on interpreting time series data on nursing home use and expenditures. These figures are inherently unstable, the object of many simultaneous policy efforts, and sensitive to fluctuation in the state economy. HCFA will be hard pressed to show that expenditures are higher than they would have been, especially since states, in addition to the waiver program, will be trying in a variety of ways to reduce them.

Second, there is more to cost-effectiveness than costs. Even if HCFA is successful in showing that expenditures rose as a result of the waiver, the states and the many other advocates of home and community based care will certainly argue that the the lives of those who used community care are better off than they would have been without the community care. In other words, they will argue that added expenditures are offset by added benefits. Since the possibility of rigorously controlled experimental findings (or even loosely controlled comparison group findings) are so limited under the waiver program with respect to patient outcomes, there will be no direct evidence to refute this claim. And intuitively, most people simply agree that patients served by community care services are better off than those not served by community care services, regardless of institutionalization.

Unfortunately, the hard evidence to support this view is limited. Again, the studies mentioned earlier have typically shown that few outcome differences could be detected between treatment and control groups. But physical and mental functioning abilities, the most frequently measured outcomes, may be insensitive; effects on family satisfaction were not typically measured; and no one who has reviewed the literature on contentment scales has come away convinced that the state of the art of measuring feelings of well-being has advanced to a stage worthy of supporting public policy.

Furthermore, there is increasing evidence that home and community based care do have a small effect on life expectancy. Results are invariably clouded by differential experimental mortality and consequent self-selection effects, but the day care and homemaker study described earlier and the Georgia Alternative Health Services Project study (Skellie, Mobley, and Coan, 1982) showed some statistically significant differences in death rates.

To summarize, we now have as temporary public policy a program which permits states to expand their home and community based care activities, to shift some of their own costs to the federal government, to fill some of the gaps in what is generally recognized as a fragmented system of long-term care provision, to remove the public financing bias which for years has favored institutional care, and to expand the beneficiary population so that some individuals not now receiving long-term care services will be eligible to have them paid for by Medicaid. Nominally, it is illegal to serve anyone but those who would be in an institution, and total expenditures may not rise. Proof of benefits is limited, but few believe we know the whole story on outcomes.

But the reality appears to be that to even strive toward strict adherence to the law, the states would have to restrict utilization of these new services to a group which is desperately in need. Doing this means keeping services away from many who appear to be legitimately in need of help. Technically, this task is difficult, politically, it is probably impossible as well as unattractive, especially given the likelihood that for technical and political reasons the law which makes it illegal to expand Medicaid expenditures may be difficult to enforce.

States are likely to differ in their degree of restrictiveness and their willingness to risk disallowance of reimbursement for some patients by expanding their Medicaid expenditures to facilitate shifting expenses from other programs. A likely response from HCFA may be to restrict overall growth of the program by demanding better evidence that new community care use will lead to one-for-one reductions in nursing home use.

In short, home and community based care services are likely to be here to stay, costs are almost certain to rise due to the complementarity problem, even though states will be aggressive in trying to offset them through more restrictive nursing home policies, and more work will (or at least should) go into devising scales which effectively measure the benefits which intuition suggests may justify the added costs.

References

Cohen, J., Public Programs Financing Long-Term Care. Washington, D.C.: The Urban Institute, Working Paper 1466-18, June 1982.

Hughes, S.L., Cordray, D., Spiker, V.A., Evaluation of a Long-Term Homes Care Program, revised, May, 1983, Northwestern University Center for Health Services and Policy Research.

Keller, E., B., Kane, R.L. and Solomon, P.L., Short- and long-term residents of nursing homes. Medical Care 19:363-370, 1981.

Krieger, M.J., Weissert, W.G. and Cohen, J., Characteristics of Medicaid Home- and Community-Based Care Program Applications. Washington, D.C.: The Urban Institute, Working Paper 3198-2, December 9, 1982.

National Center for Health Statistics, Department of Health and Human Services, Public Health Service, National Nursing Home Survey: 1977, Summary for the United States. Data from the National Health Survey, Series 13, No. 43, July 1979.

National Nursing Home Survey. Unpublished tables by The Urban Institute, 1977.

Papsidero, J.A., Katz, S., Kroger, M.H. and Akpon, C.A., Chance for Change: Implications of a Chronic Disease Module Study. East Lansing, Mi.: Michigan State University Press, 1979.

Skellie, F.A., Mobley, G.M. and Coan, R.E., Cost-Effectiveness of Community Based Long-Term Care: Current Findings of Georgia's Alternative Health Services Project. American Journal of Public Health, 72(4):353-358, 1982.

Weissert, W.G., Draft Design for Evaluation of Impacts of the Medicaid Home and Community-Based Care Waiver Program. Washington, D.C.: The Urban Institute, Working Paper 3198-3, January 10, 1983.

Weissert, W.G., Wan, T.H., Livieratos, B. and Pellegrino, J., Cost Effectiveness of Homemaker Services for the Chronically Ill. Inquiry 17:230-243, 1980a.

Weissert, W.G., Wan, T.H., Livieratos, B. and Katz, S., Cost effectiveness of day care services for the chronically ill: A Randomized Experiment. Medical Care, 18:567-584, 1980b.

Weissert, W.G., Scanlon, W.J. and O'Loughlin, S., Determinants of Nursing Home Discharge Status. Washington, D.C.: The Urban Institute, Working Paper 1466-19, June 1982.

Weissert, W.G. and Scanlon, W.J., Determinants of Institutionalization of the Aged. Washington, D.C.: The Urban Institute, Working Paper 1466 21, November 1982.

9

Organization of Long-Term Care: Should There Be a Single Or Multiple Focal Points for Long-Term Care Coordination

Diane S. Piktialis and James Callahan

Over the past decade, the United States has seen a heightened interest in problems and policy issues involved in the provision of long-term care to the elderly. The piecemeal development of long-term care programs led to care plagued by inefficiencies and coordination problems. Each public program provided funding for different services under different regulations and with different eligibility requirements.

Apart from increasing expenditures for long-term care, this has led to problems of excessive utilization of institutional care, lack of availability of needed community services, and poor matching of client needs with services. These inefficiencies have led to a public commitment to develop options for changing the existing forms of financing and organization of long-term care service delivery.

I. Long-Term Care Demonstrations

Experiments in providing alternatives to institutional care and mechanisms for coordinating community care became the major strategy of the Health Care Financing Administration in addressing the problems presented by growing numbers of elders needing services. Both single service demonstrations and community-wide coordination projects were funded. The former included demonstrations to provide adult day health care to clients in need of continuing care under Medicare Part B and experiments to assess the impact of homemaker services on clients discharged from acute care facilities who required additional services. Both demonstrations were conducted under the authority of Section 222 (B) of the 1972 Amendments to the Social Security Act. Other adult day care demonstration programs developed independently of the Section 222 experiments, notably On Lok in San Francisco.

A second type of demonstration was designed to provide a coordinated system of health and social services. Coordination of care was an important component in these experiments since, unlike nursing homes which are primarily funded by Medicaid, noninstitutional long-term care services are funded by many agencies at federal, state, and local levels. The purpose of the demonstrations was to develop more appropriate and cost effective alternatives. These projects included Triage (Connecticut); Access (Monroe County, New York); Alternative Health Services Project (Georgia); Community Based Care Systems (Washington State); and the Community Care Organization (Wisconsin).

These and other early demonstrations also attempted to provide data for a number of questions on long-term care benefits for in-home and community-based services. A review of the most prominent demonstrations in community care, day care and in-home services indicates, however, that there is only limited evidence that community-based services substitute for nursing home care. Also, even where these coordinated service packages substituted for institutional care, overall system cost reductions from using these services did not occur except in two cases (Access and Wisconsin). Also, findings on the effect of case-management on system fragmentation suggest that the effectiveness of the case management component of the demonstrations had not been systematically evaluated. With respect to patient outcomes, experts conclude that expanded coverage of community based services seemed to have a favorable impact in terms of mortality rates and increased life satisfaction, but that differences in functional capacity were not apparent. Finally, methodological problems made interpretation of results of all these demonstrations difficult.

Since this indicated a need for new demonstrations with better research designs, a second generation of demonstrations was developed to test new organization arrangements. The new demonstrations include the National Long-Term Care Channeling Project and the Social Health Maintenance Organization (SHMO). Both are concerned with using reimbursement methods to control costs and with the impact of community based services on families and other informal supporters. They include a number of additional program elements being tested for the first time. Since cost issues were paramount, the experiments will receive little public funding other than waivers under Medicare and Medicaid and both will include some type of capitation model. The Channeling Project will have a specific targeting approach to the frail elderly in order to better control costs and will introduce improved and strengthened case management systems. The Social/Health Maintenance Organization encompasses both acute and long-term care and addresses what some experts consider another shortcoming of the earlier demonstrations, namely the exclusive focus on long-term care. The Channeling project will use an experimental research design to overcome the methodological limitations of earlier studies. While these demonstrations appear to offer new, and possibly more effective models for long-term care coordination, no substantial data exist as yet upon which to evaluate outcomes for clients or for overall costs.

After a decade of long-term care demonstrations, there is a great deal of theoretical or analytic literature on organization and financing of long-term care services. Rather than expanding on these aspects, this paper examines empirical data from the Massachusetts Home Care Program. This program is a statewide case management system which presently serves 41,000 older persons. What is unique about this program is that it developed without special funding and operates without federal funding, waivers, or demonstration authority. Moreover, it is an ongoing program with over ten years of experience in providing community care to the elderly. We use the reality of this experience as a measure against which to evaluate long-term care issues and models of organization. The analysis focuses on functions at the patient management level. A second aspect is issues of single or multiple focal points for long-term care coordination.

There are certain assumptions upon which the analysis in this paper is based. These are:
1. Long-term care services are already being provided at the local level and to a considerable degree. Any federal initiative should build upon the local long-term care delivery system so as to maximize existing interorganizational community systems.

149

2. Efforts at organizing long-term care should lean toward incremental change as opposed to a single national delivery model imposed on local communities.
3. Expansion of community based services should be justified on its merits and not simply as a cost saving alternative to the nursing home.
4. Any option for service delivery must have a provision for a coordinating mechanism, such as case management, as a necessary management function.

II. A Model of Service Delivery for the Elderly Population: The Massachusetts Home Care Program

The Massachusetts home care program is itself a national model for service management and delivery that approaches long-term care from a social rather than a medical perspective. This model places long-term care services within a family and social support context and uses medical services only for health maintenance and treatment of acute illness. The Massachusetts model had been a forerunner of current national efforts to use case management as a tool for client targeting and service coordination. The program provides a basis for community care for elders on a statewide basis.

Previous research on the Massachusetts system of home care services has indicated that examining an existing delivery system can be instructive in answering important public policy questions in long-term care (Branch, Callahan, and Jette, 1981). This study focused on two primary questions: What might happen if a system of home-based services were implemented statewide and nationally? How can community-based programs be designed to target and reach the frail or vulnerable elderly population?

In order to reassess these questions and to present a measure against which to evaluate long-term care models, this section of the paper will examine more recent studies of the Massachusetts home care program along with other available data on the system. Particular attention will be paid to the characteristics of the population entering the program and indicators of outcomes such as changes in unmet need status, whether substitution of informal supporters with formal services has occurred, and overall estimates of the size of the population in need. Because the Massachusetts program is an operating statewide system and not a demonstration program, its performance is instructive.

DIANE S. PIKTIALIS AND JAMES CALLAHAN

1. Description of the Massachusetts System

History. Massachusetts' history of concern for the needs of the elderly dates back to the establishment of a Commission on Aging in 1954. In 1973, as part of a major reorganization of state government, a cabinet level Office of Elder Affairs was established, due largely to pressure by groups of the elderly and their advocates. A primary responsibility given to the Secretary of that office under its enabling legislation was the mandate to establish and coordinate home care programs throughout the Commonwealth. To fulfill that mandate, the State was divided into 27 service areas. The first two home care corporations were established in 1973 and all areas of the state were covered by July 1, 1977. By September 1983, 40,479 home care clients were receiving service through the program, a caseload representing 4.3 percent of the noninstitutionalized elderly in the state.

Home Care Concept. The Massachusetts system of home care services was designed as a social model of home care service delivery (Kane and Kane, 1978). Branch, Callahan and Jette (1981) have described the conceptualization of the Massachusetts home care model as including six basic elements:

1. *Destigmatization.* The home care concept was intended to reduce the stigma of receiving "welfare," a common association made by the elderly population with government benefits, particularly those usually provided through Welfare Departments.
2. *Local Consumer Input.* This concept includes direct involvement of the elderly and local communities in policy and decision making through representation on the board of directors. The underlying assumption is that decisions which are more responsive to the needs of the elderly will be made by local home care agencies.
3. *Reduction of Bureaucratic Obstacles.* In order to facilitate service provision, the system is comprised of private nonprofit corporations which are not subject to much of the red tape that burdens government bureaucracies, such as civil service requirements.
4. *Case Management.* The entire service delivery system was founded on the concept of case management to help the target population, elderly persons with a multiplicity of chronic health and social service needs, obtain access to services. Assessment, care planning, ongoing monitoring of client status, and a coordinated care package are all provided for the older person by the case manager.
5. *Multiple Funding Sources.* Funds for directly provided services come from a variety of sources, including Title III of the Older Americans' Act (until 1981 Title 20), Title 19 and state funds. Since 1981,

15

the bulk of funds used to purchase home care social services comes from state money. The program uses case management as a vehicle to access services funded by other sources, such as under Title 19, on behalf of the older person.

6. *Priority*. A service system set up exclusively for the elderly was intended to counteract widespread discrimination against this group frequently found in human service programs (Branch, Callahan and Jette, 1981).

The Massachusetts model of home care based on these six concepts was implemented throughout the state from 1973 to 1977. Each of the 27 home care corporations is governed by a board of directors with a majority of elderly persons, 51 percent of whom are from Councils on Aging in the communities served by the program. These corporations are the exclusive agent of the Department of Elder Affairs and offer a core service package which now includes information and referral, case management, homemaker, chore, transportation, and laundry services, home delivered meals, and companionship. The home care corporations directly provide information and referral and case management. Other social services are purchased through contracts with local providers. By June 1982, after ten years of continuous expansion, the active caseload for the home care program had reached 39,421. Expenditures in 1974 were $6 million with a caseload of 10,000, and by 1982 had reached $71 million.

Until this point, it is appropriate to describe the system as one developed under minimum regulation and with decentralized management (Branch, Callahan, and Jette, 1981). For example, each home care corporation had developed its own assessment procedures. However, since the program expanded so quickly, a number of steps were taken in 1980 to guarantee that the quality of service would remain high and that home care corporations would continue to reach the older population in need. These included required standard assessment procedures on a statewide basis, clear targeting criteria based on an individual's level of impairment, and comprehensive program performance evaluation.

2. Recent Studies: Findings on Vulnerability and Unmet Need

During the evolution of the home care program, two studies of the system have been completed, one prior to the 1980 policy and regulatory changes and one approximately two years later. Findings of both are instructive in considering how to organize long-term care.

Data from a 1979 study were used to evaluate how successfully the

Massachusetts model of home care targets services to the vulnerable elderly (Branch, Callahan and Jette, 1981). This investigation compared a sample of Massachusetts home care clients to the vulnerable elderly identified in a statewide needs study conducted in 1975 and 1976 (Branch, 1977), which described this population (about 6 percent of noninstitutionalized elderly) as the appropriate home care program target population. Comparison of home care clients found home care corporation recipients to be similar to the statewide sample of vulnerable elderly with respect to age, sex, income and education as well as in areas of unmet need or in types of formal support being received for the kinds of activities provided by home care services (Branch, 1980). The data in the investigation indicated that the Massachusetts system was successful in reaching its target population since the home care sample was generally very similar to the group the services were designed to serve (Branch's subgroup of the vulnerable).

In late 1981, the Massachusetts Department of Elder Affairs sought an updated estimate of what proportion of the elderly population the Massachusetts home care corporations should be responsible for and what types and levels of additional formal services were needed to enhance the system's response capacity. Since the state legislature at the time was interested in short and long-term budgetary projections based on need rather than demand, the Massachusetts Department of Elder Affairs contracted with the Department of Social Gerontological Research of the Hebrew Rehabilitation Center for the Aged (HRCA) to conduct a comprehensive assessment of the functioning, needs, and support options of the elderly in the State of Massachusetts. The study was intended to reevaluate and expand upon earlier data on levels of need for publicly supported home care. It is reported in summary in the following.

Methods. The 1982 HRCA study consisted of a multiple subgroup, locally based sample of the noninstitutionalized elderly. Three representative groups were studied: a sample of community residents, a sample of new clients in the home care corporations, and a sample of home care clients already receiving services. These subgroups were chosen to permit comparisons between the needs of the general elderly population and the needs of clients in the home care program and to evaluate targeting of services and the impact of services on unmet need. Data were based on self-reports on met and unmet needs in a number of critical service areas. Personal interviews were completed from January through March of 1982 with 2,674 community residents, 575 intake home care clients, and 607 clients already in the home care program, representing response rates of 90.4 percent, 96.5 percent, and 94.3 percent, respectively (Morris, December 1982).

Demographic Characteristics. Before outlining the 1982 study findings on vulnerability, unmet needs and service provision, a brief description of some key demographic variables is given to indicate some differences in the population groups studied (Table 1). Although all groups contained more females than males, an expected finding, the two home care groups had particularly high rates of females. Two fifths of the two home care samples lived in public housing in contrast to only 4.8 percent of the community population. The more recent intakes into the home care sample had the highest hospitalization rates in the previous year (63.7 percent), whereas the community population had the lowest rate (21.5 percent). As will be discussed in an analysis of referral patterns, it is not unlikely that many of the intake sample were referred to the home care program at discharge from the hospital. An analysis of sources of income and utilization of several sources of economic assistance indicated that the community residents were more financially independent, with income more likely to be from pensions, interest, investments, and wages. The home care populations were more likely to rely on SSI, and receive food stamps and Medicaid benefits. Overall, the home care recipients tended to be more more dependent on government benefit programs. However, it should be noted that this may partially be a function of the high percentage of home care clients living in public housing.

Assessment of functional vulnerability. The first major part of the study estimated the numbers of functionally vulnerable individuals defined as restricted in performing one or more activities that are central to community functioning. For this, HRCA used a simple ten-question scoring instrument including key measures of mobility, personal ADL, instrumental ADL, orientation, and activities. This instrument was able to classify as functionally vulnerable persons with physical impairments or stamina problems which severely limit their ability to get around safely or perform activities in their home environment, as well as those who require help from others with personal and instrumental activities of daily living (Morris, December 1982).

According to this definition of functional vulnerability, an estimated 20.8 percent of elderly persons in the community had deficits in their ability to carry out one or more key activities independently. Comparable estimates for home care clients were four times as high: 88.1 percent for the new intake sample and 83.5 percent for current

Table 1
Key Demographic Variables On The Massachusetts Study Of The Elderly And Their Needs

	Community residents	Home care new intake clients	Home care existing clients
Sex			
Male	41.9%	25.5%	19.4%
Female	58.1	74.5	80.6
Race			
White	97.2	94.3	95.1
Other	2.8	5.7	4.9
Residential Setting			
Private house	78.6	32.2	30.0
Apartment, private	16.4	24.5	25.1
Apartment, public	4.8	42.7	43.6
Boarding, group living	0.2	0.6	1.2
Hospitalized in last year	21.5	63.7	49.1
Report not having enough money to get by	6.4	11.5	9.4
Source of Income			
Pension, other than Social Security	37.5	23.6	18.3
Interest, investment income	34.0	14.8	16.6
Contribution from family or withdrawal from savings	9.1	8.2	12.0
Social Security	77.3	95.1	94.9
SSI	8.7	29.1	29.6
Veteran's, other government pension	12.8	11.8	13.8
Other, including wages	26.7	4.3	5.3
Public Support			
Medicare	73.0	93.8	93.7
Medex	76.9	57.0	61.6
Medicaid	13.2	36.6	37.8
Food stamps	4.0	13.6	15.0

Source: Morris, J., Department of Social Gerontological Research, Hebrew Rehabilitation Center for the Aged, *Massachusetts Elderly: Their Vulnerability and Need for Social Services*: Table 1–2 (Boston, MA. December, 1982).

home care clients. The contrast between these rates indicates that the home care program has been successful both in identifying and serving vulnerable persons. Other substantial differences between the home care and community samples were found as well. The home care populations had higher rates of problems and requirements for assistance in preparing meals, taking out the garbage, doing ordinary housework, walking up and down stairs, and getting out of their residence. They also were more likely to need a walker or cane and to have health problems which prevented them from carrying out activities of daily living.

Unmet need estimates. The study then applied an additional measure of need to the functionally vulnerable population. The majority of those functionally vulnerable receive assistance from others, families and friends being most actively involved in providing support. In order to be identified as needing publicly supported formal services, two assumptions were made. As indicated above, the first was that the person was restricted in one or more activities central to community functioning. The second was that the person be unable to identify an individual or agency who would be willing to compensate adequately for the functional deficit. Thus, assessment of need must account not only for personal characteristics such as physical and psychological functioning but also for external factors such as formal services received or response capacity of informal supporters. The determination of whether an individual had an unmet need was based on self-reports in nine areas assumed relevant to continued community living and covered by the regulations governing the Massachusetts home care population. These were:
Light housekeeping
Personal care
Laundry
Shopping for groceries
Chores
Small errands
Transportation
Managing medications
Preparing meals
The following are estimates of the proportions of persons in the community sample who were both functionally vulnerable and had unmet needs in the nine areas canvassed: 7.3 percent were both vulnerable and had unmet service needs, 4.0 percent had two or more unmet needs; only 1.2 percent classified their unmet needs as severe while 4.6 percent classified their needs as moderate (Morris, December 1982). When adjusted to include only those service needs that are met by home care corporations, the overall need for home care services dropped to 6.7 percent. This estimate of 6.7 percent is based on total need projections. A second estimate of the total proportion of

individuals requiring home care services is described as more "realistic" and adjusts for factors such as income eligibility and the likelihood that some of the more isolated populations will not come into contact with the home care program. Based on these varying definitions and adjustments, the total proportion of individuals requiring home services would vary from 5.7 to 7.3 percent of elderly persons 60 years of age or older in the community. While different measurement instruments were used by Branch and HRCA, it is important to note that Branch's Vulnerable Elders Index resulted in an estimate of 6 percent of the statewide noninstitutionalized elderly population as needing intensive supports to maintain relative independence (Branch, 1980). Thus both Branch and HRCA have identified the home care corporation's target group as being of a similar size. This finding suggests that the need for community based long-term care is in fact quite limited.

The unmet need estimates from the new intake client population who are functionally vulnerable differed markedly from the community population. In comparison to the community population, where only 7.3 percent were found to be functionally vulnerable and have one or more unmet needs, 78 percent of new intakes could be so classified (Morris, December 1982). In addition, most of the vulnerable intake sample (87 percent) had multiple unmet needs, compared to 55 percent of the community population (4.0 percent of the 7.3 percent had multiple unmet needs). An even more dramatic finding is the different rates of severe and moderate impairment (Table 2). As noted earlier, only 1.2 percent of the community population had severe unmet needs. The rate of new intakes with severe unmet needs was 23.4 or nearly 20 times the rate for the community population. When combining those with moderate or severe impairments, 65.5 percent of new home corporation clients had unmet needs that could be characterized as moderate or severe, as opposed to only 4.6 percent in the community sample. In summary, it can be stated that the Massachusetts home care program accepts a large number of clients who are both functionally impaired and in need of formal support services, including a majority of individuals whose needs can be classified as moderate or severe.

Finally, in addition to accepting clients who were clearly impaired, a comparison of the existing client population and the community population suggests that clients are receiving the necessary services. Unmet need estimates for existing clients were closer to the estimates for the community sample.

Specific unmet service needs were also evident. Of the nine service areas assessed, three areas had unmet need estimates in the range of

157

Table 2
Overall Estimates Of Seriousness Of Unmet Need Based On The Self-Report of Functionally Vulnerable Elderly Persons In Three Populations[a]

	Community residents	Home care new intake clients	Home care existing clients
Estimate of persons with moderate or severe unmet needs	4.6%	65.5%	23.5%
Estimate of persons with severe unmet needs	1.2	23.4	9.8

Source: Morris, J., December 1982.
[a]Needs assessed in the following areas: light housework, laundry, doing chores, transportation, shopping for groceries, preparing meals, personal care, managing medications, small errands.

3 to 4 percent among the community population: chores, 3.6 percent; transportation, 3.1 percent; and light housework, 3.3 percent. Estimates for all other areas were even lower. The intake sample was quite the opposite: only three areas yielded estimates lower than 20 percent. The pervasiveness of unmet need is indicated by rates of 30 percent for transportation, shopping and meal preparation, and 65 percent for light housekeeping. These figures support overall findings of the character of the at-risk population in the community and the response of the home-care program in targeting their efforts to those who are functionally vulnerable and in need of additional supports.

Informal Support System Capacity. A third aspect of the HRCA study examined informal support systems for those individuals characterized as functionally vulnerable and with unmet needs. For the community population, 82 percent of individuals who were receiving assistance from an informal support system were confident they would continue to receive this help and 62 percent believed that additional informal supports would be forthcoming if they needed them. The home care population estimates were somewhat less, with only 46 percent believing they would receive additional home care services if they needed them.

This is not unexpected given the finding that home care clients are more likely to be isolated. They are less likely to be married (16 percent vs. 51 percent) and more likely to live alone (about 70 percent vs. 29 percent; Morris, December 1982). However, as has been the case with previous studies, family and friends were found to be the most common supports for all three populations.

Service Utilization. The nature of the supports received, both formal and informal, indicated that home care services may have substituted for informal care. At intake into the home care program, service provision was similar to that for the community population in that services were predominantly informal. A comparison of the intake sample with existing home care clients, however, provides an indication of the impact of home care services on the clients. In three service areas, light housekeeping, laundry and chores, informal service provision has decreased, unmet needs no longer existed, and formal service provision had increased. These data thus suggest there has been some substitution of formal services for informal resources in these three areas. An equally important finding, however, is that this substitution does not appear to have reduced the provision of informal services in the six other areas.

Clearly, ways to maximize the assistance families provide must be an important consideration in organizing long-term care. While the cause of the substitution suggested by the data could not be clearly determined, at least three hypothetical explanations can be considered. First, the home care program retained individuals with the least resilient informal supports in these three areas. Second, family and friends found they no longer had to give care in areas emphasized by the home care program but were willing to continue care in other areas. Third, substitution may be limited to clients who came into the program in the past, when services tended to be limited to two of the three areas where substitution did seem to have occurred—homemaker and chore services (Morris, December 1982). Another possible explanation is that the home care program might have been attracting individuals where families' caretaking responsibilities are a severe burden. Whether this substitution of home care has prevented a complete breakdown of family support in these cases is an area for further study. However, it seems clear that efforts to organize long-term care must consider how to encourage families to provide assistance and supervision to complement the more skilled services the formal delivery system provides.

Another significant finding was that home care clients are not "overconsumers" of care. Information on the average number of service units, both formal and informal, received by the vulnerable population in all three samples for the two-week period prior to the study indicates that the existing home care clients have average service utilization levels that approximate those found in the community population. In all cases, the intake sample received fewer units of service than either the community or home care sample. It is also important to note that previous research on the Massachusetts home

care program found that professional care planners seemed to recommend moderately reasonable and equitable care (Sager, 1980).
Professionals frequently recommended more service than either older
persons or their families, suggesting that persons receiving long-term
care in the community are not likely to demand excessive amounts of
service and that clients and families should be actively involved in
developing care plans.

The role of home care corporations as a provider of formal services
was also analyzed. On a statewide basis it was found that home care
corporations provided three quarters or more of the formal services in
areas of light housekeeping, laundry, chores, shopping and errands.
This finding indicates a considerable market penetration of the home
care program in the provision of formal services (Morris, 1982).

A final set of data relates to the issue of how many clients now in
the home care program are not sufficiently impaired to need home
care services. Important for this discussion are the numerous studies
of inappropriate nursing home placements which claim that from 25
to 40 percent of those in nursing homes do not need nursing home
care. The HRCA study did, in fact, indicate that some individuals
should be discharged from the home care caseload but these estimates
were far lower than those generally made for inappropriate institutional placements and are all the more positive in light of the absence
of formal targeting criteria for the period 1973-1980.

Based on assessment of functional vulnerability and strength of
informal supports, it was estimated that 9.8 percent of existing home
care clients could be excluded (Morris, December 1982). It was also
estimated that an additional 2.6 percent of cases which needed only
one service and had strong informal supports should be carefully
examined. Thus between 9.8 and 12.4 percent were estimated as able
to be dropped from the caseload. This finding indicates the need for
any community based long-term care system to have clearly defined
criteria by which to screen and assess for formal service need. On the
other hand, it indicates that it is quite possible to reach a fairly limited,
needy population without having excessive demand placed on the
service system by individuals not in need of services.

3. Referral Patterns: How Do People Enter and Leave the System?

Callahan (1981) has described the long-term care system in terms of
inputs and outputs. We have examined some aspects of the characteristics of persons entering the home care system. The demographic,
functional vulnerability, and unmet need status of clients at intake

Table 3
Sources of referrals to the Massachusetts home care program (n = 6,867):
Percent distribution, May 1982 to September 1982

Referral Source	
Relatives	19%
Self	22
Hospital	22
Physician	2
Home Health Agency	14
OSS	1
Other Social Service Agency	6
COA	4
Agency Outreach	2.7
Other Home Care	1
Nursing Rest Home	2
Commission for the Blind	0.04
Other	4

Source: Monthly Home Care Program Statistics, Massachusetts Department of Elder Affairs (Boston, Massachusetts, May to September, 1982)

have been described. As a result of the home care program intervention, we saw a marked change in the existing home care caseload with a substantial drop in level of unmet need. One aspect of the system that has not been described but which is illustrative is patterns of referrals to the system as well as reasons why clients are discontinued or dropped from the program.

The high percentage of self-referrals by the elderly and their families (41 percent; Table 3) from May through September 1982 suggests the degree of market penetration described in the HRCA study and further that a destigmatized system of long-term care (one removed from the "welfare" model) does mean that elderly and their families will turn to the system when in need. The next highest share (38 percent) of referrals came from hospitals, physicians, and home health agencies. This referral pattern reflects the multiplicity of needs of the home care caseload, especially the difficulty in health as well as social areas of functioning, but also suggests that there are effective linkages between home care case managers and traditional health care providers. The only exception is the consistently small percentage of physician referrals, indicating a need to develop a greater awareness among physicians of the existence, capacity, and appropriateness of community based systems of long-term care.

Data on reasons for discontinuing clients during this same period (Table 4) indicate that about one quarter (26 percent) of clients leaving the system did so either because of increased functioning or increased

Table 4
Reason For Leaving the Massachusetts Home Care Program (n = 5,315):
Percent distribution, May 1982 to September 1982

Reasons for discontinuation	
Adequate family/friend support	12%
Service completed	14
Institutionalized	25
Moved out of state	5
Death	25
Transfer to other home care	2
Ineligible	5
Transfer to other agency	1
Other	6
Refused service	5

Source: Monthly Home Care Program Statistics, Massachusetts Department of Elder Affairs (Boston, Massachusetts, May to September, 1982).

responsiveness of the informal support systems. One could reasonably conclude that home care is an effective intervention for elders who have levels of functioning that may improve over time, such as recent discharge from a hospital, and thus can provide a less costly alternative than some form of acute hospital or short-term nursing home stay. It also indicates that home care does not always replace informal support resources. Another quarter (25 percent) of clients died, indicating that home care probably did provide an alternative to institutionalization for some individuals. The third significant finding is that another 25 percent of clients were institutionalized. While some might conclude from this figure that home care did not always prevent institutionalization, it is also quite possible that home care service substantially postponed or delayed the eventual institutionalization of a severely impaired population. Since information on the reasons for the institutionalization is not collected in the monthly statistical reports, examination of this question will require further study.

4. System Growth

As noted, the home care program in its first ten years grew from a budget of just over $1 million to $71 million, with a client count of 40,479. However, there is reason to believe that ultimate program growth is, in fact, both limited and controllable. The earlier Branch study (1977) estimated the vulnerable elder population to be about 6 percent of the noninstitutionalized elderly. Adjusting for income eligibility, the Department had set a target goal for caseload at about 5 percent. This compares with Morris' estimate of 5.7 percent overall

162

Table 5
Massachusetts home care services program 1978 to 1982: Net increase in annual caseload

Fiscal Year (July 1 to June 30)	Caseload	Percent Increase	Caseload	Percent Increase
	(Old reporting system)		(New reporting system)	
1978	19,000			
1979	27,500	44.8		
1980	33,880	23.2		
1981	36,780	8.6		
1982[a]	38,400	4.4[b]	39,421	
1983[a]			40,604	3.0
1984[c]			41,811	3.0

Source: Fiscal year 1984 Budget Request, Massachusetts Department of Elder Affairs. (Boston, Massachusetts, September, 1982).
a = Estimated   b = Actual   c = Projected

in need of home care services. Table 5 shows the actual and percentage increase in caseload for the years 1978 to 1982 (July 1—June 30). In June 1982, the caseload represented 4.2 percent of the noninstitutionalized elderly. As caseload began to approximate the overall statewide target, the program experienced a sharp decline in its overall growth rate. These declines, coupled with the data indicating successful targeting, suggest that in the long run, the growth of such a system of community based care is both limited and controllable. It is important to note, however, that the Department's regulatory changes in 1981 imposing a standard client needs assessment and clear targeting criteria also contributed to lower growth rates. In addition, there is some indication that factors in the external environment can greatly affect growth in a community based system of care. For example, Massachusetts recently implemented its own hospital cost containment law and several home care corporations are experiencing increased pressures to take on clients who would otherwise have had much longer stays in acute care hospitals. Thus, changes in the acute care sector or in income maintenance, housing and social support policies are likely to affect long-term care needs and services because of the close connection between policies in these areas (Vladeck, 1982).

5. Summary of Study Findings

The Massachusetts experience shows that a home care model of long-term care can be well targeted, efficient, and equitable. Th program serves large numbers of functionally vulnerable people. Although lack of agreement on the goals or outcomes of long-term care make it difficult to measure effectiveness, clients who had unmet needs at intake evidenced a marked decrease of those needs through services that helped compensate for functional deficits. Resources also seem to be allocated equitably, with more disabled clients found to be receiving more overall care.

Fears of uncontrollable growth for publicly funded long-term care services also appear unfounded. Service utilization data from the Massachusetts studies show recipients of home care are not over-consumers of care. Other evidence indicates that both families and clients tend to ask for somewhat less formal service than professionals recommend.

The Massachusetts experience is comparable to other long-term care demonstrations in that for most persons, informal supporters are heavily involved in the provision of care and formal resources tend to be focused on persons with weaker informal support systems. Despite some data suggesting that substitution of formal for informal supports has occurred in some areas, this substitution has not appeared to affect adversely the provision of services in the remaining need areas. Other research supports the conclusion that families provide assistance and supervision to complement the more skilled services rendered by formal agencies. The high percentage of clients leaving the system because of adequate informal resources also indicates that substitution is not widespread. Clearly, efforts at organizing long-term care must include assessment and care planning procedures which emphasize the strengths rather than weaknesses of an individual's support network as well as develop innovative ways of enhancing the family's ability to care for their disabled.

Noninstitutional programs are able to achieve considerable market penetration to serve the target population. The most reasonable explanation why home-care services are an effective entry point for the elderly is that the older client sector is able to identify with an agency concerned exclusively with the elderly. If this is valid, it is not unreasonable to suggest that entry for other subgroups of the long-term care population should be through agencies with which those client sectors identify.

The high concentration of home care clients in public housing suggests the need to think of ways to organize long-term care at the local level around units such as elderly housing projects or neighborhoods with high concentrations of the elderly rather than around individual client needs.

In light of this evidence, it is reasonable to conclude that the elderly subgroup, the largest and fastest growing segment of the long-term care population, is not exceptionally large and that overall growth of a community based system of long-term care is both limited and controllable in the long run. In view of the public preference for noninstitutional care, evidence suggests the viability of organizing long-term care in ways that are effective, efficient, and equitable. Demand for financing, particularly if informal and voluntary help is supported, will be both finite and fairly well contained. Key elements of such a system should include screening and targeting criteria, a case management component to handle assessment, care planning, and monitoring of continued appropriateness of care.

6. Future Directions

The previous section examined the Massachusetts home care program, a community based model for service management and delivery that approaches long-term care from a social rather than a medical perspective and which uses case management as a tool for client targeting and service coordination. The program's numerous strengths as a basis for community care for the elderly were documented. However, in the absence of national policy, the program has had to operate within the existing, fragmented long-term care system with its barriers to integrating health and social services at the local level. As had been noted, the services package has been limited by its focus on a narrow set of social services for an income restricted population. A lack of both formal ties with health providers and a delineated role for comprehensive care planning has prevented the current statewide system of case management from optimally assisting clients and from reducing costs in the service system as a whole.

Given these limitations and recent federal initiatives to encourage local delivery and management reforms to contain costs, several demonstration projects have developed independently in different regions of the state which build on the foundation of the social services model of home care and expand the scope of the basic Massachusetts program to include health services. These include a Channeling project site, two Medicaid Managed Health Care initiatives, Medicaid 2176 Waiver projects, and several local experiments.

With the exception of Channeling, all are state or local initiatives designed to address current organizational problems in long-term care and to provide a single entry point for elderly individuals. All developed in the absence of a national long-term care policy, indicating that even in the absence of federal intervention, various providers are seeking to expand their activities in long-term care, with hospitals the most recent arrivals on the scene. These initiatives are likely to proliferate in coming years. While some general requirements will probably be imposed by the federal government, it is unlikely that there will be a single model of organization imposed nationally, in spite of the plethora of theoretical writings on the organization of long-term care (e.g., Callahan, 1979; Callahan and Wallack, 1981; Beatrice, 1981; Diamond and Berman, 1981; Rucklin, Morris and Eggert, 1982).

In light of national trends of nonmedical and noninstitutional alternatives and the devolution of federal responsibility, states must develop criteria by which to assess the local long-term care environment and evaluate whether the long-term care service system should have a single focal point or whether clients should enter the community service network through multiple access points.

III. Single or Multiple Access Points

Much of the theoretical work on long-term care organization has commented on the question of single or multiple focal points for long-term care. The one issue on which there seems to be agreement is that some system of central intake should be required to restrict access to nursing homes at least for publicly assisted patients. Considerations of the locus for community based care are less conclusive. In his review of the literature, Callahan (1979) concluded that most experts recommend an incremental approach to change which recognizes local variation, rather than a radical national solution such as Channeling. In his analysis of case management as a long-term reform, Beatrice (1981) suggests that with a single entry point control and comprehensiveness is strengthened, but the available service resource base shrinks. Multiple access points, on the other hand, are likely to maximize resource availability.

Another debate focuses on whether accountability should rest with the medical or the social system. Some experts believe a single focal point is not possible since people will eventually enter the long-term care system through several different routes or access points. Others feel that imposition of a master plan using either model nationally would be destructive. Many are convinced that what is needed are separate systems of long-term care (acute care and a community-social model), with better linkages to facilitate information transfer and referrals for the recipient.

In a study of service management models in Pennsylvania, using either a single entry point or multiple access, Gottesman, Isizaki, and

MacBride (1979) recommend an assessment of the local delivery system, especially the relationship among providers in determining model choice.

In the following, we will examine some of the important components of the community service system to consider in conducting an environmental assessment

1. A Framework for Analyzing the Local Long-Term Care Environment

Subgroups of the Long-Term Care Population. The long-term care population consists of identifiable subgroups. the child sector, the young adult sector, the disabled adult sector, the mental health sector and the elderly sector. An analysis of the Massachusetts experience suggested that the elderly utilized the home care program because entry was through an agency with which they and their families could identify. Whether other subgroups of the long-term care population would readily utilize a system with which the elderly are identified is uncertain. Thus, Callahan (1979) has recommended establishing case management services within the different client sectors, with federally required designation by states of who is responsible for case management in each of the sectors. Studies of service management models developed by agencies serving these other long-term care populations must be done to see how well they have succeeded.

Providers. At the local level, the long-term care delivery system is comprised of a plurality of actors and interests which operate within a number of connected subsystems (Callahan, 1981). Efforts to form a single locus for long term care is likely to meet with strong opposition among the provider community since they would be dependent for most of their business on the allocation decisions of that agency. While a single locus would provide the opportunity to allocate long-term care resources more effectively by changing patterns of service utilization, those agencies which might give up control, or experience cuts due to reduced use of their services, can be expected to fight efforts to limit long term care to a single focal point. Such conflicts have already developed as a result of recent "managed health" initiatives in Massachusetts. The intensity of conflict between the home care program and local health providers over ultimate control of case management of elderly clients has influenced the state Medicaid agency to test a variety of lead agencies, based on local relationships, in their attempt to integrate Medicaid services with the state's home care program. The decision to expand models so as to use lead agencies other than home care corporations was due largely to the outcry from other interested providers.

Feasibility. Given the different subgroups of the long-term care population and the plurality of actors and interests at the community level, it is unlikely that long term care organization can be limited to a single focal point, nor do experts agree that this is necessarily preferable. However, there does seem to be agreement that any focal point must incorporate case management as a coordinating mechanism as well as adequate targeting mechanisms. The Massachusetts experience clearly supports this direction.

Sources of Change. In addition to the need for a long-term care system that can respond to various subpopulations, the current system is under pressure for change from a variety of sources relating to the elderly subgroups. Increasing growth in the elderly population needing long-term care, increased numbers of skilled service providers and of professional subgroups in this area, and strong organizations of the elderly have emerged on the local scene (Callahan, 1979). These forces and the changing federal and state initiatives in reducing nursing home beds, hospital cost-containment, and expansion of noninstitutional services have heightened interest among various provider types in becoming the focal point of long-term care for the elderly in the community. Hospitals, nursing homes, community health centers, home health agencies and social service agencies all have expressed interest in managing long-term care for the elderly. For some it is a logical extension of their current goals. For others it is a venture into a new market.

Recognizing the need to respond to variability in the local long-term care delivery system, criteria must be developed to assist states in evaluating the capacity of local providers to serve as focal points for long-term care. Here again the Massachusetts experience can be instructive.

Criteria. Any focal point for long-term care must establish mechanisms that identify key actors in the community care system and major funding sources for community services and must develop cooperative services linkage among a variety of providers. The focal point must also be able to manage long-term care through some kind of gatekeeping role that maximizes assistance provided by informal supports. A predominantly social rather than medical model of care promises to be both cost effective and efficient in meeting the long-term care population's needs.

The following criteria are offered for the purpose of estimating the respective abilities of different types of agencies to perform the necessary patient management functions in long-term care.

1. *Incentives.* What attracts providers to long-term care? Are the incentives conducive to appropriate cost effective care?
2. *Management capacity.* What is the track record of the provider in managing complex programs?
3. *Groups served.* Does the provider have the ability to serve different subgroups of the long-term care population?
4. *Incentives for recipient to use the provider.* What attracts recipients to certain providers? Are the incentives conducive to appropriate cost effective care?
5. *Scope of coordination.* Can the gatekeeper or care manager provide comprehensiveness and continuity of care?
6. *Appropriateness of care.* Will the provider emphasize a nonmedical, noninstitutional approach to care?

These criteria represent a very rough attempt to estimate the respective capacities of different providers to serve as the major locus of long-term care in the community. It is meant to be illustrative rather than definitive and serves to point out the need to evaluate organizational capabilities of the different long-term care actors at the community level.

A few brief conclusions can be drawn from an assessment of the criteria. Nursing homes are not likely to serve an expanded role in the long-term care system. Rather they will be limited to caring for that segment of the population, the sick elderly, for whom nursing home care is appropriate. While hospitals are likely to show heightened interest in expanding from acute into long-term care, the goals of large medical institutions are likely to conflict with trends to demedicalize and deinstitutionalize long-term care; their ability to coordinate a complex system of community providers is untested. Perhaps the hospital could serve as a focal point in areas that are not rich in services. Existing home care providers seem to have better strengths to provide the kind of noninstitutional long-term care that has been successful in Massachusetts. Community health centers may become effective players since they may be best equipped to provide continuity between the acute and long term care needs of patients. The description of different provider strengths and weaknesses, while useful, does not tell us what the various outcomes of locating long-term care responsibility with any provider would be. It is useful, however, in light of what we know from Massachusetts' experience in pointing out considerations states should make in identifying lead case management agencies.

2. Conclusions and Policy Implications

A comprehensive policy proposal is beyond the scope of this paper, which has examined issues in organizing long-term care at the patient management level. Decisions as to the level of government responsible for different aspects of the long-term care system are still evolving. As the federal government delegates more responsibility to states in the area of organizing long-term care programs, however, state governments will need information on what has worked in actual long-term care experiments. Analysis of the Massachusetts home care program has provided such a measure against which to evaluate organizational issues and solutions at the level of individual service management. A number of recommendations can be made based on that analysis.

If responsibility for long-term care continues to devolve to the states, the federal government will need to take some steps to ensure some degree of national equity. At the state level, some form of interagency mechanism must be developed to coordinate planning, departments, and programs around long-term care. That entity would be responsible for identifying lead case management agencies (Callahan, 1979).

Even in the absence of these clearly defined roles for the federal and state government, we can make some positive recommendations about organizing a local long-term care delivery system. First, a social model of home care can be designed to be well targeted, efficient, and effective. Based on a concept of case management to carry out the different patient management functions and equipped with clear targeting criteria, home care systems can be limited and controllable.

Such a system can be enhanced through new ways of looking at client assessment where strengths of families and informal supports are evaluated as discriminatingly as individual client needs. New ways of involving clients and families in the development of care plans can maximize the total amount of care provided to the client while minimizing the amount of formal services. Much can be done by federal and state governments to develop incentives such as tax credits or tax deductions for families to take care of their disabled relatives, in contrast to current program policies which create disincentives to caring for chronically impaired older persons at home.

The high concentration of frail elderly needing care in public housing projects suggests the need to look at new ways of organizing local level case management and service providers. Assignment of a building or neighborhood homemaker, for example, may be far more effective than authorizing a service to an individual in areas of high density.

Involvement of local consumers and citizens groups on boards or advisory councils of local long-term care agencies has great potential for ensuring accountability and assuring the agency will be sensitive to local needs.

Long-term care services are already being provided to individuals at the local delivery level and, in many cases, to a great degree. Any efforts to better organize those services will require not only the knowledge gained from empirical data, but national goals and policies for long-term care that have been sorely lacking. At a minimum, the federal government's policies should ensure availability of essential community based long-term care services based on their own merit and not simply as a cost saving alternative to the nursing home.

The home care system described here offers one approach to organizing a noninstitutional long-term care system. With a national commitment to policies and resources expansion which support this type of noninstitutional system, we will be far better able to apply what we already know to organizing more adequate noninstitutional long-term care systems for our frail elderly and disabled citizens.

References

Beatrice, D., Case Management: A Policy Option for long-term Care, in Reforming the long-term Care System. Callahan, J.J., Jr. and Wallack, S.S., eds. Lexington: D.C. Heath and Company, 1981.

Branch, L.G., "Vulnerable Elders." Gerontological Monographs No. 6. Gerontological Society, Washington, D.C., 1980.

Branch, L.G., Understanding the Health and Social Service Needs of People Over 65. Center for Survey Research Monograph, University of Massachusetts and the Joint Center for Urban Studies of M.I.T. and Harvard University, Boston, 1977.

Branch, L.G., Callahan, J.J., and Jette, A., Targeting Home Care Services to Vulnerable Elders: Massachusetts Home Care Corporations. Home Health Care Services Quarterly, 2(2):41, Summer, 1981.

Callahan, J.J., Delivery of Services to Persons with long-term Care Needs. Paper prepared for Administration on Aging Symposium, October 5, 1979.

Callahan, J.J., A Systems Approach to long-term Care. In Reforming the long-term Care System, Callahan, J.J., Jr. and Wallack, S.S., eds. Lexington: D.C. Heath and Company, 1981.

Callahan, J.J., and Wallack, S.S. (eds.), Reforming the long-term Care System, Lexington: D.C. Heath and Company, 1981.

Callahan, J.J., Single Agency Option for long-term Care. In Reforming the long-term Care System. Callahan, J.J., Jr. and Wallack, S.S., eds. Lexington: D.C. Heath and Company, 1981.

Diamond, L.M. and Berman, D.E., The Social(ss))Health Maintenance Organization: A Single Entry, Prepaid, long-term Care Delivery System. In Reforming the long-term Care System, Callahan, J.J., and Wallack, S.S., eds. Lexington: D.C. Heath and Company, 1981.

Gottesman, L.E., Isizaki, B., and MacBride, S.M., Service Management: Concepts and Models. The Gerontologist, 19(4):378, August 1979.

Kane, R.L. and Kane, R.A., Care of the Aged: Old Problems in Need of New Solutions. Science, 200; 913, 1978.

Morris, J., Hebrew Rehabilitation Center for the Aged, Department of Social Gerontological Research, Massachusetts Elderly: Their Vulnerability and Need for Support Services and the Role of the Commonwealth's Home Care Corporations. Report submitted to the Massachusetts Department of Elder Affairs, April 17, 1982.

Morris, J., Deparment of Social Gerontological Research, Hebrew Rehabilitation Center for the Aged, Massachusetts Elderly: Their Vulnerability and Need for Social Services, final report submitted to the Massachusetts Department of Elder Affairs, December 17, 1982.

Rucklin, H.S., Morris, J.N., and Eggert, G.M., Management and Financing of long-term Care Services: A New Approach to a Chronic Problem. New England Journal of Medicine, 306(2):101, January 14, 1982.

Sager, A., Learning the Home Care Needs of the Elderly: Summary. Paper prepared for Levinson Policy Institute, The Florence Heller School for Advanced Studies in Social Welfare, Brandeis University, Waltham, Massachusetts, March 1980.

Vladeck, B., Understanding long-term Care. New England Journal of Medicine, 307:890, September 30, 1982.

Massachusetts Department of Elder Affairs, Fiscal Year 1984 Budget Request, September, 1982.

10

The Financing of Long-Term Care: Practices and Principles

William Pollak

A number of demographic and social trends that are examined extensively in other papers presented in this volume suggest that long-term care expenditures will increase significantly over future decades. Changes in technology will also play a role. On the demand side, changes in medical technology that increase life expectancy may compound other demand-increasing forces by increasing the age-specific incidence of chronic illnesses. It is possible, however, that this age-specific incidence as well as the impairments they create, will decline and partially offset the increased demand resulting from lengthened life spans. As Manton persuasively argues, the evidence is unclear (Manton, 1982).

Technological change will also exert a "supply side" influence on the course of expenditures. Long-term care would seem less suscep-tible than acute care to the cost impact of expensive technical inno-vations. At the same time, there is little likelihood of technical changes that would significantly increase productivity in the labor intensive core of long-term care services. The most important influ-ence of technical change on the supply side of long-term care, there-fore, may result from its impact on other sectors of the economy. Technical change will increase productivity in those sectors and raise real wages throughout the economy—including the long-term care sector, where the effect of rising wages on costs is unlikely to be offset by proportionate productivity increases, however. The costs and prices of long-term care services are therefore almost certain to rise more rapidly than prices in general.

Although the influence of some factors is open to debate, most observers envision changes in utilization and unit costs that will increase expenditures on long-term care, even as general budgetary stringency is increased by related and unrelated forces.

One reasonable response is to search for new funding sources that might satisfy the evident need for more long-term care resources—to venture into the "devil's briarpatch" in Fullerton's words (Fullerton, 1981). That response may, indeed, be the most useful one. However, given the importance of long-term care it is worth examining a variety of approaches to its financing, including some that build from a less immediate concern than the search for revenues. That concern must be addressed, but it can follow from as well as lead the discussion.

The possibility of impairment in old age confronts us all. Long-term care financing is the budgetary reflection of how we publicly meet and share burdens that are present no matter how we choose to deal with them. Perhaps by examining the content of current arrangements and considering at least one distinct alternative, policy options may become apparent that would be obscured when starting from a more pragmatic base. That possibility is the basis for the following discussion.

I. Practices, Principles, and Problems

1. Practices: What is Financed, How is it Financed, and for Whom is it Financed?

Most public resources devoted to long-term care are used to finance institutional services in intermediate care and skilled care facilities. Although noninstitutional services (e.g., home health care, and homemaker chore services) are provided on a small scale in many parts of the country, they are financed extensively only in a few states and in some localities, often as elements in long-term care demonstration projects. An estimated $1.2 billion was spent on these noninstitutional services by public programs in 1978; this figure represents only 8 percent of total spending on nursing home care and 14 percent of public expenditures on nursing home care (Health Care Financing Administration, 1981).

Most public funding for institutional long-term care flows through the federal/state Medicaid program which in turn is financed by the various general revenue sources of federal and state governments. However, institutional care that is partly financed by government also is typically financed in part by contributions of those receiving care.

Thus, single individuals receiving Medicaid institutional benefits must contribute virtually all of their financial assets and income to the financing of care. What the public sector finances, therefore, is only what the individual cannot finance. Similarly, married couples with an institutionalized member whose care is partially financed by government must contribute all of their resources except for an amount reserved for the maintenance of the noninstitutionalized spouse in the community.

The public financing of noninstitutional services is far less easily summarized—even with the broad-brush approach adopted here because of the large number of programs involved. Medicare home health benefits are financed by the payroll tax, while home care benefits under Title XX and Medicaid regular and demonstration projects are financed out of general revenues. The financial responsibilities of users of subsidized noninstitutional services vary, but tend to be minor in both ongoing programs and in demonstration projects.

Institutional care at public expense will, essentially, be provided for anyone medically certified as needing such care who cannot, even while using all personal resources, finance the full cost of care. Because of the high cost of institutional care, eligibility extends well up the income scale to an exact level determined by the reimbursement level at which care is paid for by the state. Currently, about 60 percent of the nursing home population are Medicaid patients (Fox and Clauser, 1980). Among those whose stays are long, this percentage is probably significantly higher because of the greater likelihood that assets will be exhausted by long stays.

As for financing, it is more difficult to summarize eligibility standards for noninstitutional than for institutional care because of the greater variety of programs involved. In all programs, services are provided only to those certified to have a need created by a medical condition and/or a functional impairment. Eligibility for Medicare noninstitutional services is independent of the user's income, whereas eligibility for noninstitutional services under Medicaid depends on income and assets being below levels established by the states. It is important to note, though, that many people who would receive Medicaid assistance if they were institutionalized (because their income is less than the cost of care) are ineligible for Medicaid financed noninstitutional care because their income exceeds the regular Medicaid income eligibility levels. Separately funded programs that finance noninstitutional services through Medicaid and/or Medicare waivers tend to have no eligibility cut-off based on income or have a much higher cut-off than Medicaid does.

175

2. *Public Financing of Long-Term Care: The Principle Implicit in Current Policy*

Rationales used in many areas to explain and/or justify public intervention abound: for example, responding to externalities or inadequate consumer information; controlling monopolizing behaviors; and providing so-called public goods that will not be provided by the market even when cost-covering demands exist. Although some of these rationales have been used to justify public financing of long-term care, none is consistent with the particular long-term care policies that we now have.

Numerous public policies, however, have as their primary rationale an equity objective. A subset of these are policies justified by society's evident desire to insure some minimum standard of living for all of the population. The income maintenance or welfare programs, such as SSI, for example, insure that people who can live independently attain the minimum standard by providing them with an income deemed sufficient to cover the cost of maintaining the standard.

Current long-term care policy is possibly best understood in this context. Our nation is committed to the maintenance of at least minimum living standards. Long-term care policy expresses that commitment when impairments, by elevating the cost of maintaining the minimum standard, make payment levels of the income maintenance programs inadequate. The particular forms that long-term care policy will take, when fashioned under this principle, are enlighteningly discussed by Krashinsky (1981).

Several of the characteristics of current long-term care policy that were identified earlier are consistent with this view of its underlying rationale. Consider, for example, the financing for long-term care: most funding comes through Medicaid. This program, which evolved and has been administered in parallel with categorical welfare programs, was basically designed to serve the welfare population and is financed by the same general revenue sources. Indeed, only a small fraction of long-term care financing comes from sources dissociated from welfare.

Equally revealing are the parallels between most of long-term care and welfare policy in their approaches to eligibility and to the criteria that determine the amount of assistance provided. In both cases, assistance ("care" in long-term care) is provided only to those who, in the absence of the program, cannot achieve the standard with their own resources. And, in both cases, there is a strong tendency to limit benefits to the amount by which the requirements of the minimum standard exceed the beneficiaries' resources.

176

These characteristics also suggest that long-term care policy is consistent with another characteristic typically associated with programs designed to insure a minimum standard of living. This is the tendency to meet those standards at least public cost—whether or not the policies that minimize public costs minimize social cost and are efficient in the economist's sense.

Administrative location, eligibility, financing of the public subsidy, and client financial burden in long-term care all are consistent with the maintenance of the minimum-living-standards principle argued here as underlying current policy. The general restriction of benefits to institutional care (with small but increasing exceptions) also is consistent with the "least-public-cost" feature of programs that maintain minimum living standards. Nursing homes are generally regarded by potential residents and their families as undesirable. The limitation of benefits to care in an unattractive setting discourages use. The frail are less likely to seek care, and families, in order to avoid institutionalizing their relatives, will provide substantial care themselves, often resorting to the (institutional) benefit only when overwhelmed by the physical and/or financial demands, including foregone income, of providing care at home.

Thus by providing an institutional benefit, society meets its felt obligation to place a floor under the well-being of the frail elderly. However, by limiting the benefit to institutional care, the public burden is constrained by a program characteristic that expands the fraction of the care burden that will be borne by the frail and their families. Such policies may, in fact, approximate the least-public-cost principle of meeting the commitment to the maintenance of living standards for those who are impaired.

The fit of this interpretation with experience is borne out in the debate over expanding benefits to cover noninstitutional services. Proponents generally specify an impressive list of benefits that will flow from such a shift: improved health and well-being for the frail, extended duration of family care, and reduction in unnecessary institutionalization. I leave out the claim that public costs will be reduced because I, and an increasing number of others, think the claim is false (General Accounting Office, 1982). Proponents less frequently and less explicitly mention two other effects of the increased provision of noninstitutional care that might be viewed positively. First, social costs would probably be reduced by a policy that makes more equal the subsidization of two forms of care that frequently are substitutes. Second, as noted above, public costs would probably rise in spite of the more efficient use of substitute forms of care, because the resulting increase in use of formal noninstitutional

177

care shifts burdens from informal caretakers to the public sector. This increased public cost, though, can be viewed positively to the degree that it is felt that more of the burdens of impairments should be shifted from the frail and their families to society in general.

The expansion of long-term care policy to more adequately cover noninstitutional services is likely to yield benefits that are impressive. It also would probably increase public outlays. The fact that to date the latter consideration has dominated discussion and public action suggests that conformity of current policy is consistent with the maintenance-of-minimum standards rationale presented earlier.

3. Problems: Their Relation to the Operating Rationale for Public Long-Term Care

Several problems are repeatedly cited in writings on long-term care. Prominently mentioned in many discussions is the matter of rising costs, usually public costs. It seems certain that with the elderly increasing as a fraction of the population, and with the older groups among them rising as a fraction of that fraction, our society will face long-term care burdens that will rise relative to other responsibilities. Furthermore, if these burdens are shouldered as they should be and, one hopes, will be, public outlays on long-term care will rise, and will rise as a percentage of GNP unless, as seems quite unlikely, the burden shifts significantly from the public to the private sector.

In this scenario, the precise sense in which rising costs are "problematic" is not always made clear. If production efficiency or productivity can be raised, or if the locus of production can be shifted to reduce public costs, or if the private sector should shoulder more of the care burden, then failure to do any of these would make cost increases indeed problematic. However, none of these aspects figure prominently in discussions of cost escalation. Similarly, if it were felt that the quality of care was excessive, or that we should not provide care to all the future frail elderly who need it, then these too might be considered sources of a cost problem. But those are not plausible assertions.

This is not to argue that we should ignore policies that will encourage efficiency or an equitable sharing of burdens. Rather, it is to suggest that anticipated cost increases in long-term care are in largest part the inevitable consequence of meeting needs created by demographic and technical changes. Unless we choose to neglect those needs we will face those costs. The problematic matter, then, is not costs but the assembling of resources to meet them. And that is a finance problem, one of several to which we turn in the next section.

Two other frequently cited problems are the impoverishment imposed on those who use the Medicaid institutional benefit, and the general, though incomplete, restriction of benefits to institutional care. Both of these problems were argued earlier to be consistent with the maintenance-of-minimum-standards rationale and the administrative location of long-term care policy. These arguments will not be repeated here. Instead, it is useful to note, without making any forecast, recent increases in the financing of noninstitutional care. The increases have been modest in volume, often in demonstration rather than normal program contexts, and frequently encumbered by constraints designed to minimize violations of the "at-least-public-cost" character of mainstream long-term care policy.

But the important fact is the increased funding of noninstitutional care even though, as it occurs, it is strongly questioned. This trend, and the tension it produces, should not be surprising when policies seemingly rooted in the maintenance of minimum standards evolve into policies covering more than sixty percent of the population, including the parents of much of the middle class and many who, prior to the onset of old-age impairments, were themselves of the middle class.

II. The Financing of Long-Term Care: An Alternative Rationale and Its Implications in Practice

There are many rationales by which public intervention can be justified other than the maintenance of minimum standards. If one of these is particularly relevant to long-term care, its neglect in the design of current policy may explain some of the pressures now pulling long-term care out of its former mold. More important here, attention to the implications of another rationale may suggest a discontinuous shift in policy or, if continued incremental change is more desirable, may facilitate and shape the evolution of policy and make it more consistent with our goals. For these reasons, we turn now to a second rationale for public financing of long-term care and later consider its implications for policy.

1. The Market Failure Rationale

All people face the risk of someday needing long-term care, with the possibilities ranging from minor needs of short duration to the need for intensive personal care and treatment for several years. A significant part of the long-term care risk is financial. It therefore is reasonable for people to purchase insurance from firms that can profit from the pooling of risks. Buyers can correctly be viewed both as making a small but certain sacrifice in order to reduce the costs of an uncertain but unusually burdensome event, and as sharing the costs associated with a costly eventuality that only some will suffer.

Given the reasonableness of insurance for long-term care, why has coverage not been bought and sold? It is a plausible guess that demand for such insurance was much weaker years ago than it would be today. The period during old age when people needed care was, on average, probably shorter. More important, the frail elderly person was more likely to have had a child or sibling whose family included an adult who was not employed and available to provide care. Care in the past, therefore, was more available from the family and when available, was probably provided by them at a smaller real sacrifice, and therefore with less imposition by the old on the young, than is true today.

Low demand, thus, may in part explain the past absence of long-term care insurance. Whatever the validity of this partial explanation of a historical phenomenon, the government did, by providing long-term care services, meet a need against which people could not insure. More important for this discussion, the evolution and growth of publicly provided long-term care now inhibits the private marketing of insurance. For with known and free "coverage" of the worst eventuality, the demand for private insurance is reduced.

Other factors further reduce the likelihood that the market would respond effectively to long-term care insurance demands. These factors are analyzed by Bishop in a paper on which this discussion is based (Bishop, 1981). Two considerations would seem to make such insurance reasonable only if purchased over a long period, even though benefits would typically be concentrated late in life. First, the high average cost of care would tend to make premiums prohibitively expensive if charged over only a short period. Second, the varying risks presented by different people would become more measurable late in life as the proximity of need increases. While this reduces problems of adverse selection, it also makes it far less useful as an insurance program, and would make premiums still more prohibitive for those who most need coverage.

Premiums paid over many years, therefore, would seem essential for marketed long-term care insurance. But other problems plague this option. Because of the long term of the insurance and because the insured risk is a service whose price is enormously difficult to forecast, private insurance premiums would have to be elevated, possibly to prohibitive levels, to cover the insurer's risk. Furthermore, given both the complexities of managing the benefit side of long-term care insurance and the mobility of the population, a firm would have to be geographically widespread if the enterprise were to be profitable. Few, if any, private firms could simultaneously manage such complexity and geographical breadth.

Finally, there is the problem of moral hazard. It is a problem that must be dealt with in public long-term care programs and is discussed below. Here it is sufficient to note that the felt large magnitude of moral hazard in long-term care further reduces the probability of market response.

Coverage for long-term care, thus, is something which many and possibly most people would like to purchase. Yet the market is unlikely to respond both to the demands that would exist in the absence of public programs and to the residual demands under existing programs from both those who are not covered and from those who, though covered, would prefer benefits that were less impoverishing and less institutional than those now provided.

The market's lack of response to long-term care insurance demands provides a strong rationale for public intervention, and one that is different in character from the maintenance of minimum standards rationale. The implications of this market failure rationale for the scope and financing of benefits merit attention and are considered below. Here it is worth stressing that although "efficiency" (the minimization of social costs) remains an objective, the market failure rationale, unlike the "minimum standards" rationale, does not dictate that *public* costs be minimized, however problematic that may be in the contemporary context.

2. Implications of the Market Failure Rationale

The implications of the market failure rationale are developed here in a discussion that moves from the abstract and idealized to the concrete and applied. Only in the final section are suggestions for policy change explicitly derived.

It is possible to design an "ideal" program consistent with the market failure rationale and independent of programs now in place. Although numerous practical and political considerations prevent its implementation, the ideal is of heuristic value in analyzing desirable program characteristics and identifying dilemmas.

In this perspective the problem to which public long-term care responds is the occurrence of uninsurable, impairment-created needs which are greater than the needs which people feel can or should be borne by the individual and his or her family. The ideal program should respond to those needs efficiently and equitably. The uninsurability of long-term care and the cited need for compulsion suggest that a program based on the assumption of market failure should be universal in coverage.

Consider the benefit side of such a program. The impairment of needy individuals should be measured, and the dollar resources required to meet the needs should be identified. The family status of the individual should be noted and the burdens thought appropriate to be borne by any family should be ascertained. This may include financial contributions of the individual or family as well as the amount of physical assistance thought to be appropriately provided by a spouse or possibly a child or sibling. A cash grant equal to the difference between measured need and appropriate individual and family contributions should then be awarded. It should be noted that board, housing, and other expenses that are part of the price of institutional residence, but not part of the cost of care, would not be part of this grant.

If impairment-created needs can be measured, and if contributions appropriately borne by the family can be agreed upon and established, the equity of such arrangements is self-evident. Society in general would then bear, for those suffering impairments, that part of the burden thought inappropriate to be borne by the individual and the family.

The efficiency of this arrangement, as well as the form it assumes, though less evident, merit attention. With augmented income, the frail individual and his family can choose among forms of care unbiased by subsidies that separate price from cost differently for institutional care, formal noninstitutional care, and informal care.

If, alternatively (as now), subsidies are used in place of grants and only institutional care is subsidized, institutionalization is encouraged even when its social cost may be higher than alternatives. If both institutional and noninstitutional formal care are equally subsidized, the bias toward institutional care is eliminated but there is an incentive to use formal rather than informal care even when the social cost of the informal care is lower. The efficiency of a cash grant system relative to its alternatives derives from shifting actual care tasks towards informal systems when they are the preferred (least social cost) mode, even as, consistent with an equity objective, it shifts burdens from the impaired and their families by providing cash resources. This significant virtue is still further enhanced to the degree that society sees a social benefit in family and informal care even beyond the benefit felt by those directly involved.

An example may clarify this point. Under policies that subsidize only institutional and formal noninstitutional care, a two-worker family with a disabled grandmother may choose either to institutionalize her or to use substantial formal noninstitutional services in order to keep the grandparent in their home. The latter solution, although possibly preferable to institutional care, may have a higher social cost and be less satisfying than a third alternative that is possible only with a cash grant (or cash-grant like) program: having one spouse work part-time, using some, but less, formal care to supplement increased private efforts and using the grant to compensate for lost market income. Although the family actually provides care, the public grant stabilizes family income and shifts the resource burden associated with care from the family to society.

The increased efficiency of cash grants might be viewed as particularly valuable if, by enabling the substitution of informal for formal care, it makes home care that would otherwise be more expensive less costly than institutional care.

The implications of the market failure or insurance rationale for the financing of long-term care can also be argued to be apparent in this ideal context. If general distributional concerns are adequately met by the tax transfer system, then a long-term care program should be financed by a tax arrangement which approximates actuarial fairness in its distribution of burdens. Given that care burdens (exclusive of housing, board, and other costs not properly counted as care costs) are not income related, this would seem to suggest a flat head tax. Of course, the redistributional demands on the tax transfer system might be altered with recognition of the long-term care cost, a phenomenon which could be responded to by alteration of those systems, or by a departure of the long-term care finance arrangements from actuarial equity.

3. Implications in a More Constrained Context

Important practical considerations that obstruct implementation of the "ideal" program just discussed are considered here in order to identify remaining implications that may have practical relevance when existing programs are incorporated in the discussion.

In an ideal case, cash grants would be equal in value to the excess of measured care needs over "appropriately provided" physical and financial family assistance. There may be some problems in measuring impairments, and there certainly are disagreements about the service needs (and, therefore, resources) associated with given impairments. Even more problematic, however, is assistance "appropriately provided" by the family.

The notion of grading benefits to assistance providable by the family is logically reasonable, and would be as desirable under insurance as in a public program. People would generally not want insurance coverage against the entire risk associated with impairments. Indeed, so long as the risk of financial or physical care burdens is less odious than the premiums required to insure against them, people would prefer that the risks not be covered. And, since the burden of some care risks is associated with the family situation, this implies a preference for benefits that vary with the family situation.

For example, if long-term care insurance were marketed, most people would probably prefer coverage that did not provide benefits for less than severe impairments when a spouse was present. I would expect this to be the dominant preference because I imagine that most people would prefer the combination of spouse-provided care, spouse-borne burdens, and low premiums to an insurance package that combines high premiums with the opportunity to receive services even when a spouse is present.

The same reasoning applies to a public program. Benefits could be awarded to meet total care needs, independent of family situation. However, people would probably prefer that the tax cost of a public program, like the premium for insurance, not be inflated by the coverage of risks that, given costs, they both would prefer to bear themselves (or think their family should bear) and think that others, in similar circumstances, should also bear. In other words, they would like benefits that complement what they feel family (and friends) can and should do.

The notion is reasonable, but its implementation with cash grants is impossible—a point developed with insight by Krashinsky (1981). Perhaps there would be agreement that if an able spouse is present, benefits are appropriate only for care needs above some level of intensity. Similarly, if no family were available, the benefit should reflect total care needs. But after that, matters become elusive. What people think their own and others' families should do, under given circumstances, is likely to depend on such matters as the familial and geographic proximity of relatives, competing claims on their time (for example, jobs, child-rearing responsibilities, and caring for other relatives), the subjective benefit or cost of their providing care, the availability of housing space, and so forth.

There certainly would be arguments concerning how such considerations should influence benefits. And, even if disagreements could be resolved, there would be problems in codifying and measuring the "considerations" in order to establish an appropriate cash benefit. But these significant obstacles to a cash grant program are less fundamental than the moral hazard problems to which the program would be exposed. For with the magnitude of grants adjusted to complement family capability to provide care, as judged by considerations listed above, observed family behavior and stated preference would reasonably alter in a way that would indicate reduced capability.

For example, labor market participation by the child of a frail old person would alter if working yielded not only a salary, but also a long-term care cash benefit. Observed work and other behaviors and stated preferences would not, as desired, neutrally indicate family care capacity, but rather, the reduced capacity induced by the distorting effect of the cash grant.

In-kind service benefits, as Krashinsky, Bishop and others have noted, can reduce this problem (Krashinsky, 1981; Bishop, 1981). This is particularly true if the in-kind benefit is useful only in meeting an insured-against need for a skilled treatment service. Because demand for such a service is minimally influenced by price, moral hazard distortions are minimized. However, noninstitutional services not only aid the impaired but also, by substituting for family care, relatives of the impaired. Consequently, an in-kind long-term care benefit that includes noninstitutional services faces the moral hazard posed by the cash grant program, although somewhat reduced in degree.

The dilemma can be resolved only through cost sharing. By raising the cost of formal care, cost sharing reduces the likelihood of in-kind benefit utilization that is excessive by the standard implicit above. Cost sharing, therefore, should be an element in the financing of a broad benefit long-term care program. However, because cost sharing that is unrelated to client income would limit access for the poor, cost sharing should be income related.

Further issues in the design of long-term care cost sharing are discussed at length by Pollak and Bishop (Pollak, 1979; Bishop, 1981). Both point out that residents of institutions should, at a minimum, pay for housing, board, and other non-care costs that are not part of the (insured) long-term care risk. Therefore, cost sharing for institutional as well as for noninstitutional services should be significant elements in the financing of public care that is justified by a market failure rationale.

A universal program of institutional and noninstitutional service benefits partly financed by income related fees is a reasonable compromise response to the market failure rationale for public long-term care: a compromise forced by an inefficiency of cash grants that would be revealed in excess public costs. As noted earlier in a different context, the inefficiency (and possible inequity) of a service or in-kind program arises because formal services are subsidized while informal care is not. This may suggest that informal care also should be subsidized, a notion advanced by Bishop and promoted by others.

The problems with this "adjustment" to an in-kind program are similar to those discussed with respect to cash grants. Thus, just as cash grants that meet total need are excessive, so too would be payments to all families that provide care or other services. Yet if it is accepted that payments to families providing care should vary among families, other dilemmas are posed. How do we distinguish between family assistance that can reasonably be expected and family help that should be reimbursed because it is above that level? To the degree that the response depends on the circumstances of families and their members, moral hazard problems are raised identical to those discussed in the earlier analysis of cash grants.

III. Implications: Suggestions for Policy Change

This paper began by arguing that existing arrangements for the financing of long-term care are most easily understood as society's mechanism for maintaining minimum living standards for the frail elderly. The paper then explored the implications of an alternative rationale, i.e., market failure, with the hope that they would suggest constructive departures from current policy.

This possibility is explored here in a discussion that successively considers program benefits and cost sharing, eligibility, and the financing of the subsidized portion of long-term care.

1. Benefits, Cost Sharing, and Eligibility

Benefits. With respect to benefits, the outcome is disappointing. Cash grants, as suggested by the market-failure rationale, could reduce burdens on the impaired and their families while maintaining efficiency by not encouraging the substitution, at lower social cost, of formal for informal care as occurs under all alternative arrangements for financing benefits. Because of severe moral hazard problems, however, cash grants would inevitably increase public costs by more than is justified by the insurance rationale. That is, cash grants not only are dubious politically, they also have economic failings which make their use inappropriate even under a market failure rationale.

Changing policy by increasing noninstitutional benefits and making more equal the subsidization of noninstitutional and institutional care is also suggested by the market failure rationale. The probable efficiency of that shift would likely be revealed in more appropriate (and, sometimes, lower cost) care as well as in more adequate care and a greater public assumption of long-term care burdens. Although, as is increasingly acknowledged, these changes would probably increase public costs, they are, at the same time, probably justified by the efficiency objective of the market failure rationale; the benefits of the additional care probably exceed costs, and the shifted burdens are consistent with the sharing of burdens people might seek were they to insure (General Accounting Office, 1982).

Of course, the expansion of noninstitutional benefits is a change that many have sought without the aid of an explicitly altered rationale. The additional support derived here, therefore, may not be a particularly significant contribution. Perhaps, however, an altered and widely accepted rationale would encourage acceptance of a policy change that, though it increases costs, increases benefits by more; but that unlikely expectation is more appropriately discussed below.

Cost Sharing: Noninstitutional Care. Here the shifting of burdens that might accompany expanded noninstitutional services merits additional attention. Evidence that families and other informal supports persist as the primary providers of long-term care casts some doubt on fears that formal services will be substituted for informal services. However, families are less dominant than they once were in the providing of long-term care (Bane, 1983). Furthermore, they have "persisted" under policies that subsidize only an unattractive alternative to their care. With cheaper access to an attractive alternative (home care), use and pressure to use formal services is bound to increase and this is desirable, as noted above. However, beyond some level, increased use would probably be both inefficient (substituting higher for lower social-cost care) and inequitable (shifting more burden to the public than is appropriate).

Cost sharing is a justified finance mechanism under a market failure rationale, and may be essential in fostering appropriate use of noninstitutional services. If related to income, cost sharing can also be equitable and incorporated without unduly limiting access. Interestingly, and possibly because they represent modifications of the Medicaid program serving low-income populations, many home care demonstration projects have eschewed cost sharing even when eligibility has extended to relatively high income groups. This may be an

187

unfortunate precedent that obstructs or complicates broader adoption of home care benefits. The absence of cost sharing elevates costs and makes programs less attractive. Additionally, eschewal of cost sharing in demonstration programs makes a later transition to cost sharing much more difficult. Thus, at the time of the author's involvement, cost sharing in the "channeling" programs was severely constrained because with it the programs would have been more costly for users than existing pilot and demonstration programs that provide services at zero or nominal cost.

2. *The Financing of Long-Term Care*

In summary, demographic, social, and technological trends all are likely to increase expenditures on long-term care over the next several decades. For many people the financing of these expenditures is the primary long-term care problem. In that context, as well as in the more immediate budgetary climate, the preceding arguments may seem academic. The policy directions they derived from a market failure rationale would increase the number of beneficiaries, expand noninstitutional benefits, reduce cost sharing on institutional care, and impose significant cost sharing on noninstitutional care; these changes, taken together, seem certain to increase rather than decrease long-term expenditures.

Implementation of such changes would, therefore, seem impossible. Indeed, it almost certainly is—unless something identified here makes accessible sources of funding that would otherwise be inaccessible.

Earlier discussion suggested that although many people would like to insure themselves against long-term care risks, they cannot because the market fails to respond to their demands. However, many of these very demands are also neglected by current policy, which primarily benefits those for whom public long-term care serves to maintain minimal living standards. If there is a possibility of addressing existing problems, it may depend on an articulation of the demands now unmet, and the design of arrangements to meet them.

Any discussion of major change in the financing of long-term care, however, must clearly recognize the largely income maintenance and intragenerationally redistributive function served by current policy. The following considers two policy approaches. Both would fit the market failure rationale, and both would tend to satisfy the unmet demands which it identifies. One is a universal long-term care program that largely replaces current policy; the other is a policy which would meet unmet demands by complementing current policy. In discussing both, it is assumed that the redistributive impact of current policies that are respectively encompassed and complemented will be retained.

Financing of a Universal Coverage Program. A single universal program would serve all the frail elderly, regardless of income. Benefits would depart from current practice in ways discussed above while financing is considered in this section.

The disadvantage of a universal program would probably be its discontinuous increase of budget costs. Its primary advantage, compared to alternatives that also meet unmet demands, might be symbolic and psychological. A universal program could be characterized and promoted as an "insurance" type program. Alternatively, and more accurately (if "contributions" are spent immediately rather than funded) it could be characterized as the programmatic means through which the younger generation meets the care needs of the elderly, obtaining in return the guarantee of similar assistance in old age. In either case, a program which both meets a widely felt and much feared need and which is widely recognized as the public long-term care program would constitute a significant break from current policy. It might make resources available that cannot be obtained for a "patching up" of current arrangements that are either unseen, or are seen as welfare rather than as long-term care policy.

There clearly are limits to the resources which even a reasonable and accepted purpose assures, as recent debate over Social Security amply demonstrates. However, there may be more consensus on the inadequacy of long-term care benefits than on the deficiency of OASI payments. The substantial public resources now devoted to long-term care should also be noted. If incorporated in the financing of a universal program, their use might make the benefits of the program loom quite large relative to the incremental revenues which its implementation would require.

The financing of a long-term care program involves (1) client cost sharing and (2) the financing of the subsidy. Here cost sharing is briefly examined in the context of a universal program. Earlier it was argued both that cost sharing should be an important element in the financing of all types of long-term care, and that cost sharing should be income related. The latter requirement may be problematic in a universal program, particularly if its financing suggests that all who contribute throughout their lifetimes get access to equivalent benefits.

A solution, however, is not elusive. Cost sharing terms that are independent of client economic position could be devised to meet revenue and rationing needs in the universal program. A back-up program, such as Medicaid, could then meet distributional concerns by paying a part of client shares that would be determined by client income, much as Medicaid now complements Medicare in the financing of acute care for the indigent elderly.

In light of the earlier discussion, it is suggested that the income independent cost sharing terms of the base program be less severe with respect to institutional care than the cost sharing terms now implicit in Medicaid policy. This suggestion derives from the presumption that many of the non-poor would be willing to sacrifice some income during their work life in exchange for the avoidance of impoverishment which institutional care financed by Medicaid now imposes.

The subsidy part of a universal long-term care program could be financed in innumerable ways with myriad varied details. This brief discussion considers only a few and these only in broadest outline.

Conceivably, a program could be financed with revenue from a single levy, much as Social Security is, at this writing, entirely financed by a tax on earnings. A universal program, however, would by definition have to incorporate people who now receive publicly financed care, and services something like those now provided. The current provision and financing of those services out of general revenues involves a substantial and appropriate downward transfer of resources. It is difficult to see how that distributional impact could be even very approximately retained if an entire universal program, promoted as a "social insurance type" program, were financed by a levy appropriate to that function.

An alternative is suggested by a program characteristic that makes a single source inappropriate. Any universal program would (1) incorporate the income maintenance functions served by current policy, and (2) provide and finance services that compensate for market failure. This suggests that benefits serving the former redistributive function within a new program should be financed by "old" revenues that already flow to long-term care. Analogously, the increment to the program that largely does what failed markets cannot do would be financed by a revenue source appropriate to that function and the distribution of the program's incremental benefits.

Gross benefits would presumably not be income related; but because of the progressive distributional impact of current policy, the incremental benefits derived from the shift to a universal program would be positively related to income. A reasonable guess is that incremental benefits would increase with income over the range of incomes over which benefits are now received, and then would be flat as a function of income. A plausible finance option would, therefore, be a proportional tax on income above some minimum up to a maximum income at which revenue approximates the actuarial value of incremental benefits. A full assessment of these options would obviously require a more detailed picture of the program to be financed and the distribution of its benefits, as well as a weighing of political considerations which are relevant to but beyond the scope of this paper.

Financing of a Complementary Program. A universal program of the type just suggested would confront considerable political opposition. Furthermore, existing policy does meet a major part of the total social demand for public long-term care. A program that complements rather than incorporates existing policy by serving those now left unsatisfied deserves attention. Such a program would have benefits designed to satisfy preferences that are met neither by Medicaid nor by private insurance: preferences for a benefit package that includes a broad noninstitutional as well as institutional benefit, and that provides protection against complete impoverishment in the event of institutionalization. If the benefits were financed by taxes, then all people would be required to pay, and all would presumably be potentially eligible both for the complementary program and for Medicaid. The two programs together would then resemble the universal program just discussed; they require no additional discussion.

A complementary program, however, could also be offered on a voluntary basis. Among those who might voluntarily enroll are individuals who anticipate no benefits from current policy, those who perceive functional inadequacies in what they would receive from current policies, and those who, independent of functional considerations, would willingly pay to avoid dependence on a welfare program.

A voluntary program might "sell" in the political arena because, unlike a universal program, it would not require an increase in taxes. How well it would sell in the market would depend on the attractiveness of its benefits, the strength of the desire to avoid welfare medicine, and the level at which required payments (premiums) were set. The last poses a number of puzzles. Only the most significant is examined here.

Premiums might be established that are actuarially fair in financing gross benefits in the complementary program. Sizeable voluntary enrollment with such premiums would have strong positive significance. Enrollees would benefit from an improved program and public costs in the back-up (Medicaid) program would fall. Two related considerations might suggest lower premiums. First, enrollment with premiums that finance gross benefits might be negligible. Second, the reduced Medicaid costs associated with enrollment constitute an external benefit. Consequently, rates sufficient to finance the gross costs of the complementary program are in a sense too high, and lower rates might be justified by efficiency considerations.

Note though, that lower premiums introduce their own problems. Income related premiums on a voluntary program are problematic. Suppose therefore, that uniform premiums are established that in total fall short of expected gross benefits by the amount that Medicaid costs are reduced. Enrollment would then confer an implicit transfer that would rise with income. The transfer would be negative at low incomes, where the foregone Medicaid benefit would be above average, and would be large and positive at high incomes, where individuals would get a subsidized benefit and sacrifice nothing since they would be foregoing no Medicaid benefit. Utilization patterns induced by the pattern of implicit transfers could only worsen these distributional consequences.

A complementary program with high premiums might yield significant benefits. However, the high rates might excessively constrict utilization and prevent the capture of significant efficiency gains. Low rates pose the threat of unacceptable distributional effects. A compromise might be acceptable—although difficulties in avoiding the equity-efficiency conflict in a voluntary program constitute an argument for the compulsory approach.

Other aspects of a voluntary program to complement Medicaid are also problematic. It can be noted that the government operates first and second class programs in some areas: OASI and SSI, for example, in the area of income support. Nonetheless, the development of a first class long-term care alternative for the middle class would certainly reduce pressure to improve Medicaid and would be opposed by many, even if the middle class paid the full (gross) costs of the program targeted on their demands.

This particular problem is avoided in a program notion developed by Fullerton (1981). Caught between demographic trends, the desire for better long-term care, and the impossibility of generating new tax revenues, Fullerton presents more clever suggestions than can be summarized here. One essentially is a "complementary" program of the type just discussed; but it is considerably simplified and separated from government. People would be granted tax benefits during their work life for savings that are earmarked for long-term care. At retirement these funds could be used to purchase private long-term care insurance or long-term care services. The program has the merits of a "complementary" program, cleverly avoids a host of problems, and merits consideration. However, it is very important to stress that, to the degree that it is supported by tax benefits, the program is subject to the same distributional objections just raised against the complementary program.

IV. Conclusions

Several problems in long-term care seem associated with the welfare character and origins of current policy. The problems become more apparent as policies increasingly serve a different function: meeting impairment-created needs against which people cannot insure. The relative significance of long-term care demands from this source is probably increased by social and economic changes.

A program with broader (universal) coverage of the population, wider benefits, and appropriate cost sharing might match the future mix of long-term care demands better than incremental adjustments to current policy; but it probably would also further increase public costs. A voluntary program that complements existing policy sounds like a good idea and some policy suggestions along that line have been made. However, it is not clear that such a program could be made appealing enough to attract enrollees without subsidies that would have a significant regressive impact.

Perhaps a distinct, universal long-term care program genuinely deserves attention on the off chance that its incremental public costs would not spell its political doom. The needs to which it would minister are widely felt, and the burdens imposed by those needs cannot be avoided. Unsatisfactory programs do not reduce burdens; they only increase social burdens or lodge them disproportionately on the frail and their families. It is possible that a program which acknowledges the burden, distributes it equitably, and manages it humanely and efficiently could be sold. Public long-term care expenditures for the elderly, though very large, are only about ten percent of OASI expenditures. Possibly in some future negotiations over social security benefits, some income benefits could wisely be traded for improvements in our long-term care arrangements.

References

Bane, M.J., Is the Welfare State Replacing the Family? The Public Interest, Winter 1983.

Bishop, C.E., A Compulsory National Long-Term Care Insurance Program. In Reforming the Long-Term Care System, James J. Callahan, Jr. and Stanley S. Wallack, eds., Lexington: Lexington Books, 1981.

Fox, P.D. and Clauser, S. B., Trends in Nursing Home Expenditures: Implications for Aging Policy. Health Care Financing Review, Fall 1980.

Fullerton, William D., Finding the Money and Paying for Long-Term Care Services: The Devil's Briarpatch. In Policy Options in Long-Term Care. Judith Meltzer, Frank Farrow and Harold Richman, eds. Chicago: The University of Chicago Press, 1981.

General Accounting Office, The Elderly Should Benefit from Expanded Home Health Care But Increasing These Services Will Not Insure Cost Reductions. GAO/IPE-83-1, Washington, D.C.: Government Printing Office, 1982.

Krashinsky, M., User Charges in the Social Services: An Economic Theory of Need and Inability. Toronto: The University of Toronto Press, 1981.

Manton, Kenneth G., Changing Concepts of Morbidity and Morality in the Elderly Population. Health and Society, Vol. 60, 1982.

Pollak, William, Expanding Health Benefits for the Elderly. In Long Term Care, Vol. I, Washington, D.C.: The Urban Institute, 1979.

194

Participants*

Faye G. Abdellah, Ed.D.
Deputy Surgeon General and
Chief Nurse Officer, PHS
Rockville, Maryland

Richard Adelson, D.D.S.
Special Assistant to the Chief Medical Director
V.A. Central Office (107)
Washington, D.C.

Ms. Maureen S. Baltay
Arlington, Virginia

H. David Banta, M.D., M.P.H.
Assistant Director
Division of Health and Life Sciences
Office of Technology Assessment
U.S. Congress
Washington, D.C.

Ms. Donna R. Barnako
Director
Government Relations
National Council of Health Centers
Washington, D.C.

Colonel Julius Bedynck, M.D., Ph.D.
U.S. Army

Ruth Bennett, Ph.D.
Deputy Director
Center for Geriatrics and Gerontology
Columbia University
New York, New York

*All positions noted here were current at the time of the conference.

Robert L. Berg, M.D.
Professor and Chairman
Department of Preventive, Family and Rehabilitation Medicine
The University of Rochester
School of Medicine
Rochester, New York

Robert Binstock, Ph.D.
Director
The Policy Center on Aging and Stulberg
Professor of Law and Politics
Heller School
Brandeis University
Waltham, Massachusetts

Queta Bond, Ph.D.
Director
Divisions of Health Sciences Policy and
Health Promotion and Disease Prevention
National Academy of Sciences
Institute of Medicine
Washington, D.C.

Abraham Brickner, Ph.D.
Director
Health Services Research and Development
Cleveland Clinic Foundation
Cleveland, Ohio

Mr. Thomas E. Brown
Project Director
Community Long Term Care
Spartanburg, South Carolina

Ms. Debora Burch
Research Assistant
Office of Technology Assessment
Biological Applications Program
U.S. Congress
Washington, D.C.

James J. Callahan, Jr., Ph.D.
Director, Levinson Policy Institute and
Deputy Director, University Health Policy Consortium
Brandeis University
Waltham, Massachusetts

Robert Cook-Deegan, M.D.
Congressional Science Fellow
Office of Technology Assessment
U.S. Congress
Washington, D.C.

Karen Davis, Ph.D.
Johns Hopkins University
School of Public Hygiene and Public Health
Baltimore, Maryland

Ms. Nancy N. Dubler, LL.B.
Director
Legal and Ethical Issues in Health Care
Department of Social Medicine
Montefiore Medical Center
Bronx, New York

Lois K. Evans, Ph.D.
Chairman of Nursing Practice and Nursing Education
Health Care Institute for the Aging
Washington, D.C.

Edward W. Fox
Director, Group Claims
Group Insurance Department
The Prudential Insurance Company of America
Roseland, New Jersey

Paul B. Ginsburg, Ph.D.
Deputy Assistant Director for Income Security and Health
Congressional Budget Office
Washington, D.C.

Samuel Gorovitz, Ph.D.
Department of Philosophy
University of Maryland
College Park, Maryland

John M. Grana, Ph.D.
Senior Policy Analyst
Center for Health Affairs
Project HOPE
Millwood, VA

Mr. George E. Greenberg
Senior Program Analyst
Office of the Assistant Secretary for Planning and Evaluation
Washington, D.C.

Judy Miller Jones
Director
National Health Policy Forum
Washington, D.C.

Mr. Stanley Jones
Principal
Health Policy Alternatives, Inc.
Washington, D.C.

Robert L. Kane, M.D.
Dean of the School
School of Public Health
University of Minnesota
Minneapolis, MN

Rosalie A. Kane, D.S.W.
RAND Corporation
Santa Monica, California

Gretchen S. Kolsrud, Ph.D.
Program Manager
Biological Applications Program Office
of Technology Assessment
U.S. Congress
Washington, D.C.

Ms. Sarah Kestenbaum
Special Assistant
Subcommittee on Health and the Environment
U.S. House of Representatives
Washington, D.C.

Mr. Michael B. Lanahan
Vice President
American Health Capital, Inc.
New York, New York

Mr. Steven Lazarus
Senior Vice President
Baxter Travenol Labs, Inc.
Deerfield, Illinois

Ms. Teri L. Louden
President
Louden & Company, Inc.
Chicago, Illinois

Mr. Robert G. Lynch
St. Michaels, Maryland

David B. McCallum, Ph.D.
Fellow
Institute for Health Policy Analysis
Georgetown University
Washington, D.C.

Lawrence H. Miike, M.D., J.D.
Berkeley Springs, West Virginia

Mr. Douglas W. Nelson
Assistant Administrator
Division of Community Services
Department of Health and Social Services
Madison, Wisconsin

Robert J. Newcomer, Ph.D.
Deputy Director
Aging Health Policy Center
University of California, San Francisco
San Francisco, California

Mr. Budd Norris
President
Upjohn HealthCare Services
Kalamazoo, Michigan

Mrs. Helen B. O'Bannon
Consultant
Harrisburg, Pennsylvania

Diane S. Piktialis, Ph.D.
Assistant Secretary
Office of Programs, Department of Elder Affairs
Boston, Massachusetts

William Pollak, Ph.D.
Associate Professor
School of Social Service Administration
University of Chicago
Chicago, Illinois

Ms. Barbara Selfridge
Deputy Associate Director
Special Studies Division
Office of Management and Budget
Washington, D.C.

Ms. Barbara W. Sklar
Director, Geriatric Services
Mt. Zion Hospital and Medical Center
San Francisco, California

Kay A. Smith, Ph.D.
Senior Analyst
Biological Applications Program
Office of Technology Assessment
U.S. Congress
Washington, D.C.

Richard Thorenson
Biological Applications Program
Office of Technology Assessment
U.S. Congress
Washington, D.C.

Mr. Gordon R. Trapness, F.S.A.
President
Actuarial Research Corporation
Falls Church, Virginia

William G. Weissert, Ph.D.
Senior Research Associate
The Urban Institute
Washington, D.C.

Louise Williams, Ph.D.
Senior Analyst
Biological Applications Program
Office of Technology Assessment
U.S. Congress
Washington, D.C.

T. Franklin Williams, M.D.
Professor of Medicine
University of Rochester
Monroe Community Hospital
Rochester, New York

Acknowledgements

The editors gratefully acknowledge the numerous individuals and organizations that made this book possible—especially the following:

- Guidance for development of the workshop from the planning Committee: Dr. Queta Bond, Director, Division of Health Promotion and Disease Prevention, Institute of Medicine; Judy Miller-Jones, Director, National Health Policy Forum; and Dr. Gretchen Kolsrud, Program Manager, Biological Applications Program, Office of Technology Assessment;
- Assistance from Dr. Larry Miike, rapporteur, whose summaries of the discussion were invaluable in the preparation of this book;
- Support from the Office of Technology Assessment—Technology and Aging in America, Robert A. Harootyan, Project Director;
- Editing assistance from Margaret Higgins Radany, Institute for Health Policy Analysis;
- Technical assistance from Claudia Cole, Jennie Best, Barbara Stickley and Sharon Pollard and,
- Most of all, ideas from the participants and speakers at the workshop.